IN PRAISE OF
COMEDY

Books by James K. Feibleman

DEATH OF THE GOD IN MEXICO
CHRISTIANITY, COMMUNISM AND THE IDEAL SOCIETY
IN PRAISE OF COMEDY
POSITIVE DEMOCRACY
THE MARGITIST
INTRODUCTION TO PEIRCE'S PHILOSOPHY
JOURNEY TO THE COASTAL MARSH
THE REVIVAL OF REALISM
THE THEORY OF HUMAN CULTURE
THE LONG HABIT
AESTHETICS
TREMBLING PRAIRIE
THE DARK BIFOCALS
ONTOLOGY
THE INSTITUTIONS OF SOCIETY
INSIDE THE GREAT MIRROR
THE PIOUS SCIENTIST
RELIGIOUS PLATONISM
BIOSOCIAL FACTORS IN MENTAL ILLNESS
FOUNDATIONS OF EMPIRICISM
MANKIND BEHAVING
THE TWO-STORY WORLD
GREAT APRIL
MORAL STRATEGY
THE REACH OF POLITICS
THE WAY OF A MAN

Co-Author of

SCIENCE AND THE SPIRIT OF MAN
THE UNLIMITED COMMUNITY
WHAT SCIENCE REALLY MEANS

JAMES K. FEIBLEMAN

IN PRAISE OF
COMEDY

A Study in Its
Theory and Practice

HORIZON PRESS   NEW YORK

TO

BRUCE MANNING

There is no Jupiter, I tell you so;
Vortex has whirled him from his throne, and reigns
By right of conquest in the Thunderer's place.

ARISTOPHANES, *The Clouds*

Let thor be orlog. Let Pauline be Irene. Let you be
Beeton. And let me be Los Angeles. Now measure
your length. Now estimate my capacity. Well, sour?
Is this space of our couple of hours too dimensional
for you, temporizer? Will you give you up? *Como?*
Fuert it?

Sancta Patientia. You should have heard the voice
that answered him.

JOYCE, *Two Tales of Shem and Shaun*

I want to tell the truth about something about what
yamma yamma yamma.

IVAN T. DOWELL

The voice of the turtle is heard in our land.

Old Testament

Preface to the 1970 Edition

THE FIRST edition of *In Praise of Comedy* appeared in 1939. At that time I was new to lecturing, and when some members of a ladies' club invited me to address them I accepted eagerly.

Just before I was introduced I gathered that there had been a misunderstanding. My book was called a joke book and I was presented as a very funny fellow. I heard such bits as "just wait until you hear him . . .," ". . . you will split your sides," and "he will have you in stitches," and the like.

I confess I was left in something of a predicament; but when in trouble, I thought, the only way out is the truth. I had written what I believed was an earnest contribution; why not say so? I went on to explain that comedy is no laughing matter (no one laughed, by the way), and I tried to soften the rebuke my remark contained by ending a brief talk on the nature of comedy with a few of the jokes I had put in the book for purposes of illustration. By that time, however, they were afraid to laugh.

When I told the ladies that comedy is a serious business they must have been bored and disappointed; but I was right: not only is comedy serious business, it is also big business. One of the changes that has occurred in recent decades is that comedy has spread widely throughout the culture. You have only to listen to what goes on and to look around you in everyday life as well as in what (I regret to say) is called "the entertainment industry," to know that this is the case. Salesmen, waiters and bell boys have their sense of humor, while taxi drivers, soda fountain clerks and short order cooks are specialists. As for the more formal varieties, the New York stage, for instance, has been taken over by the musical comedy, a blend of sentimentality and humor. What few Broadway plays are left are mostly comedies, and there is no writer of tragedies who can compare in skill and success with Neil Simon with his three comedies playing simultaneously. On television, except for the reshowing of old movies, comedy dominates the field. There are weekly "situation comedies," so called, and there are dozens of very good "stand-up" comedians on all the guest shows. Even the advertisements are funny, and some of them very funny indeed.

Comedy is not confined to those bantering exchanges with which most Americans have learned to lighten their daily chores so that even the most casual encounters have an element of wit about them, nor is it confined to the performing arts. For the insupportable burdens of poverty, illness and death are made somewhat more bearable by resort to the endless varieties of mordant humor. Nothing is spared, nothing so sacred that it cannot be a reason for laughter. And, I would argue, the effects of such an approach are desirable. Very often when a situation is so desperate that it generates some kind of intense emotional discharge, it is better to laugh than to cry.

From the time when I first took an interest in comedy, life in the United States became more hazardous and more threatened. There was a second world war, and then, after a brief decade of comparative calm, wars and crises have followed one upon another. The amount of humor in the culture has rapidly increased to ease the strains and stresses. It is of course highly contemporary humor, having been produced to meet a need.

Looking back, however, it is easy to see that comedy was always important to us. Comedy *is* the American genius; there is something peculiarly local about it, and this has been so since the very beginning. There is in our country a strong and unbroken comic tradition, from Mark Twain to Petroleum V. Nasby and Bill Nye, from Ellis Parker Butler's *Pigs is Pigs* to the comic strips of the "funny papers," from Joe E. Lewis and Buddy Hackett to Guy Marks, not to mention the classic figures of the middle period, such as Charlie

Preface

Chaplin and W. C. Fields. Eugene O'Neill was the only dramatist who tried to write tragedies, but tragedy, alas, is not a native product.

Comedy sometimes manages to survive long periods of cultural change. Certainly the plays of Aristophanes and Shakespeare are still with us, but these are the exceptions and it is not for nothing that Homer's comedy, *The Margites,* was lost. By and large, comedy is too contemporary to last; for it criticizes adversely the shortcomings of current customs and institutions and the empty pretensions of fashionable heroes, and it goes when they go.

Not what comedy *does,* then, but what it *is* is what counts. The best kind of criticism is a call for improvement, and comedy is the best kind of criticism; thanks to its cutting-edge, the same mistakes are less likely to be made again. Meanwhile, comedy serves another purpose, for what it is not strong enough to replace, it renders endurable. The most civilized people are those who are able to make fun of themselves. Social life is enriched by comedy and protected from dictators, for with it life can be serious but cannot be solemn. Thanks to a sense of humor, all experiences can be appreciated in depth. When we recognize that instances of the good, the beautiful and the true exist in our own time but are not confined to it, we are in a position to give only half of our attachment to what things are like here and now; and half attachment is quite enough to prevent us from giving ourselves altogether to a period and a set of practices which must certainly perish. Comedy, in other words, provides us with a comfortable ringside seat, and a good view, just above the heat of the battle.

— JAMES FEIBLEMAN

New Orleans
February 1970

Preface

In connection with the effort to orient the reader toward the understanding of the theory of comedy here presented, certain problems have arisen. For instance, it is the fault of the many one-sided treatments that rational understanding seems to clash with intuitional appreciation. There is the viewpoint of logical analysis according to which comedy is relegated to its place on a plane with tragedy where it becomes part of the general theory of aesthetics. And there is the other viewpoint according to which comedy consists in the emotional reaction of laughter to situations themselves intrinsically neutral. But comedy is susceptible both of more exact definition and of wider penumbral meaning than is usually supposed. The task has been to show that the two conceptions of comedy are not contradictory but rather mutually implicative; and this has required an historical as well as a logical approach.

Another important problem should perhaps be mentioned. Novelty seems to be continually at odds with tradition, so that the claims of either appear to vitiate those of the other. In one sense there is nothing new in the world, and so the plan has been to show by means of an historical survey how something approaching the theory of comedy here set forth has been foreshadowed—or else mistaken—by traditional thinkers and actors of the subject. Yet there is another sense in which everything that happens is novel, and therefore the opportunity has been taken to compare this theory with other contemporary notions as to the true nature of comedy, and to seek for illustrations among a variety of living comedians.

The question of treatment has also had to be resolved. The work does not contain any pretensions to elaborate scholarship, but neither on the other hand is it a joke-book, being suggestive rather than exhaustive of the different kinds and varieties of humour. It should probably be stated at the outset that secondary as well as original sources have been consulted freely, a practice which calls for some explanation. In philosophy, pedantry has too long been identified with invention, scholia mistaken for texts. There is, however, a profound difference between them; for pedants must turn to live in the past, while inventors look forward to the future. Only the accident that both are somewhat removed from the vivid immediacy of the actual present has led them to be classified together.

The reconstruction of the past, however brilliant, is not to be confused with the recovery of ideas. The two pursuits have their separate purposes: the efforts of the savants provide a necessary preparation for the theorist who must have his feet on the ground. Were great works of scholarship intended to lie useless on library shelves; to close controversies on their respective topics; or to be put on required reading lists for reluctant undergraduates? It is to be hoped that some educators at least are wrong, and that none of these is their main purpose. Surely no one expects the reading of commentaries to replace the inspection of original material, but the former do accelerate and support further consideration. To verify every assertion made by scholars would mean to be held down indefinitely to the contemplation of facts, to the exclusion of all theoretical speculation. Instead, it should be possible to take the statements of such men as E. K. Chambers and F. M. Cornford as within certain limits authoritative, and to proceed from these authorities to show the metaphysical implications which are independent of historical contexts. Scientific principles take their start from empirical findings and are held strictly accountable to them yet go beyond them, and the same relations hold between aesthetics and historical scholarship. For it is abstract and independent principles, which must be true for any date and place, that both science and philosophy are seeking.

Every proposition implies the assertion of its own truth, an implication presupposing the being of an objective set of conditions which the proposition attempts to represent but to which, of course, it may or it may not truly correspond. True

Preface

knowledge is knowledge of the truth, but there is also the familiar fact of widespread error with regard to any topic. Whether or not the present approach to comedy has succeeded in making the acquaintance of those universal factors which are requisite for comedy is not for me to judge. The philosophy here supported is that of axiologic realism, and the validity of the deducibility from it to comedy, exemplified in the following pages, must be supported finally by the impartial demonstration of the degree of self-consistency attained in this work and by further grounds of allowance which only a continuous application to actuality can provide.

Certain portions of Chapter IV appeared in *The Journal of Philosophy* as "The Meaning of Comedy," and my thanks are due to the editors for permission to reprint this material here.

J. F.

NEW ORLEANS
October 1938

CONTENTS

CHAPTER I

A Survey of the History of Comedy

I. ANCIENT COMEDY

A THOROUGHGOING history of comedy would require several volumes, if not a whole library. Since the purpose of this study is not to exhaust the history but rather to discover a theory of comedy which will prove permanently and ubiquitously true, it will employ the method of sampling. The plan is to select from the historical material available (and much of the history of comedy is of the most evanescent kind) suggestions as to the wide range of facts which any valid theory would have to include within the reach of its principles. Thus the survey is compelled to be restricted to the most significant examples of comedy.

Explicit instances of comedy are probably as old as humanity. Although evidence on which to base any judgment concerning the earliest of human ages is extremely scarce, it is safe to conclude from what scant remains have come down to us that comedy was already in existence in the most primitive times. Of informal comedy, little or nothing is known. But in the earliest known formal arts it is safe to say that comedy was already in evidence. The cave drawings of the Paleolithic period offer evidence of caricature, as do also the small stone statuettes.[1] The reindeer hunter was primitive, yes, but that is only another way of saying that he was simple and uncomplicated. He was also an artist with a sense of humour, and his artistry is by no means to be underestimated. "The works that he has left us are superior to the greater part of the production

---

[1] E.g. the statuette of a woman found in the Cavern of Willendorff in Austria, illustrated in Elie Faure, *Ancient Art* (New York, 1921, Harper), p. 4.

of the Inoits, to all those of the Australians, and especially to those of children."[2]

"A tendency to burlesque and caricature . . . is one of the earliest talents displayed by people in a rude state of society. An appreciation of, and sensitiveness to, ridicule, and a love of that which is humorous, are found even among savages, and enter largely into their relations with their fellow men. Primitive warriors amused themselves by turning their enemies and opponents into mockery . . . caricaturing them in words. . . . When the agricultural slaves were indulged with a day of relief from their labours, they spent it in unrestrained mirth. And when these same people began to erect permanent buildings, and to ornament them, the favourite subjects of their ornamentation were such as presented ludicrous ideas. . . . In fact, art, itself, in its earliest forms, is caricature; for it is only by that exaggeration of features which belongs to caricature, that unskilled draughtsmen could make themselves understood."[3]

It is certain, however, that in primitive times, no separation was made of comedy and tragedy. Comedy may be very old, but the separation of comedy from tragedy in formal works of art is a comparatively recent occurrence. This is only what should have been expected. Early comedy and tragedy inextricably fused in works of art mark the first recognition of the shortcomings of actual life simultaneous with the acceptance for their positive content of things just as they are. Formal comedy was certain to have been a later development than formal tragedy. Formal comedy could not have arisen until there had occurred in men's thoughts considerations of the limitations of actuality and hence of the possibility of some sort of progress.

In this connection, the origin of the fool or buffoon, which is assigned an early date, is significant. The invention of intoxi-

[2] Op. cit., p. 14.
[3] Thomas Wright, quoted in Carolyn Wells, *An Outline of Humour* (New York, 1923, Putnam), p. 25.

cating drinks, which certainly must have given occasion for much unrestrained merriment, was aided and abetted, but at the same time somewhat tempered, by the presence of the official fool. He was usually physically deformed and by profession remained sober, so that while his body stood as a living symbol of imperfection arousing laughter, his words must have stung by pointing satirically to the imperfections of others which had been kept, and it was hoped could remain, better concealed than his own.

The art of the earliest civilization, Egypt, is, as Faure says, religious and funerary. Religion, as we shall later see,[4] is always serious and never amusing. We have no right to expect that a civilization whose entire hopes and aspirations were pointed toward an existence beyond mortal life could be interested in learning about the shortcomings of this actual world. Human existence was governed by considerations of a life above and beyond actuality, and hence did not concern itself with the future of actuality at all.

Nevertheless, there were great masses of humble people whose lot of oppression did not entitle them to share to any great extent in the future life. And since it was largely from this class that the artists were drawn, we may imagine that although they felt the awe and the tragic inevitability imposed on Egypt by royal oppression and priestly usurpation, being artists they must also have awakened now and again to the comedy of the human situation. Sir Gardner Wilkinson tells us that they did. In Thebes there is a picture of a drinking party, with the women as drunk as the men, the whole enlivened by definite caricature.[5] This must have been an early drawing; but as late as 1000 B.C. there was a papyrus drawing made of a cat with a shepherd's crook driving a flock of geese.[6] There are a number

[4] Cf. p. 38.

[5] For these facts I am indebted to Wells, *An Outline of Humour*, pp. 27–9.

[6] See also the drawing entitled "Too late with the basin," in James Parton, *Caricature and Other Comic Art* (New York, 1877, Harper), p. 34.

of other drawings, some of drinking parties but mostly depicting animals performing human tasks, now taking the place of King and High Priest,[7] now playing chess. Egypt had a long and scarcely interrupted history, and as the form of her culture became more strongly set and the likelihood of change passed out of all Egyptian conjecture, comedy disappeared altogether from the banks of the Nile.

A civilization without any traces of humour is hardly to be believed. In the sculptured remains of Assyria and Babylonia, there is little or no humour to be found. The people of these civilizations are known to have been stern; they devoted as much time to war as to commerce and indulged in very little else. Thus we may conclude that although there must have been some comedy in such a fertile field, it may have either been surreptitious or suppressed at the time, or else have been later lost. In all events we know so little about these cultures that the absence of comedy in the scant remains can hardly be considered significant.

The same situation which we found to be true of religious Egypt held also for the ancient Hebrews. For them as for the ancient Egyptians religious aspects of life could not be separated from other aspects. Life was essentially religious in all of its phases. Customs and institutions were regarded as indistinguishable from religious ritual, a condition which inevitably leads to preoccupation with the protection of the vested interests of those in charge of the religious life. It is the first business of the officials who administer a fixed and rigid order to see that it is not criticized or attacked. Therefore comedy is perforce discouraged. Dogmatic religions, like absolutistic political systems, never allow for the rational and the critical, for the air-clearing services which are so incisively performed by comedy and laughter.

The Old Testamentary Prophets, who were the revolutionaries of their day, did not indulge in any comedy lighter

[7] See the drawing entitled "A condemned soul," a pig being ferried by dogs, in ibid., p. 33.

than irony.[8] It was a heavy and bitter kind of irony, designed to call back to high seriousness those who had fallen toward sensual indulgences and false gods and away from the true faith. By this same token, however, we can discern behind the Prophets those masses whose faith had been shaken by unknown events, and who had, temporarily at least, abandoned themselves to trivial levity. Thus laughter is discouraged by the Prophets and sadness put in its place. The lighter and more critical side of life was given no justification by these teachers, to whom it meant not improvement (since to religious dogmatists this has no meaning) but decline.

With the writer of Ecclesiastes, the ancient Hebrew position with regard to comedy was intensified. He thought that there was not much sense to comedy: "I said of laughter, It is mad: and of mirth, What doeth it?"[9] Later, the same author makes his position even clearer. He identifies sadness with wisdom and comedy with foolishness. Foolishness is the action of one who has not thought very much about life.[10] Foolishness, in the opinion of the Preacher, has no purpose. The whole of Ecclesiastes, however, is the complaint of one who is viewing life under only one aspect, namely its tragedy, its disappointment, its sorrow. He is judging the world in a final manner from the narrow perspective of a single mood; and so despite the validity of that mood and the beauty of the poetry which he has written, the Preacher's identification of all comedy with trivial levity and the laughter of fools is misleading and false.[11] The most trivial foolishness certainly has its place, and comedy at its highest, as we shall see in a later chapter, is very close to tragedy. At any rate, wisdom can be reduced exclusively neither to the one nor to the other.

[8] Cf. Isaiah xiv and 1 Kings xviii.
[9] Ecclesiastes ii, 2.
[10] Ecclesiastes vii, 2–6.
[11] The Jews have a peculiar affinity for comedy, of which they do not seem to have been aware and which goes unrecognized to-day. Cf. Chapter V, p. 245.

In Praise of Comedy

2. ARCHAIC GREEK COMEDY

In the Homeric *Hymn to Demeter*, the daughter of Celeus who first makes the goddess smile is named Iambe. To "iambise" someone meant to make him the object of an invective lampoon. Early iambic poetry was certainly satirical, and its formal use was probably in association with the festivals of Demeter. The known iambic poets, Archilochus, Simonides, Hipponax, wrote satiric poetry and indulged in coarse and bitter satire and personal abuse. Certainly their work contained a large element of comedy; yet the poets conceived of shortcomings as limited affairs only, and they took no large view of comedy.

The kind of comedy which is probably as old as any consists in the thoughts, feelings, and antics of drunken persons. To over-indulge in alcoholic drinks is to be able to relax, if only for a while, from the rigidities of current customs and institutions which have come to be regarded as immutable laws of nature and hence as insuperable obstacles to freedom of action. The intoxicated man feels free to do whatever strikes his exaggerated fancy; he is liberated for the moment, or at least supposes that he is, and in this condition he has the sympathy of others who feel the confinement of the bonds but who for some reason or other cannot choose the same way out. Those more restricted hold moral objections; those less restricted prefer to remain sober and to attempt to alter the customs and institutions to something nearer their chosen ideal. But the drunkard himself remains a perennial object of comedy. "Go through the ship with a cup," Archilochus in the seventh century exclaimed, "take the covers from the hollow casks and draw the red wine from the dregs; for we cannot keep sober on this watch."

The beast-fables attributed to Aesop, the hunchback, are among the first successful poetry which can be called comedy. The use of animals in comedy was already familiar through the poem on women by Simonides of Amorgus, in which he compares the different classes of women to various animals: the swine, the fox, the dog, etc. One class, of course, was considered worse than another; but Simonides required an animal to stand for the female virtues, and then he chose the bee, most likely because of its unflagging obedience and labours.

The use of comparisons between animals and humans, often to the detriment of the latter, has been a characteristic of comedy from earliest times to the present. The anthropomorphic reading of the refinements of certain animal gestures and habits: the plans of the beavers, the mimicry of the monkeys, and the patience of the elephant, have long appeared funny. Likewise though less often the bestialities of some humans, the coarseness of crude persons, the inhumanity of the insane, and the actions of the intoxicated, have appeared to be amusing. Logic only becomes operative when things are carried past their limits and this condition is brought about as much by bestial man as it is by anthropomorphic animals. Humanity has its animal nature in common with the beasts, yet its claims on higher psychic levels together with its ambitions at ordinary levels lie so far above the animal that evidence of the failure to attain its ambitions as well as evidence of its lower associations always seem amusing. The failure of things as they are to approximate to things as they ought to be is here involved in the object of comedy.

It may be parenthetically remarked that from Aesop to modern writers, and from East to West, certain natural objects, and particularly certain animals, have long appeared *ipso facto* as funny. Frogs are one example of this. The *Batrachomyomachia*, Aristophanes' comedy *The Frogs*, the Vedic Hymn in which the frog is a Brahmin priest, Garrick's scorn of what passed for a diet in France,[12] the American soldier's name for Frenchmen, mark a long tradition. Similarly with the oyster, Jonathan Swift once remarked that "he was a bold man who

[12] "Beef and beer give heavier blows
Than soup and toasted frogs."

23

first ate an oyster"; Lewis Carroll's poem, "The Walrus and the Carpenter," the satiric references to evolution by Whitehead ("from oysters to apes, and from apes to modern man"),[13] and even the topics of contemporary poems,[14] mark the perennial value of this type of comedy. The reason probably is that chiefly those living beings which most resemble men, e.g. monkeys, and those which least resemble men, e.g. frogs and oysters, are funny when caught in any analogous human situation. In either case, there is much exaggeration and the stretching of human notions past their logical limitations.

The epics of Homer contain sure evidence of a sense of humour in Homer himself. The *Odyssey* especially is a fund of comic appreciation. The adventures of Odysseus with Nausicaa, her disreputable father Alcinous, and her bossy mother Arete betray a deep feeling for comedy, as has been pointed out by Samuel Butler.[15] On the basis of the intimate knowledge of women and money displayed therein, Butler argues that the *Odyssey* must have been written by a woman, since no man would know so much about these topics. The adventures of Odysseus and his companions in the clutches of Polyphemus and their escape is fine comedy, also. After Polyphemus is blinded in his only eye, and the heroes get away under the bellies of the sheep, he calls to his companions for help with the name that Odysseus gave him, οὖτις, which is to say "nobody," and is thus left to his fate. The wiles of Odysseus are always amusing, as are also the remarks of Thersites and the situation of Penelope and her suitors, themselves rudely

[13] A. N. Whitehead, "Remarks," in *The Philosophical Review*, vol. xlvi (1937), p. 181.

[14] "Was it the oysters
Or the insidious
Influence of the moon?
Heavenly bodies in conjunction
At any rate. . . ."

(From an unpublished poem by Louis Gilmore.)

[15] Samuel Butler, *The Humour of Homer and Other Essays* (London, 1913, Fifield), pp. 59 ff.

24

comic. Parts of the *Iliad* are true comedy, especially the antics of the gods of Olympus. But indeed the whole of the *Odyssey* forms a vast comic pattern, and the protagonist one with an ideal goal, whose adventures and misadventures in the course of its pursuit necessitate many compromises. His cunning efforts to reach home form a symbolic representation of the whole question of dealing mediately with the shortcomings of actuality.

The *Achaioi*, as Homer calls them, who entered Greece about 1500 B.C., already possessed some harvest songs. The Ionic authors and the Homeridai of Chios drew on orally-transmitted legends. The most ambitious comedy of early times, which was like the tragedies most likely based upon traditional songs and legends, was the *Margites*, a comedy written by Homer, and dated about 700 B.C. The *Margites* has unhappily been lost, but we know that Margites, the hero of the poem, was a foolish youth who "knew many things and knew them all badly," a condition which got him into all sorts of difficulties. The earliest comedy which has survived is the *Batrachomyomachia*, or the Battle of the Frogs and Mice. It appears to be a parody of the highly serious Homeric epics, and makes use of the familiar animal analogies. The style of Homer and some of the episodes of the *Iliad* and the *Odyssey* are there held up to gentle ridicule.

Greek comedy originated in the fertility rites and ritual dramas of agricultural life.[16] Phallic processions designed to secure the success of crops and drive away malign influences passed into performances by amateur actors. Aristotle said that "Comedy originated with the leaders of the Phallic Songs, which survive to this day in many of our states."[17] The worship of Dionysius, with which was later associated the worship of Bacchus, was accomplished by much reckless and drunken

[16] For much of the information in this and the following section I am indebted to Francis Macdonald Cornford, *The Origin of Attic Comedy* (Cambridge, 1934, University Press).

[17] *Poetics*, 1449a9.

licence; laughter, song, and dance were part of the ritual worship accorded these deities.[18]

The followers of Dionysius were satyrs, and were accordingly disguised as half-man, half-goat, and the satyr-dramas survived as mythical burlesques. The satyr choruses of some of the classic Greek tragedies and *The Cyclops* of Euripides contain much of absurdity and comedy. The *Ichneutae* or *Trackers*, found in Egypt, is a fragment of a satyr-play by Sophocles. Old myths were employed, but only such as lent themselves to comic treatment, and the heroic protagonists were prevented from verging on tragedy by the absurd comments of the satyr chorus. The satyr-dramas were half-way between comedy and tragedy but contained large comic elements.

The term comedy is probably to be derived from the Greek name for the festal processions which were part of this ritual worship as it became more formal and fixed. A *Komos* was a festal procession, hence κωμ-ῳδία.[19] "In Comedy the emphasis still falls on the phallic element and the fertility marriage" and "has been marked all though history by an erotic tone, and in its lower manifestations relied openly on the stimulus of sex attraction."[20] In particular the κῶμος or Revel of Dionysius implied a Γαμος or general union of the sexes, and without such a Gamos it would have failed of its purpose.[21] The grotesque representations and hysterical orgies of the followers of Dionysius, in which the mummers disguised themselves as animals with horrible masks, were left at first in the hands of amateurs. The Bacchic processions of Megarid especially were said to have been popular, and were supposedly introduced

[18] The origins of formal comedy are discussed here. The spirit of ridicule also touched in an irreverent way upon sacred things. See the caricatures of Jupiter and the oracle at Delphi, reproduced in Parton, op. cit., pp. 29–30.

[19] Cornford, op. cit., p. 20. Or perhaps from κωμάξειν, to revel, despite Aristotle's explicit denial. See the *Poetics*, 3.

[20] Op. cit., p. 68–9.

[21] Gilbert Murray, *Aristophanes* (New York, 1933, Oxford Press), p. 6.

into Attica early in the sixth century B.C. The Megarian comedies, the first to have plots,[22] were given regular performances but were at first unwritten. But gradually they passed into the hands of writing professionals. Official recognition finally substituted a regular Chorus for the amateur performers in 488-7 B.C. Comedy had a place in the Great Dionysia after the first victory of Chionides in 486.

Epicharmus of Cos, later of Megara, is said to have introduced the element of plot and made theatrical comedy an affair of connected scenes. These, together with the mimes of Sophron and later mythological dialogues or pantomimes, ushered in the formal comedy of classic Athens: Cratinus, Crates, Eupolis, and others. Cratinus was already making contemporary politics the object of his satiric wit. Quintilian remarks of the Old Comedy that it had "the charm of a most elequent freedom of language" and was "chiefly employed in attacking follies."[23] Of this group of comic writers, and indeed of Greek comedy as a whole, Aristophanes was the master.

3. Classic Greek Comedy

Aristophanes did not greatly alter the framework of the early Greek religious ritual dramas, which had been taken over into comedy. The fertility drama of the year-god, the marriage of the Old Year transformed into the New, interrupted by the death and revival of the hero: this is the classic theme of Aristophanic comedy, as Professor Cornford has well shown.[24] The stock characters of Aristophanes were "at first serious, and even awful, figures in a religious mystery: The God who every year is born and dies and rises again, his Mother and his Bride, the Antagonist who kills him, the Medicine-man who restores him to life. When the drama lost its serious magical intent, probably the Antagonist and the Doctor were the first to become grotesque . . . these two figures gave rise to two pro-

---

[22] Aristotle, *Poetics*, 5.
[23] *Instituto Oratoria.*   [24] Cornford, op. cit.

27

In Praise of Comedy

fessional types, the Swaggering Soldier and the Learned Doctor, the false pretenders to superior courage and more than mortal wisdom."[25]

The modern comedy of the formal theatre had, then, an origin as profound as tragedy; it proved to be concerned with the most serious and fundamental aspects of human life. In the course of the religious spectacle which was so seriously regarded, it was logical that the first figures to be taken as comical should be those which tended to impede the successful progress of the New Year's struggle. Failures, such as the Antagonist who challenged the New Year, and the Doctor who restored him to life, were interruptions in an otherwise orderly triumph. Thus they appeared only as ludicrous.

The themes of tragic dramatists were set for them by myths. Tragedy is concerned to show the inevitability of value. The themes of comic dramatists were taken from contemporary life. Comedy is concerned to show the inevitability of logic.[26] Tragedy deals with the past, and by inference with the future, with a timelessness. But comedy's concern is with the present. The weakness of any contemporary social life is as much in evidence in men's characters as in the current customs and institutions. Thus Aristophanes' comedies concentrated on character. But it was a character of a classic type, having only as much latitude and variety as was permitted by the stock masks of the old figures in the religious drama, traditional properties brought up to date by being given contemporary names and aimed at contemporary foibles. The presence of masks in the Greek comedy is a clear indication of their formal property. Whether the attempt of the Greek comedians to work through the most immediate details of actuality to a set of truths and values which are independent of actuality and so eternally applicable was a conscious one or not is of no importance. Such a procedure is always the method of art, and its use is particularly evident in the plays of Aristophanes. Character

[25] Cornford, op. cit., p. 202. See also pp. 188–9.
[26] Cornford, op. cit., p. 199.

was with Aristophanes a typical phenomenon. As a consequence, there was nothing of the psychologistic or subjectivistic cast to it. Character was, so to speak, a mirror of the customs and institutions whose shortcomings Aristophanes was intent on exposing. For Aristophanes well recognized the purpose of comedy: the exhibition of the shortcomings of actuality in the name of the logical order.

Comedy points to what actually happens, as Aristotle said, in the interests of what may happen. "The reign of Zeus stood in the Greek mind for the existing moral and social order; its overthrow, which is the theme of so many of the comedies, might be taken to symbolize, as in *The Clouds*, the breaking up of all ordinary restraints,"[27] restraints broken, however, not in the interest of anarchy but of a wider and more inclusive order. The rôle of anarchy is to mediate between the old order and the new, since the old must be destroyed before the new can be ushered in. It is this anarchic-mediated period which is the topic of comedy, this period when "whirl is king."[28]

The Clouds is not structurally the greatest of Aristophanes' plays, but its subject-matter most closely illustrates the purpose of comedy. The Greek realistic doctrine of the Idea is the target of the attack, and Socrates appears as the rather absurd Learned Doctor.[29] But that the play is a kindly attempt to introduce the search for truth as opposed to the craftier intentions of the Sophists is still somewhat in doubt. Elsewhere Aristophanes has made it plain that for him the comedian is a man of principles who has no respect for the opportunist willing to compromise with actuality in order to gain unlofty ends.[30] Aris-

---

[27] Cornford, op. cit., p. 33.

[28] *The Clouds*, 1468.

[29] Cornford, op. cit., p. 156 ff.

[30] "Dexterous and wily wits
Find their own advantage ever;
For the wind where'er it sits,
Leaves a berth secure and clever
To the ready navigator;
That forsees and knows the nature
Of the wind and weather's drift;

tophanes, it would appear, was not ridiculing the Theory of Ideas, but merely the wrong interpretation of that theory.[31] The Ideas were not meant to be considered as though they went floating about like clouds. Again, Aristophanes may have been gently introducing to his Athenian audience the new "natural" explanation of phenomena. The questioning of theological explanations was suspect, but the buffoon, then as now, could get by with statements that would be regarded as treason if seriously uttered.[32]

The pursuit of comedy always flourishes during periods of excessive unrest and change, troublous times of wars and revolutions. For at such a time more than at any other is it possible to see and to point out the contradictions and disvalues of actuality. Then also is the opportunity for great hope in the future: that it will be moulded nearer to the ideal logical order. Aristophanes lived during the Peloponnesian War; there are explicit references to it in *The Wasps*.[33] "We see, in the main from Aristophanes, that the transition from the earlier type of Attic comedy went hand in hand with the circumstances of the Peloponnesian War. The *Ecclesiazusae* and the *Plutus*, as is noted by Rogers, "are the only extant comedies which were produced after the downfall of the Athenian empire.' "[34]

Cornford has shown how the comedies of Aristophanes were

> And betimes can turn and shift
> To the sheltered easy side;
> 'Tis a practice proved and tried,
> Not to wear a formal face,
> Fixt in attitude and place,
> Like an image on its base;
> 'Tis the custom of the seas,
> Which, as all the world agrees,
> Justifies Theramenes."

(Translated by J. H. Frere. Theramenes was an unscrupulous politician.)

[31] James Feibleman, *Christianity, Communism and the Ideal Society* (London, 1937, George Allen & Unwin), pp. 128–9.

[32] *The Clouds*, 380.   [33] 700 and 707.

[34] Lane Cooper, *An Aristotelian Theory of Comedy* (New York, 1922, Harcourt, Brace), p. 24.

built upon old ritual formulas, from which they had only slightly divested themselves by a process of transformation. Professor Gilbert Murray[35] has completed the picture by demonstrating that these plays were severe and serious attacks upon the shortcomings of the customs and institutions of the Athens of the playwright's own day. Aristophanes fought against Cleon, the unscrupulous demagogue, and against war (*Knights*, *Peace*, *Lysistrata*); against the unavowed class-struggle which was responsible for the corruption of the jury courts (*Wasps*); against the precious excesses of the exaggerated realism of Socrates and his circle (*Clouds*); against the dramatic innovations of Euripides, the experimental technique which compared so unfavourably with the more solid work of Aeschylus (*Acharnians*, *Thesmophoriazusae*, *Frogs*); and against the imperialistic ambitions of the Athenians in remote Sicily (*Birds*). The comedian cries out for change, because there is always the possibility of a better order, but when the change comes, usually in the form of an anarchic war, he cries out upon war, too, until his very cries are stifled by the unhumorous force of the masses struggling to find their new place in the social world.

George Meredith observed of Aristophanes that "He hated with the politician's fervour the sophist who corrupted simplicity of thought, the poet who destroyed purity of style, the demagogue, 'the sawtoothed monster,' who, as he conceived, chicaned the mob, and he held his own against them by strength of laughter, until fines, the curtailing of his comic licence in the chorus, and ultimately the ruin of Athens, which could no longer support the expense of the chorus, threw him altogether on dialogue, and brought him under the law. After the catastrophe, the poet, who had ever been gazing back at the men of Marathon and Salamis, must have felt that he had foreseen it; and that he was wise when he pleaded for peace, and derided military coxcombry, and the captious old creature Demus. . . . Aristophanes might say that if his warnings had been followed

[35] *Aristophanes.*

there would have been no such thing as a mercenary expedition under Cyrus."[36]

Throughout his comedies, Aristophanes was pleading for the good life. But the pleadings of the comedian are always in terms of the criticism of current shortcomings.[37] Thus whenever the conservatives of this world are able to detect the serious intent of comedy they hasten to prohibit it. There is nothing less tolerant of humour than a new social order. As Mr. Will Rogers once observed of Soviet Russia, "they haven't got what you might call a constant critic." But Russia now is beginning to laugh a little. The fascists, however, will never laugh; the stern countenances of Hitler and Mussolini forbid it because they are afraid of its consequences. They know that men with a sense of humour can never surrender their reason to absolute authority, and this is just what dictators demand.

We cannot leave the greatest of Greek times without acknowledging the divine comedy of Plato. Plato was not a professional comedian; he was a serious philosopher; but he was a dramatist too in the form he gave the *Dialogues*, and often he turned to comedy to make a specific point. Socrates always had a twinkle in his eye and frequently his tongue in his cheek as he led his listeners on to their own confusion and the consequent revelation of the truth. There is one grand comedy, the *Symposium*, which places its discussions at a banquet, where Aristophanes himself is listed as one of the invited guests. The banquet ends when Socrates, who at dawn is beginning to discourse on the difference between tragedy and comedy, suddenly realizes that all his hearers are drunk or asleep under the table. The whole is suffused with that delicate handling of the most profound

---

[36] George Meredith, *An Essay on Comedy*, p. 64.

[37] The high point in the toleration of criticism was reached in that passage in *The Acharnians* in which Dicaiopolis defends the Lacedaemonians against the unfair treatment which has been accorded them, then dressed as the Euripidean prince, Telephus, shows how the Megarians, reduced by the Athenians to starvation, had justifiably appealed to Sparta for help. *The Acharnians*, and Murray, op. cit., pp. 30–3.

topics which is the privilege of all those who wear their erudition lightly yet without triviality. Above all, Socrates felt himself free, a situation which was not to last.

The change in the viewpoint of Plato is obvious, a change which, as Professor Murray observes, was not uninfluenced by the disintegrating social conditions of the day. "In the early dialogues of Plato there is still a spirit of gay enjoyment in confounding the bourgeois and turning received ideas upside down. But the War was at work with its disasters, its brutality and cynicism, its revivals of superstition." Regrettably it must be observed that in certain respects Plato's attitude grimly sided with irrational authority. Hence followed "the outbursts against the wicked sophists in Plato's *Gorgias* and *Republic*; the arrangements for a religious inquisition and the execution of atheists in the *Laws*. A phrase that was a harmless jest in 423 might easily become deadly denunciation in 399."[38]

Athens was never the same after the Peloponnesian War and neither was Athenian comedy. The Old Comedy had cut deep to a criticism at the philosophical level of being. The Middle and New Comedy, from Antiphanes to Menander, became more romantic, and its criticism lighter and more superficial. The loss of the chorus because of lack of funds, combined with the new law prohibiting direct attacks on living persons, was sufficient indication that the decline of comedy could be taken as symptomatic of the decline of Greece in general. Antiphanes was still aware of the high function of comedy; he knew that intellectually speaking it had more difficult tasks to perform than had tragedy. The tragedian, he observed, can fall back upon myths which are familiar to any audience, but the comic writers lack such props; their problem is more logical. "We have to imagine everything," he says, "new names, what went before, what happens now, the change of fortune, and the opening of the play."[39]

By the time we reach Menander the change is complete.

[38] Murray, op. cit., p. 101.
[39] Quoted in Lane Cooper, op. cit., p. 33.

Not sex ritual but romatic love forms the subject-matter of his comedies; and the intricacies of his plot are intended to divert rather than to criticize. The social implications contained in the comedies of Menander are those of a defeated people and an uncertain life. No props of external organization remained to the individuals of Menander's time. Religion was a matter of habit, politics a dangerous complication mostly in the hands of foreigners, and slavery the preponderant lot of humanity. Menander's reply was that of an amused and moderate Stoic: he exhibited the antics of individuals, mainly of women enmeshed in the contemporary imbroglio, and that is all; and for the persons of his own time he had a melancholy smile.[40]

The New Comedy is the comedy of manners, with the happy ending of united young lovers; its reformatory and revolutionary implications are practically nil. Not without reason did the Roman translators choose the New Comedy for their purposes; for by the time of Menander there was little left to Greek comedy which was not suitable to the uses of the derivative Roman stage.

4. Roman Comedy

There was hardly a Roman activity which did not become influenced to a large extent by its Greek equivalent. Roman comedy, however, did not grow immediately out of Greek comedy. There was an interim period during which Roman comedy took its own primitive start, similar to the earlier origins of Greek comedy. The so-called Fescennine verses were a native Italian form of comic poetry, sung by masked dancers at vintage, harvest, and other rustic festivals.[41] They most likely originated in the primitive religious rites, whereby the phallic[42] motive was invoked to encourage fertility and to drive

---

[40] Cf. Murray, op. cit., chap. x.

[41] *Encyclopaedia Britannica*, ix, p. 199.

[42] *Fescenninus* has been traced to the Latin town of Fescennium, but its derivation is more probably *fascinum*, or phallus.

out evil forces, and were accordingly abusive and obscene. Centuries later Augustine quoted "Varro's description of how the phallus was carried at the Liberalia on carts, at first through the villages of Italy and later into Rome itself. 'By such means,' he adds with pious horror, 'the God Liber had to be placated for the success of the crops, by such means must malign influences be driven from the fields.' "[43]

In the Idylls of Theocritus and the hymns of Callimachus and in other pastoral poets the formal humour of the Roman civilization begins.[44] Throughout the hymns of Callimachus we find the "irrepressible laughter of the gods" at the grotesque efforts of the heroes, and a parody of the Homeric Thetis requesting Hephaestus for Achilles' armour, with the child Artemis and the Cyclops substituted for the Homeric figures. The ludicrous contrast occurs again in the story of Praxinoa's child pulling hairs out of the chest of Brontes the giant while sitting on his knee, hairs which we are told (much to M. Couat's puzzlement) never grow again.[45] Theocritus was more concerned with the serious purpose of portraying the advantages of the peasant life, but when he does indulge in comedy it is already a departure from the Greek (although under Greek influences)[46] in that his comedy is concerned with morals and manners, more specifically with the psychological comedy of housewifely busybodies and the plight of rejected suitors.[47]

It is easy to detect in these early Roman instances of comedy the marks of a derivative civilization. It was Greek comedy in its decline that influenced the early Roman comedians; dramatists of the New Comedy like Menander and Philippides were

[43] Augustine, *Civitate Dei*, vii, 21, quoted in Cornford, op. cit.

[44] There is much extant evidence of the existence of a broad informal humour which spared nothing and no one. Crude wall drawings have been found which caricatured everything from local politics to Christian martyrdom, drawings similar in nature to those which we find on our own fences to-day.

[45] Auguste Couat, *Alexandrian Poetry under he First Three Ptolemies* (London, 1931, Heinemann), pp. 284-6.

[46] Op. cit., p. 444, n. 1.

[47] Op. cit., pp. 444-5.

found by the Romans to be the most congenial. Thus Roman comedy began, as it flourished and declined, by being held down very sharply to the details of its own day, without striving, as Aristophanes did, for example, to discover eternal truths and values which should be as significant in any day as it was then.

The Attelane farces[48] were of ancient date, and were acted by amateurs, until the first century B.C., when they took their place as formal comedies following the performance of tragedies, much like the Greek satyr-dramas. The actors wore masks and played stock characters, but these latter were more of Roman rural characters (the simpleton, the glutton) than of the Greek symbolic type. One mask of Dossenus, a clever hunchback, may have been derived from the Greek buffoon; it foreshadowed the court fool and the jester, the figure of Punch.

The first impetus was given to Roman comedy by the translation of some of the classic Greek comedies by the Roman or Campanian, Naevius, toward the end of the third century B.C. His own attempts at comic theatre led to his imprisonment, and after him the attacks of the comedians on current politics were either absent or heavily disguised. The influence of the subject-matter of the later Greek comedies, together with the atmosphere of suppression which prevailed in earliest Roman times, destined Roman comedy to be of an amusing but more homely and less far-reaching sort than was Greek comedy. There is no trace of any Roman comedian who even aimed at the heights of comedy which Aristophanes succeeded in achieving. Comedy breathes best in a free air and at great intellectual levels. Rome was only partly able to supply these.

Plautus, the greatest Roman comic dramatist, was as much a translator from the Greek as he was an original dramatist. His plays were based on translations from Menander and other writers of the New Comedy. But he was also much influenced by the *Atellanae Fabulae* in which he may have taken part. His adaptations from the Greek were full of Roman allusions:

[48] *Atellanae Fabulae*, probably originating in Atella, an Oscan town between Naples and Capua.

A Survey of the History of Comedy

places and characters which would be familiar to the Roman audience. But the Greek models which he took over were already part of a tradition in decline. His plots were the conventional romantic affairs of the New Comedy, and are comparable to the romantic plots so popular in the modern theatre and cinema: "boy meets girl, boy loses girl, boy gets girl." Despite much wit and humour, despite the valid though petty criticism of local foibles, Plautus' comedies fail of greatness. His comedies are robust enough; but as essential comedy, that is, as the derogation of the shortcomings of the actual life of his own day in favour of an actuality as it ought to be, they leave much to be desired.

Terence, the literary friend of Scipio, wrote comedies much in the manner of Plautus, on Greek models modified to suit the Roman taste; but he substituted for a certain crude vigour, which was largely the value of Plautus' work, a fastidious and correct style. From those fragments which have survived to us of Menander's comedies we may fairly conclude that the adaptations of Plautus and Menander from the Greek were comparatively coarse and crude affairs. The gentle but stoic immobility, the refinement and the philosophical ideas, which are so much in evidence in the plays of Menander are overlooked by Roman imitators who learned from the Greek writers of the New Comedy only their heavily-plotted outlines and coarse-grained characters.

By the last century B.C. the *fabulae Atellanae* had become transformed into the *fabulae togatae*, formally written comedies dealing with rural life and characters. The *togatae* owed less to Greek influences. In sharp contrast with these, there were the urbane writings of the poet Horace, whose comedy was based on the detection of small faults and the celebration of amusing pleasures rather than on the higher criticism which we have come to expect from the great comedians. Petronius, a more uproarious comedian than Horace, is yet like him in urbanity, and specialized chiefly in the *Satyricon* in satirizing the *nouveau riche* of the Roman provinces. The comedy of Horace and

37

Petronius and their kind is not profound; it dances over the surface of manners and customs in a critical mood, yet remains deeply approving of the fundamental moral and social structure of the day. It calls for little improvement of any radical kind.

Whatever definite call for improvement there was came from the new religious movement of the Christians. That there was no comedy in the leadership of Christ or from within the Christian movement is easily understandable. The religious leader comes to affirm and not to deny. He holds each thing sacred for just what it is, for what is positive about it and not for what it comes to replace. Consequently he is not in a position to view events humorously. The humour of the day issued from those urbane citizens who were able to raise themselves just enough above the society in which they played a part to see that although it was fundamentally sound it yet possessed some minor shortcomings. But Christ came to destroy humour for a while; as Swinburne observed:

> Thou hast conquered, O pale Galilean,
> The world has grown grey with thy breath.

The decline of Roman comedy in the first centuries A.D. was in two directions: toward the petty and scurrilous wit of contemporary fashions, as exemplified by the poet Martial, and toward the bitter attacks on the corruptions of the day without any hints toward improvement, attacks in which humour was seldom present, as exemplified by Juvenal. In theatrical comedy the rise of mimes and later of pantomimes witnessed the decline of the spoken comedy and the gradual elaboration of gestures, until words disappeared altogether and a kind of ballet with music in which women participated (*fabulae salticae*) took their place. The theatre in its degenerate form of comic mimes finally fell a prey to the "bishops and barbarians," and only the sterile *spectacula* remained to the end to salt the bread. Roman comedy ended in pure licentiousness, without the affirmation of anything. Finally when a mute and open obscenity was substituted for what had once been the prerogative of an Aristophanes or even of a Plautus, comedy itself was for the time being at least a thing of the past.

5. MEDIAEVAL COMEDY

Late Roman audiences insisted that the actors in their comedies, including the fat and middle-aged fool, should play before them entirely naked. Comedy bears more than any other activity the marks of the day, and Roman comedy was significant. Christianity awoke in the profligate Roman world, and naturally cast the full brunt of its disapproval upon the licentious and dissolute theatres. World-movements in their origins are positive and militant; they meet with much opposition, not least of which is the laughter of the sceptics, who have been deprived of one world-order before they have been offered another and who tire of anything serious. A perfect example is the reception given Paul in an Athens which had grown weary of everything except novelty.[49] Thus world-movements whether puritanical or not appear unable to reconcile themselves with comedy until they have become so thoroughly established that they no longer need to fear criticism.

Christianity from the first was opposed to the Roman theatre and to comedy in general. Great social movements, whether religious, political, or whatever, although logical entities in themselves and thus independent of place or date, are, like great individuals, very much moulded in their origin by the omissions and over-emphases of the times. These marks of their origins are carried with them throughout their career as an integral part of their logical organization. Thus Catholic Christianity arose and became a world order during the extraordinary decline of the Roman political organization. This decline being marked by dissolute and degenerate immorality of a particularly perverse nature, it was dialectically logical that the Church should take the opposite turn, and become extremely puritanical, and, in its old age, even prurient.

[49] Acts xvii.

In Praise of Comedy

The theatres were closed as early as possible by the Christian authorities, and the actors, who were put under severe social bans and regulations, turned to the road to earn a meagre living as wandering minstrels. The origin of the minstrels is hard to determine. Certainly they were known to the European peoples before the coming of the Christian civilization. The duties of these bards were to sing the praises of the tribal chieftain to the accompaniment of the harp at feast times, in hall or tent.[50] "At the banquet with which Attila entertained the imperial ambassadors in 448, the guests were first moved to martial ardour and to tears by the recital of ancient deeds of prowess, and then stirred to laughter by the antics of a Scythian and a Moorish buffoon."[51]

It was these as well as the disorganized actors turned minstrel with which the Church had to contend. In the fifth century, the *spectaculae*, who were in social disgrace, gave way to the wandering minstrel, performing his own *spectacula* on street corners before remnants of his old audience. These in turn later became the official court harpers of the Teutons and Anglo-Saxons. In some quarters, the Church relaxed and Bede complained of "those who make mirth in the dwellings of bishops."[52] But generally the Church was determined. As Chambers observed, "There is the ascetic tendency to regard even harmless forms of secular amusement as barely compatible with the religious life."[53]

The minstrel life was not an easy one, and the minstrel fought back with the only weapon at his command: humour. Minstrel songs became sharp criticism: songs against bad rulers, songs against the clergy. At first the battle was a severe one for the minstrels. "To tramp long miles in wind and rain, to stand wet to the skin and hungry and footsore, making the slow *bourgeois* laugh while the heart was bitter within; such must have been

[50] For much of the information in this chapter I am indebted to E. K. Chambers, *The Mediaeval Stage* (London, 1903, Oxford Press). The reference here is to vol. i, p. 28.

[51] Op. cit.., vol. i, p. 35.

[52] Op. cit., vol. i, p. 32.

[53] Op. cit., vol. i, p. 33.

the fate of many among the humbler minstrels at least. And at the end to die like a dog in a ditch, under the ban of the Church and with the prospect of eternal damnation before the soul."[54] But meanwhile "they were the satirists, satirists mainly of the hypocrisy, cupidity, and evil living of those in the high places of the Church, for whom they conceived a grotesque expression in Bishop Golias, a type of materialistic prelate, in whose name they wrote and whose *pueri* or *discipuli* they declared themselves to be."[55]

About the twelfth century, the wandering minstrel began to give way to the *trouvère*, who were the educated nobles and merchants devoting themselves to composition in the vernacular. Minstrelsy was at its height from the eleventh to the thirteenth centuries. During this time, the minstrels served the purposes of comedy well: speaking for nationalism, like the gleeman Minot;[56] satirizing by means of mimicry in one country the customs of the next;[57] and in general furnishing the method of contemporary criticism. The *trouvère*, however, benefited by the invention of printing, and the minstrel henceforth declined to the status of a mere reciter of songs written by the *trouvère*.

Besides the minstrel and *trouvère*, the restlessness of scholars gave rise to another form, the Goliards. The Goliards were wandering clerics, scholars travelling from one university to another, more given to wine, women, and dice than to studies. They wrote many famous ballads, of which the most famous, *The Confession of Golias*, "is a song of the open road, of the vagabond life, of taverns and hard drinking, of sport and mocking irreverence, of love, of spring, of gamesters, of poverty, of sorrow and defiance. Its gods are the pagan gods—Venus, Bacchus, and Decius, god of dice. Christianity is all but forgotten."[58] From these tonsured heads came "much parodying,

---

[54] Op. cit., vol. i, p. 48.   [55] Op. cit., vol. i, p. 60.
[56] Op. cit., vol. i, p. 76.   [57] Op. cit., vol. i, p. 82.
[58] Nathan Schachner, *The Mediaeval Universities* (London, 1938, George Allen & Unwin), p. 368.

too, of the most sacred things. Nothing was too holy, nothing too powerful, for the Goliards' satiric verse: not Popes, Bishops, the Vulgate, the solemn accents of the liturgy, the Lord's Prayer, the Mass; not even the Virgin was exempt. . . . All authority, whether of Church or State, was fit matter for their mocking wit."[59]

> To my mind all gravity
> Is a grave subjection;
> Sweeter far than honey are
> Jokes and free affection.
>
> All that Venus bids me do
> Do I with erection,
> For she ne'er in heart of man
> Dwelt with dull dejection.[60]

It is not possible to talk about comedy in the Middle Ages without giving a word to those informal and semi-formal outbursts of comic interplay which were so integral a part of the times. The gallantry that characterized all relations between the sexes and the courts of love contained large elements of play that can only be described as a sophisticated kind of light comedy. In the thirteenth century, for example, there were "castles of love," built and defended by noble ladies and their waiting-women, and fortified by "sable, purple cloths, brocade of Bagdad, and ermine." The castles were assaulted by men armed with fruits, perfumes, flowers, and spices.[61] No doubt chivalry knew its serious souls who took their most casual relations heavily, but these must have been if not outnumbered then at least in the majority by only a small margin. In a relatively stable order of things, comedy tends to degenerate into wit, but this was a decline which the Middle Ages fought to a standstill. Enough malice remained to give point to the jokes, and to all forms of comedy that were indulged in by everyday

[59] Op. cit., p. 369.
[60] Trans. by J. A. Symonds, in *Wine, Women and Song,* quoted in op. cit., p. 366.
[61] G. C. Coulton, *Life in the Middle Ages* (Cambridge, 1930, University Press), vol. i, p. 90.

A Survey of the History of Comedy

folk. Although the Church was unaware of it, comedy as the avenue of free opposition was partly responsible for the long life of the established religion. Unconscious recognition of this fact is contained in the characterization of buffoons as a renegade "tenth order,"[62] in a sermon of Berthold von Regensburg in the thirteenth century.

Besides the minstrels, who were the inheritors of the dispossessed and disgraced *spectaculae* of the Roman theatre, there was another way in which ancient comedy came to be the property of the Middle Ages. The primitive and pagan fertility festivals which, as we have noted, influenced the formation of the theatrical Greek comedies and later the Roman comedies, too, still existed in a modified version among the village folk of Western Europe. As Chambers observes, "the traditional beliefs and customs of the mediaeval or modern peasant are in nine cases out of ten but the *detritus* of heathen mythology and heathen worship, enduring with but little external change in the shadow of an hostile creed. This is notably true of the village festivals and their *ludi*. Their full significance only appears when they are regarded as fragments of forgotten cults, the naïve cults addressed by a primitive folk to the beneficent deities of field and wood and river."[63]

By the Middle Ages, most of the frenzied religious fervour was out of such celebrations, however, and "the instinct of play found a foothold at the village feast in the debris which ritual, in its gradual transformation, left behind."[64] Village festivals of one sort or another: the May-Day Festival, the sword dances which were so popular throughout continental Europe, and the Mummers' Play, all performed under the open or tacit hostility of the Church to which these festivals made innumerable concessions, were the versions in which formal comedy survived from paganism to the peasantry. The May-Day games, for instance, lost much of the erotic flavour of the spring celebration and became reconciled with the

[62] Op. cit., vol. iii, p. 61.
[63] Op. cit., vol. i, p. 94.   [64] Op. cit., vol. i, p. 147.

43

demands of the Church. The symbolic dumb show of certain sword-dances, in which one of the dancers was slain and brought back to life by a doctor, led finally to the Mummers' Play.

In some ways the most interesting form of comedy in the Middle Ages is this Mummers' Play. The Play was divided into a prologue, a spoken welcome to the spectators, and the introduction of the actors; the action, in which someone is slain and then restored to life by a doctor; and finally the introduction of some supernumerary characters and a collection. One characteristic note of comedy, in evidence from archaic Greek comedy straight through to our own times, is that tragedy (i.e. death) occurs but is never wholly accepted or taken seriously. Men are slain obviously enough, but the dead always arise to fight again, having evidently experienced little or no discomfort in cheating death. The instrument by which this miracle is accomplished is the magic doctor of Greek comedy, the comic doctor of the Mummers. The doctor is invariably a comic character.[65] He always brags about "his travels, his qualifications and his remedies," and his cures follow as a matter of course.

The introduction of needless characters at the end of the Play is the surest evidence of its ancient origins. Certain characters must be introduced even when there is no dramatic justification for it; so what does the rural playwright do? He naïvely introduces the characters one by one and lets it go at that! Beelzebub appears long enough to recite:

> Here come I; ain't been yit,
> Big head and little wit.[66]

The Mummers' Play, like other mediaeval folk festivals and dramas, was finally taken over for Church purposes, and in the form of the miracle play presented the legend of St. George and the Dragon. This was a tardy development and it lasted as late as 1732.

The sword-dance and the Mummers' Play are summer

[65] Op. cit., vol. i, pp. 210, 213.   [66] Op. cit., vol. i, p. 215.

affairs, but there were also the winter celebrations: the Christmas plays. Both summer and winter festivals are "moments in the cycle of agricultural ritual." The winter festivals were taken over from peasant custom by *bourgeois*, churchman and courtier. Chief among these was the so-called Feast of Fools, which flourished in the thirteenth century, and died out by the fifteenth. It consisted in a mock church ritual, a parody of the regular services; and symbolized the periodic revolt of the minor clergy: sub-deacons, vicars, chaplains, and choir-clerks. "That it should perpetuate or absorb folk-customs was, considering the peasant or small *bourgeois* extraction of such men, quite natural." The Feast of Fools "was largely an ebullition of the natural lout beneath the cassock. Familiarity breeds contempt, and it was almost an obvious sport to burlesque the sacred and tedious ceremonies with which they were only too painfully familiar."[67]

Let us listen to a report of a Feast of Fools, as quoted by Chambers. " 'Priests and clerks may be seen wearing masks and monstrous visages at the hours of office. They dance in the choir dressed as women, panders, or minstrels. They sing wanton songs. They eat black puddings at the horn of the altar while the celebrant is saying mass. They play at dice there. They cense with stinking smoke from the soles of old shoes. They run and leap through the church, without a blush at their own shame. Finally they drive about the town and its theatres in shabby traps and carts; and rouse the laughter of their fellows and the bystanders in infamous performances, with indecent gestures and verses scurrilous and unchaste.' "[68] If further evidence be needed of the essentially anti-religious nature of the Feast, it may be pointed out that there was always a leader who was called "abbot" or "king," and that the ceremony was the inverse of the mock king of the divine sacrifice of primitive religion.[69] Even the lay-brothers, the cooks and

---

[67] Op. cit., vol. i, p. 325.   [68] Op. cit., vol. i, p. 294.
[69] Sir J. G. Frazer, *The Golden Bough*, vol. "The Dying God" (London, 1923, Macmillan).

45

gardeners, "put on the vestments inside out, held the books upside down, and wore spectacles with rounds of orange peel instead of glasses."[70]

The history of mediaeval comedy is the account of a constant effort on the part of the Church to suppress all gaiety and criticism, and of the way in which these tended to burst forth despite suppression. Early movements do not need humour, which is a destructive force. But when movements begin to exhibit contradictions, humour is required to expose them and to introduce the notion of their susceptibility to attack. Although one hears of "the sin of dancing" condemned by preachers as late as the early thirteenth century,[71] and "dissolute laughter" was considered a "light default" in nunnery discipline, yet laughter "by way of recreation" was allowed to nuns when begun by the sovereign elder sisters.[72] One hears of war more among civilians than soldiers, of solemnity more among laity than clergy. The phrase "merry monk" was not uncommon,[73] and at least one archbishop is remembered for his wit.[74] Recognition of the part played by the devil has always been an occasion for comedy. We find tangible evidence of such recognition in the Middle Ages in the brutal and grotesque "bestiaries" which were carved on the pillars and portals and choir stalls of the mediaeval churches. "Grinning apes, sly foxes, and those unclassified animals that occasionally devour their arch-enemy, man, indicate, we are told, the dynamic force of evil, and prove the lurking presence of the great Manichean heresy. Imps and demons are not excluded. The Devil broods over the vastness of Notre Dame, and shares with St. Genevieve a perpetual watch over Paris. He has his place in the hierarchy of creation."[75]

Those in authority would dispense with the buffoon, who

[70] E. K. Chambers, op. cit., vol. i, p. 317.
[71] G. C. Coulton, *Life in the Middle Ages*, vol. i, p. 90.
[72] Op. cit., vol. iv, p. 317.   [73] Rabelais.
[74] Coulton, op. cit., vol. i, p. 79.
[75] Agnes Repplier, *In Pursuit of Laughter* (Boston, 1936, Houghton Mifflin), p. 10.

A Survey of the History of Comedy

does not find it in his rôle to accept current evaluations. The unity of gaiety and criticism which is comedy in the Feast of Fools was a wave that swept up to the heart of the Church itself. This feast was never more than grimly tolerated until such a time as it could be discontinued, or rather transformed. For the custom never really died out, its satisfactions having been too much appreciated by the town folk, especially the young. Thus in the middle of the fifteenth century there arose the lay organizations of young people known as *compagnies des fous* or *sociétés joyeuses*,[76] to take over on the calends the function of the suppressed cathedral festivals.

The duties of the *sociétés joyeuses* consisted in the seasonal feasts, including what remained of the former Feast of Fools, local *faits divers*, and even the moral tradition of the *charivari*.[77] They also played *sotties*, which have been compared to the modern revue.[78] In the sixteenth century, the festival passed into a court revel "in which, behind the accretions of literature and pageantry, can be clearly discerned a nucleus of folk-custom in the entry of the band of worshippers, with their sacrificial *exuviae*, to bring the house good luck."[79] During the reign of the Tudor Kings there was appointed for royalty, for Universities, and for Inns of Court, an "Abbot of Unreason" or "Lord of Misrule" to hold sway over the Christmas celebrations, doubtless an inheritance from the Feast of Fools. Thus the folk festival and its symbolic ritual finally reached the bourgeois, the nobility, and even the court. Comedy survived through the Middle Ages despite "the relentless hostility of the austerer clergy to the ineradicable *ludi* of the pagan inheritance."[80]

Mediaeval comedy comes to a close with the liturgical plays. Religious plays and, somewhat later, moralities, arose in which "a barred human instinct" showed itself "within the hearts of

---

[76] Similar bands had already existed in Athens in the fourth century B.C. See Cornford, *The Origin of Attic Comedy*, p. 44.
[77] Op. cit., vol. i, p. 379. [78] Op. cit., vol. i, p. 381.
[79] Op. cit., vol. i, p. 400. [80] Op. cit., vol. i, p. 419.

47

its gaolers themselves."[81] These were Christmas (or Birth) and Easter (or Resurrection) Plays, which in their decline assumed an allegorical form. The comedy in them, with some exceptions,[82] was confined to the life of Mary Magdalen before her reform,[83] and to the perennial quack doctor of all comedy.[84] There is no trace of comedy in the guild and parish plays into which the liturgical plays declined. With the rise of the interludes, which were brief plays, given before royal patrons and on the road by professional players, we reach the end of mediaeval comedy.

Dante's great poem has been called the apotheosis of the Middle Ages; it is not for nothing that it is a comedy. *The Divine Comedy* is all-embracing, a comedy because a criticism of Dante's own times, and divine because Dante showed as few others have that although comedy is native to this vivid world, it is in a sense raised above the battle and with its raillery has a place in the logical order of eternal values. In Dante's poem there is to be found comedy at every level. Vossler has observed that in the Cantos of the *Inferno*, xxi-xxii, the crude but powerful comic play of the devils is reminiscent of the satire of the mystery plays,[85] or, perhaps better, of what we have described above as the Feast of Fools. Yet there is no laughter, only a judgment that is in itself beyond good and evil, in the struggles of men to attain to their true goal; and the divine comedy consists in the fact that in their efforts to

[81] Op. cit., vol. ii, p. 3.

[82] A "divine comedy" with emphasis on the grotesqueries of the devils was performed in skiffs on the Arno, but the wooden bridge collapsed under the weight of the spectators, and many were drowned. "The wit of the survivors came to the conclusion that the people who had been so eager to get fresh news from the other world were having it now at first hand and quicker than they could have expected." Karl Vossler, *Mediaeval Culture*, W. C. Lawton trans. (New York, 1929, Harcourt, Brace), vol. ii, p. 127.

[83] E. K. Chambers, op. cit.., vol. ii, p. 33.

[84] Op. cit., vol. ii, p. 91. The *Mercator* probably is "the inveterate quack doctor of the spring folk drama."

[85] Op. cit., vol. ii, p. 126.

raise themselves above their limitations and to contemplate this actual world *sub specie aeternitatis,* they remain human after all and that necessarily "a trace of earthly weakness and worldly levity clings to them still."[86] Not the devils alone but the Middle Ages turn to Dante for the symbolic presentation of their truth, and

> Per l'argine sinistro volta diènno
> ma prima avea ciascun la lingua stretta
> coi denti vèrso lor duca per cenno;
> ed elli avea del cul fatto trombetta.[87]

6. RENAISSANCE COMEDY

European comedy survived with the aid of three traditions: folk drama, religious liturgy, and classical survival. Translations of the classics were not common in the Middle Ages although they existed. Terence was an influence for centuries, even if Plautus was known first. The latter in translation was to have a greater influence later. But these were largely forces bearing on the theatrical form of comedy. Comedy itself underwent an essential kind of renaissance. The spirit of the times made fun of the gross absurdities of mediaeval life, causing them to appear old; it tore away the pretences and by its mocking laughter rendered customs and institutions which formerly had been reverenced ready to be abandoned. "The *Sophrosyne* of Comedy," as Cornford remarks, "is the spirit of genial sanity, in all its range from the flicker of lightning reason and the flash of wit, through the large humour of common sense, down to the antics of the fool, making ironical play with every form of absurdity."[88] The reawakening to the presence of profuse actuality with all its qualities to be experienced

[86] Karl Vossler, *Mediaeval Culture,* vol. ii, p. 309.
[87] *Inferno,* XXI.
> "To leftward o'er the pier they turned; but each
> Had first between his teeth pressed close the tongue,
> Toward their leader for a signal looking,
> Which he with sound obscene triumphant gave."
> (H. F. Cary, trans.)
[88] Op. cit., p. 211.

in a welter of contradictions, which was the Renaissance, knew comedy in all these varieties. But it was chiefly the sanity of common sense that prevailed. The late mediaeval man had to return to reconciliation with life in this world, which the Church had condemned, and for this purpose common sense was a competent method, *"la vertu moyenne,* that average rectitude which human nature had never signally lacked, and which, if it fails to make this the best of all possible worlds, saves it from being the worst."[89]

There was much evidence of the reawakening in the fourteenth century. The subject-matter of the French *fabliaux* and the Italian *novelle* consisted in the humorous episodes of ordinary life. The *fabliaux* were gay, crude, and vigorous; chiefly they were amoral, and they took as a special target the topic of woman, perhaps as a reaction against the mediaeval chivalric customs. The Italian *novelle* were the first European novels in prose, and their outstanding representative is Boccaccio. *The Decameron* (written shortly after the Black Death had by its decimation punctured the regimen of the Middle Ages for once and all) was the first of the great human epics which the Renaissance was to usher into literature.

About the same time there lived the man whom Coleridge has called the best representative in English of the Norman-French *trouvères,* Chaucer. Chaucer, however, was a focal point of the new learning; he was influenced by classical survivals and also by Boccaccio and Petrarch. Although much influenced too by Dante, he was convinced of the goodness of this world, the definite product of a new turn of interest. The comedy of *The Canterbury Tales* is broad and keenly observant of those small virtues and petty vices which are what we call human. In the late fourteenth century there lived in France another comic poet, Villon. Villon was a true comedian in the fullest sense of the term, an essential rebel, in full revolt against all the customs and institutions of his time. A great poet also, he undercut the contemporary and the common-

[89] Repplier, op. cit., p. 24.

place to focus attention upon the problem which comes to vex all those who regard this actual life as of final importance. From a preoccupation with life after death which the Church had taught, the Renaissance saw the beginning of a new preoccupation: the problem of time. If the vivid qualities and experienced sensations of this life were real, why did they pass so quickly?

> Dictes-moy où, n'en quel pays,
> Est Flora, la belle Romaine;
> Archipiada, né Thäis,
> Qui fut sa cousine germaine;
> Echo, parlant quand bruyt on maine
> Dessus rivière ou sus estan,
> Qui beauté eut trop plus qu'humaine?
> Mais où sont les neiges d'antan!

Villon's laugh is always bitter, but the business of time, he seems suddenly to have realized, is to play one vast and continual prank upon everything actual and finite.

The German legend of Tyl Eulenspiegel, recorded in the chap-book of that name by Murner, is the German equivalent of the man who actually lived in France, although there is of course no actual connection. Villon and the German rascal, although differently motivated, seem to have had much the same effect in their respective countries. Unwilling to pay the debts owed to innkeepers and tradesmen, unsympathetic with the old, amorous of the young, outcast yet beloved and cursed —these are the lot of the romantic rebels who serve the classic purpose of comedy. For it is they who must relieve for the common man the dull monotony of his life; who must show him that the conventional laws, customs, and morals, which he has obeyed blindly for so long that he has come to regard them as interwoven with the nature of things, are made only to be broken. The rôle of the comedian is also that of the liberator.

It is hard to believe that Erasmus and Rabelais are contemporaries; from the gentle satire of Erasmus to the robust rioting of Rabelais is a far cry, and well illustrates part of the range of humour. Both satirized the dogmas and ritual of the Catholic Church, to which Rabelais in his own fashion added the abuses of politics and many individual foibles as well. But there is in Rabelais an affirmative aspect which is to be found in few other comedians. The rippling flow of the vast catalogues, which show Rabelais alive to everything, remind one of nothing so much as of the contemporary *Work in Progress* by James Joyce. There is more in Rabelais than was ever dreamt of in the philosophies of those cautious professorial scholars who shrink from the warning, so brutally presented by that great humorist, that the refinement of culture is apt to mean the desiccation of culture unless we manage while striving for the form of the upper levels of being to retain the content of the lower as well.

The great Spanish comedy of the sixteenth century is *Don Quixote*. The book which Cervantes ostensibly intended as an attack upon the absurdities of mediaeval chivalry has come to symbolize in a sublime manner the comedy of humanity itself—almost the homily of all limitations and finitude. The grand old man tilting against windmills will always remind us of the folly—and somehow the magnificence—of the limited human being endeavouring to resolve all his contradictions in a finite world where some limitation, and hence contradiction, is necessary. But Don Quixote was more than a reformer; he was also a divine clown. "For it was by making himself ridiculous that Don Quixote achieved his immortality."[90] As Unamuno observes, Pilate sought to make the Crucifixion into a comedy, but the people clamoured for tragedy, whereas "the human tragedy is the tragedy of Don Quixote, whose face was daubed with soap in order that he might make sport for the servants of the dukes and for the dukes themselves, as servile as their servants. 'Behold the madman!' they would have said."[91]

The classic revival was a revival only in the sense of renewed

[90] Miguel de Unamuno, *The Tragic Sense of Life* (London, 1931, Macmillan), p. 306.
[91] Op cit., p. 315.

attention to the classics, for these were at no time entirely forgotten. There are traces throughout the Middle Ages of Greek and Roman comedies which were read and recited if not performed from time to time. Terence was known as early as the eleventh century, and Aristophanes was performed at Oxford and Cambridge in the middle of the sixteenth. Plautus had been adapted for the Italian stage in the fifteenth century, and his influence spread throughout Europe. The Aristotelian distinction between comedy and tragedy had come to be the accepted norm: "Tragedy is narrative which concerns persons of high degree, is written in a lofty style, and beginning happily comes to a sad conclusion. Comedy, on the other hand, concerns itself with ordinary persons, uses humble and everyday language, and resolves its complications in a fortunate ending."[92]

The new religion of Protestantism, although later to assume a puritanical form, did not oppose at first the enjoyment of sensual pleasures. Indeed comedy was endorsed as a weapon to be employed against Catholicism, and in the sixteenth century, in England at least, fun was made of the high clergy.[93] The Renaissance was characterized by a revival of interest in the vividities and disorders of actuality. The old strictures of the mediaeval Church were sloughed off, and since the Church had represented whatever order there was, the limitations of the old order had come to be identified with order itself. Hence order was conceived as something which was essentially too confining. There was a renewal of interest in the sensible realities of the actual world here and now, and this world was filled as always with contradictions and disvalues, with unattained goals and interrupted striving. Thus the social order was new but in a sense non-revolutionary, and there was more play than criticism in comedy. Comedy was rendered the greater in that its criticisms began to be directed against the nature of things as they were found to be, and not

[92] Chambers, op. cit., vol. ii, p. 209.
[93] Chambers, op. cit., vol. ii, p. 220.

against the foibles of customs and institutions, although the latter came in for a light-hearted share.

The feeling of sheer play, however, permeates all Elizabethan and pre-Elizabethan comedy, from *Ralph Roister Doister* and *Gammer Gurton's Needle* to the comedies of Shakespeare. The Elizabethans "were never without their simple pleasures. They had the Cotswold games. They had their May Queen as of yore, and at Christmas time their Lord of Misrule, who made no trouble because he no longer ruled. He was merely carried into Church when the service was over and carried out again. They had bears to bait. Every township kept a bear for this laudable purpose. We are told that one petty borough which had the misfortune to lose its bear sold the Church Bible to buy another. Villages too poor to afford a bear were perforce content with humbler sports. A cat hung up in a leather bag as a target for crossbows, or a cock in an earthenware vessel to be stoned, or a few doves to be 'sealed' (blinded) for the sake of their strange, disordered flight."[94] The domestic or court fool was also the luxury of all those houses which could afford one, and the vari-coloured garments, the *marotte*, the bells and hood was an "all-licensed" and not an informal affair, although the symbolic hunched back must have been a common enough spectacle.

Adventure precludes laughter. The discovery of the actual world was a high adventure and did not admit of any sympathy for the poor. The number of paupers was tremendous due to the practice of enclosures and the destruction of the guilds. Poverty did not go unnoticed by the comedians. The comic poet, Nicholas Breton, observed the fact; but by and large the leading motive of comedy was the abundance of actual life and not the conditions of the living.

The Elizabethan playwrights are too many and too well known to require discussion here. Sufficient to point out the new technique, which was the Renaissance contribution to formal comedy, of mixing comedy and tragedy in the same

[94] Repplier, op. cit., p. 46.

plays. This method heightened the effect of abundance which was felt rather than realized, and though the tremendous formalism of the classic comedy had gone, there was "a definite aimlessness; a disorder that preserves the form of law."[95] Shakespeare covers the range from sheer nonsense to meaningful humour: the sarcasm of Iago, the burly comedy of Falstaff, the fantasy of Feste and of Edgar, the nonsense of his court fools. *Twelfth Night* and *Love's Labour's Lost* are comedies in the main, but it is in such a play as *Hamlet* that the contrast between comedy and tragedy is important, the critical understanding of what ought to be giving tremendous import to the emotional acceptance of what has to be. Both criticism and acceptance rested, however, upon an abundant knowledge of what actually is, which was the work of the Renaissance.

7. SEVENTEENTH-CENTURY COMEDY

The joyful return to an acquaintance with actuality in all its sensible affects which had characterized the Renaissance was succeeded by a century of consolidation. In the seventeenth century reason was largely thrown to the winds, and for the most part this meant abandoning common sense (which is a limited kind of rationality backed by a limited kind of experience), also. In England the comedians, who were particularly facile and superficial, seemed unaware of the measure of their acceptance of prevailing custom and opinion; they did not avoid criticism but rather saw no reason for it, and so limited themselves to the comedy of gaiety, licentiousness, and frivolity. The laughter was healthy enough but lacked significance. On the Continent, however, things were different. The classic influences had a stronger hold there; and in France Molière who might have been of the same sort as the British turned into a comedian of a higher order. In Italy there took place one of the strangest phenomena ever to represent comedy:

[95] C. C. Everett, *Poetry, Comedy and Duty* (Boston, 1890, Houghton Mifflin), p. 197.

the *Commedia dell' arte*, an influence which spread strongly also to France.

There rages much controversy as to whether the *Commedia dell' arte* had its origin in the Attelane farces of classic Rome or in more recent mediaeval sources. Was the Zani of the *Commedia* the Sannio of the Attelane plays or was he not? The problem remains open to speculation.[96] Suffice to point out, however, that the similarities are in some ways remarkable, and that there is a family resemblance between these two and the Old Comedy of Greece. There were certain stock characters and stock masks common to all three. The buffoon or clown whose nonsense contains cryptic wisdom, the magic doctor whose pomposities point to quackery but who successfully refuses to take death seriously, and the swaggering captain whose authority is not as strong as his bluff, all of whom began in the vulgar comedy of the folk which Aristophanes repudiated, have swirled around that great Greek writer and reappear again in Atella and in Renaissance Italy.

The fact that the *Commedia dell' arte* may have repeated these patterns without owing them to any direct influence would make their appearance an even more remarkable affair. For it would mean that certain forms of comedy begin to take on the authority of identification with certain inalienable forms of human behaviour, irrespective of place and date. The *Commedia dell' arte* had a genius all its own, however, and besides carrying on certain traditional stock masks and characters may be credited with having invented certain new ones which it came to regard as equally traditional. Some of the actors were intelligent and self-conscious comedians, and one who was a harlequin, Visentini, once said in words that are almost a definition of comedy itself,

Pour ce qui nous regarde, je vous prie de songer que nous sommes des étrangers, réduits pour vous plaire à nous oublier nous-mêmes.[97]

[96] Cf. Constant Mic, *La Commedia dell' arte* (Paris, 1927, Schiffrin), pp. 208 ff.

[97] C. Mic, op. cit., p. 19.

But as with the Atellane farces the comedy survived and triumphed over the comedians, and there are instances aplenty of famous actors in the Italian comedies who went through life by the names of the masks in which they played. There was little or no comedy in Germany of a strength sufficient to leave important traces, and the same may be said of France, with the exception of one man. Cyrano de Bergerac was a mediocre figure whose romantic appeal has been explored by Rostand. There was Boileau also; and there were some others. But none existed either on the Continent or in England to compare with Molière. Molière was a tragic figure, like every great comedian. Perhaps it is not possible to be a great comedian without the contrast of a dismal and even tragic private life. Profound comedy is a matter of publicity, but it seems to require the instrument of an off-set tragic privacy. Certainly Molière's life was unhappy enough for any great comedian, and comedy often appeared to him to be a matter of painful necessity.

Il y faut plaisanter;—he said—et c'est une étrange entreprise que celle de faire rire les honnêtes gens.[98]

The significance of a work of art is roughly commensurable by the number of important influences to which it has been susceptible. If a great many leading movements of the day succeed in leaving their mark upon a work without triumphing over the work's own peculiar characteristics which still manage easily to dominate, then the work is truly great. Molière's comedies rank highly by this test. They were strongly influenced by previous comedians, from Menander and Plautus to Boccaccio and Scarron, yet they survived these derivations— plagiarisms even. Whole scenes have been lifted from predecessors, yet the resultant whole is unmistakably Molière's. In France under the early reign of Louis XIV humanism was consolidating its gains. Life was very vivid, but the human

---

[98] Speech of Dorante in *La Critique de l'Ecole des Femmes*, Sc. 7.

beings in it consisted in large part of a network of errors which the comedies of Molière carefully unravel.

Typical of the change from the symbolism of the Middle Ages to the naturalism[99] of those centuries in which modern Western civilization was in its teens, is the change from the magic doctor to the modern quack. The magic doctor was a comic character because he symbolically restored the dead to life in order to demonstrate the ineffectuality of death upon the true values, but the doctor in Molière's comedies becomes an entirely different affair. For in *Le Médecin malgré lui* the doctor is comic because of the ineffectuality of his pretensions to cures and to esoteric medical knowledge. With Molière the ancient tradition has not been revived but has taken a new turn. The doctor was always a comic character because death was not taken seriously and the dead could always be restored to life. But with Molière it is the actual contemporary medical profession that is being held up to ridicule. This represents a lesser criticism and therefore a decline in comedy as compared with the Greeks. The shift is sadly indicative, although Molière continues to stand out as a strong figure.

The happy Elizabethan acquaintance with the pleasures of this actual world were rudely interrupted some years later by Cromwell's victories. The Restoration, which thought vainly that it had restored the abundant sense of life, was unaware that a deep undercurrent of design which had existed before was now missing. Criticism there was to be sure, but of trivialities only, and marked by cruelty rather than by sympathy. The comedies of the Restoration sound as though they were written by thieves set to catch thieves rather than by those who wished indirectly to affirm the eternal values. Cruelty, pain, and torture have often occurred in formal comedies but only for the incidental grotesqueries which attended them, and never for their own sake. The Elizabethans had their petty cruelties, but

The gallants of the Restoration who went for amusement to see the chained maniacs of Bedlam, and the women prisoners flogged

[99] Or, metaphysically speaking, from realism to nominalism.

at Bridewell, and a stallion baited by dogs, were on as wrong a track as any generation that trod before or after them.[100]

The comic writers, Congreve, Vanbrugh, Farquhar, Wycherley and others, had what Molière did not have: a keen perception of the smallest details of daily life. The British were empiricists in comedy, and then as now missed the larger issues: the general principles at work which had to be pointed out to them later. But they could find the little faults, the contemporary evils, with an unerring eye. Their shortsightedness, however, refused to allow them to see these evils as contemporary; they rather preferred to read them as human. Contemporary foibles were human foibles, to be recognized because never to be obliterated. Life had always been, it was, and it must always be a sordid affair of pettifogging. Such was the view of the Restoration. They could see no further; and consequently exchanged the enjoyment of comedy, with its incidental improvements, for the pursuit of pleasure.

As a consequence, "Society did not lack vigour, nor literature talent; men of the world were polished, writers inventive. There was a court, drawing-rooms, conversations, worldly life, a taste for letters, the example of France, peace, leisure, the influence of the sciences, politics, theology—in short, all the happy circumstances which can elevate the intellect and civilize manners. There was the vigorous satire of Wycherley, the sparkling dialogue and fine raillery of Congreve, the frank nature and animation of Vanbrugh, the manifold inventions of Farquhar, in brief, all the resources which might nourish the comic element."[101]

But what was the result? Exactly the opposite of what we should expect. Taine understood the situation so well that he must be quoted again. "Nothing came to a head; all was abortive. The age has left nothing but the memory of corruption; their comedy remains a reportory of viciousness; society has only a soiled elegance, literature a frigid wit. Their manners

[100] Repplier, op. cit., p. 68.
[101] H. A. Taine, *History of English Literature*, trans. N. Van Laun (Chicago, no date, Donahue), vol. i, p. 639.

were gross and trivial; their ideas are futile or incomplete. Through disgust and reaction a revolution was at hand in literary feeling and moral habits, as well as in general beliefs and political institutions. . . . The Englishman discovered that he was not monarchical, Papistical, nor sceptical, but liberal, Protestant, and devout. He came to understand that he was not a roisterer nor a worldling, but reflective and introspective. He contains a current of animal life too violent to suffer him without danger to abandon himself to enjoyment."[102]

Only to a century as hidebound with legal restrictions and moral restraints as the nineteenth would there appear to be anything to regret about the loss of that freedom which was so coercive in the seventeenth century. To-day we have the freedom and seek to retain it with the addition of some legal security. The Restoration appears to have had little else worth saving.

8. EIGHTEENTH-CENTURY COMEDY

The Renaissance marked a reaction against the limited rationality of the mediaeval Church, and the centuries of the revival of learning were also times of the discovery of the vivid values of actuality. The partial reaction of the seventeenth century consolidated the gains. The necessity for some kind of rationality is as deep as the understanding of nature, and the Reformation showed that even a mistaken rationality is better than no order at all. Reason, as it came to be conceived in the eighteenth century, was a contentless affair indeed. That conception of reason which holds it to be a substitute rather than a framework for values is apt to be restricting rather than liberating and thus itself antirational. The eighteenth century was a time of confusion for comedy. Comedy, as we have seen, wishes to criticize the limitations of what has been, in favour of what ought to be; but the fulfilment of this purpose requires an outworn system which is still standing and some sort of programme for the future which is yet to be introduced. Mediaeval

---

[102] Taine, ibid., vol. i, pp. 639-40.

and limited realism was already destroyed and there was no point in again pushing over straw men. *"Les philosophes"* (who were incidentally not really philosophers at all) maintained a naïve conception of sweet reasonableness which could be ridiculed well enough but which was not sufficiently strong to furnish the material for the ridicule exercised by great comedy. In such an atmosphere of ideas, comedy was apt to be both bewildered and too deeply bitter to be very funny.

This period marks the sharp decline of the superb *Commedia dell' arte*. The classic comic figures and masks which had been revived from ancient times, and which were destined to live again in another form, could not survive the dry air of the age of reason. "Quant aux fous et aux farceurs de l'ancienne comédie, ils ne purent supporter l'air du siècle de la Raison. . . . L'esprit du siècle de Voltaire et de Montesquieu était imbu de verité et de logique, et les joyeuses absurdites des masques italiens ne pouvait lui convenir."[103] Voltaire, who was also a comic writer, nevertheless represented the new comic spirit; the forms of the old comedy could not adapt themselves to it, and so perished. Goldoni, who was the most successful comic dramatist of eighteenth-century Italy, imitated Molière in writing of and for the middle classes, although his criticisms are less severe than the Frenchman's.

The most original comic figure of this period in Italy, and in some ways one of the great comic figures of all times, was the lover and adventurer, Casanova. Although chiefly pre-occupied with the pursuit of women, there was hardly an activity of the day in which Casanova did not have some interest or participation. He insisted that his love affairs, which were rarely sentimental, were always of benefit to women and a commentary on the infantilism of all other adult men. His adventures in the glove-manufacturing business, in high French finance, and in other prosaic as well as exotic enterprises, proved his life to be a comedy of the highest order. In so far as he ever took contemporary activities seriously, it was always

[103] C. Mic, op. cit., p. 234.

to show what rot the accepted systems were. Casanova implicitly understood the logic of ethics. Outwardly he claimed to uphold the customs and laws of the day and to be a rigid moralist, well aware that otherwise his kind of life would not have been possible for him. We cannot all be cheats and liars and philanderers; for then the system itself would break down. Casanova seems to have felt this. It is an amazing fact that he understood the function of his life perfectly, and admitted that Horace had always been his guide-book.[104] To be a philosopher is a wonderful disguise for an adventurer. Although his definition of philosophy was somewhat unorthodox,[105] he yet understood its nature, and always sincerely regarded himself as a philosopher. He even made a pilgrimage to the home of Voltaire, whom he held in great admiration.[106]

In Germany comedy did not in this period reach as high a point as it did in France. There was the *Jobsiade* of Kortum, the comic epic about a student who did everything but study, a proper enough subject for humour in Germany; and there was the humorous satire of Wieland, *Die Abderiten*; but little else worthy of note.

Comedy always has to have something formal to attack, some conventional norm the criticism of whose shortcomings can serve as the starting-point of humour. The great French comedians could find nothing of this nature in contemporary customs or political institutions. But there was a new philosophy, the mechanical materialism of the French Encyclopaedists and their followers, and this was chosen by the wits of the day as the object of their satires. Particularly worthy of mention is the comic drama of Destouches, which was a direct attack upon *les philosophes*. We have already mentioned Voltaire, whose *Candide* took its start from the ridicule of the dogmatic optimism of the *Théodicée* of Leibniz, who thought that he had been able to prove by reason alone that this is the best

[104] *The Memoirs of Giacomo Casanova di Seingalt*, trans. Arthur Machen (London, 1922, Casanova Society), vol. vi, p. 189.
[105] Op. cit., vol. iii, p. 154.   [106] Op. cit., vol. vi, pp. 187–210.

A Survey of the History of Comedy

of all possible worlds. *Candide* remains, however, like all superlative comedies, of permanent humorous value over and above the criticism of the particular contemporary object of its attack. This survival value is always found in comedy, which merely takes off a contemporary foible as the occasion for writing, and which goes beyond it to the fundamental criticism of some human limitation presenting itself as ineradicable. The value which uses contemporary points of departure is thus able to manifest itself unchanging by means of one changing form or another in every succeeding generation.

Comedy of the highest order is always crusading for a state of affairs so perfect that it can never be achieved. The comic purpose is so completely an affair of propaganda in this sense that it never appears to be propaganda at all. Eighteenth-century English comedy had retained its lustiness, but the growth of the democratic spirit was accompanied by a prosaic attitude toward life, a dull matter-of-fact-ness and an increasing reformatory tendency. Sheridan alone in the theatre succeeded in producing one or two plays out of a total of four that are worthy of ranking with England's best. Mrs. Malaprop of *The Rivals* is a justly celebrated character who has called attention permanently to the humour in the wrong use of long words that sound as though they ought to be correct. Sheridan's retreat from the theatre to politics was more of a loss to the theatre than a gain to politics. He was too scintillating to be profound for long. As Repplier observes, he could speak for three days at a time in Parliament, but probably made more remarks than were apposite in his casual conversation, as when he observed concerning the vanity of his patron, the Prince of Wales, "What his Royal Highness particularly prides himself upon is the late excellent harvest."

For the rest the comic theatre was interesting but hardly important. There was Samuel Foote whose wit was too personal to remain once the personalities criticized had died. There were what Goldsmith derided, the "Tradesmen's Tragedies," realistic domestic plays of no particularly great quality. England

63

was swamped with what Allerdyce Nicoll has termed the "humanitarian drama of sensibility."[107] But besides these, Fielding's *Tom Thumb* is worthy of mention as a satire on the absurd convention of the contemporary popular tragedies. John Gay's *The Beggar's Opera* is in some ways the most honest piece of comedy that the eighteenth-century theatre has to offer. The suggestion that there is some honour among thieves was not as new as the notion that there is class consciousness and a sober knowledge of social function among them. And the further hint that the superior classes are not all they are supposed to be, made by contrast, shows the play to be true comedy in a fine and complete sense.

In general, Bernard Shaw has observed, "On the stage, comedy as a destructive, derisory, critical, negative art, left the theatre when sublime tragedy perished. From Molière to Oscar Wilde we had a line of comic playwrights who, if they had nothing fundamentally positive to say, were at least in revolt against falsehood and imposture, and were not only, as they claimed, 'chastening morals by ridicule,' but, in Johnson's phrase, 'clearing our minds of cant, and thereby shewing an uneasiness in the presence of error which is the surest symptom of intellectual vitality.' "[108]

For the most part, however, the eighteenth-century theatre in England marked a definite decline. It became self-conscious and ingrown, its criticisms "literary" or inconsequential. "Farce, ballad-plays, pantomimes, dancers, performing animals of all kinds, became immensely popular even in the regular theatres—perhaps because of the new audience, the honest citizens and their wives, who now thronged them."[109]

Before leaving the theatre a word should be said about the puppet-shows of Punch and Judy. Of obscure Italian origin,

[107] *Lesser English Comedies of the Eighteenth Century* (Oxford, 1931, University Press), p. x.
[108] Bernard Shaw, *Back to Methuselah* (New York, 1931, Brentano), p. xciv.
[109] *Eighteenth-Century Comedy*, W. D. Taylor ed. (Oxford, 1929, University Press), p. ix.

the traditional play of Punch and Judy was known in England in the seventeenth century but obtained terrific popularity in the eighteenth, dwindling soon thereafter to a modest position in the English theatre which it occupies to this day. Professor Cornford points out that the puppet-play of Punch bears unmistakable resemblance to the traditional folk-plays which characterized the festivals of the primitive fertility rites of classic Greek and Roman times.

However, it was not the theatre in the eighteenth century which most perfectly expressed the ideas of the times. It was rather literature, or, shall we say literature and Hogarth, because there were no other painters or draughtsmen quite in his class. Hogarth's work is extremely funny, and yet, as Walpole said, "He observes the true end of comedy—reformation." Of Samuel Johnson, it can be noted that he expressed, or rather by believing so profoundly in it, ridiculed the uncompromising empiricism of the prevailing English philosophy. Whatever could not be smelled, touched, heard, or tasted obviously could have no existence. He refuted Berkeleyan idealism by kicking a stone, and he had a simply terrifying notion of what was normal and what was not in the way of customs and morals. From this distance of years, the solidity of Dr. Johnson seems to be without foundation, and we are in a position to appreciate his true, though largely unconscious humour.

A new type of humour now appeared in England: the prose comedy as contained in the novels by Fielding and Smollett, and the prose satire as written by Sterne. Fielding, with one eye on the lost *Margites* of Homer, preferred to call his novels "comic epics." Fielding's novels began by making fun of the solemnities of Richardson; he then turned, in his maturest work, *Tom Jones*, to make fun of the customs and morals of contemporary life in general. Fielding had been trained for the law, and in his last novel he took as the object of his ridicule the constitution of England. Smollet, somewhat more influenced by the picaresque novels of Spain, threw the brunt of his attack in random fashion and did not succeed in hitting anything very profound. Into his work, too, there began to creep the sober vein of sentimental romanticism which should be a topic for rather than a method of humour.

Sterne more than the writers of the "comic epics" was the one who in the eighteenth century attacked in candid fashion the customs and institutions of the day. There is nothing about Sterne's books, and especially *Tristram Shandy*, which appears to be exactly what it ought to be, nothing that a serious adherent of custom, a conventionalist, could approve. Even the typographical set-up is messed about, as though to indicate that tradition can expect little compromise in the contents of the pages. Sterne, like T. E. Lawrence, wants "to show what rot the systems are." Sterne's disorder is not accidental; he was a careful worker, and once said that he had destroyed more than he had ever allowed to be printed. His effects, whatever they were, were intended. He was a fully conscious, albeit not the greatest, votary of Whirl, the vortex of humour which clears the air for new customs and institutions and the building up of new traditions by the simple method of making a ludicrous hash of the old. "Obviously a god is hidden in *Tristram Shandy*, his name is Muddle. . . . quite to reveal his awful features was not Sterne's intention; that is the deity that lurks behind his masterpiece—the army of unutterable muddle, the universe as a hot chestnut."[110] As Foster recalls, it was Dr. Johnson who wrote in 1776, "Nothing odd will do long: *Tristram Shandy* did not last!" There must have been others less sentient who had a foretaste of "my Uncle Toby's immortality."

9. NINETEENTH-CENTURY COMEDY

By the nineteenth century the battle against the old restrictions of the theological Middle Ages had been won so long that

[110] E. M. Foster, *Aspects of the Novel* (London, 1927, Arnold), p. 146.

the issue itself was entirely forgotten. Freedom there was, more freedom than prevailed even in the eighteenth century or the seventeenth, but there was also something else. There was a complete retrenchment within the walls of this new freedom, which was itself constitutive of a new kind of restriction. One of the first things to be ruled out was the possibility of any kind of change. The perfect order had been discovered, or rather the perfect freedom, and woe to him who spoke critically of established customs and enshrined institutions. As a consequence, there was gaiety in the nineteenth century, but there was no comedy. For instance, Taine, who recognized the universal nature of comedy, observed that comedy "consists in leading by an agreeable path to general notions,"[111] and Meredith, as we have seen, laid down the rule that comedy was not to disturb anything fundamental.

Gaiety was allowed, yes, for it is one of the lasting tributes to the human being that under any and all circumstances he manages to retain some minimal quantity of gaiety, of good spirits and laughter, which adversity cannot entirely suppress. But somehow there is louder laughter when there is deeper criticism, and we find that the periods of great comedy are also revolutionary times. "The greatest height of heroism to which an individual, like a people, can attain is to know how to face ridicule," said Unamuno,[112] but the people of the nineteenth century were hiding behind the sanctuary of their "time-honoured" customs and institutions, and were not ready to face ridicule. Despite this situation, and not because of it, some comedy managed to get itself enacted and written.

The English comedy of this period may properly begin with Byron. Byron was a true comedian, but he was romantic and he was bitter. His contacts were chiefly with abandoned periods and forgotten ideals, whereas his criticism of contemporary foibles seldom cut very deep, not because of any frank policy

---

[111] H. A. Taine, *History of English Literature*, trans. N. Van Laun, (Chicago, no date, Donahue), vol. i, p. 618.
[112] Op. cit., p. 315.

of avoidance, but because Byron was a child of his times and it did not occur to anyone then that anything very important could be challenged.

The outstanding exception to these remarks was Charles Dickens. His attacks upon the corruption of the jails and the orphanages and similar social abuses of the times were in favour of a basic humanitarianism rather than of any broad world outlook. Nevertheless they were attacks and they were funny, and they did have far-reaching social consequences. These were of two kinds, we may say. First, the necessary social reforms in the operation of jails, poorhouses, and orphanages were shortly forthcoming, and this after all was one of the main and direct purposes of many of Dickens's books. Secondly, Dickens in the course of the process succeeded in eliciting some immortal comic characters whose foibles are universal and whose quirks are human. Mr. Micawber, a few figures from the *Pickwick Papers*, and many others, will not soon be forgotten. Dickens is easily the great humorist of the nineteenth century.

This achievement marked the top so far as nineteenth-century humour is concerned; but there was also a bottom, plumbed by the practical jokes (of which the century was so fond) of Theodore Hook, and the obvious and tortured puns of Thomas Hood. Hood's jokes, many of which resulted in serious and painful consequences of a public nature, seem to have had little excuse for being. Hood's puns, however, were redeemed somewhat by his belated but earnest attack upon the scandalous poor laws in *The Song of the Shirt* and similar poems.

Comedy in England found its proper and natural home with the Hollands who ran a sort of salon for the leaders of the Whig party. Events appear more amusing to the "outs" than they do to the "ins," and comedy is ever on the side of the minority party. To those in power it is not amusing to be ridiculed, and to those securely in power (which, theoretically at least, in a democracy can never be) it is unpatriotic or at the very least merely uninteresting. But the wits held forth gaily at Holland House, and not least among them was Sydney Smith, a clergyman who is chiefly remembered for his sense of humour. Others might have been amusing but Smith's comedy was, as George Ticknor has noted,[113] "logic in masquerade." Even Whigs come to power sooner or later, however, and then comedy passes to other political affiliations. Holland House humour still gives off a faint air of professionalism which raises its claim to a higher kind of comedy, a status to which it was entirely unequal.

Of the comedy of Lewis Carroll it is hard to make an estimation. Originally written for children, it proved to be adequate to its audience, and has outlived that generation. The social criticism in Carroll's work is deeply imbedded, but it is present, and there are moments in *Alice in Wonderland* which have rarely been excelled by any other comic writer. Nevertheless, despite this high praise, the work of Carroll has its limitations and as a whole appears to bear the unmistakable stamp of sanctimonious superficiality which impressed everything in the English nineteenth century. Much the same criticism can also be levelled at the comic opera writers, Gilbert and Sullivan. Their particular objects of attack were the foibles of the British, and while they did not spare their ridicule, it is all done with the lightness that indicates that no genuine harm is meant. The collaborators shared the apparent conviction that although they were daring to make fun of insular customs and institutions they could not be taken too seriously because the British way of doing things was the inevitably right and final way.

Samuel Butler, in his satire *Erewhon* and its successor, and in the *Note-Books*, is in some ways most typical of the period with which we are dealing. Butler was alive to the weaknesses of the ruling middle class; he was also seriously affected by the Darwinian theory; both appear with their bones exposed in his pages, although there is nothing political about the

---

[113] Repplier, op. cit., p. 151.

former. Alas, however, the character of the stolid Butler protrudes also, and behind all his wit and penetration lurks an inevitable belief in the British which no amount of comedy can ever dispel. Butler was capable of insights which surpassed his loyalties. He was an advocate of the supremacy of reason, but his unawareness of the fact, made understandable by the confused psychologism which prevailed undisputed during the period in which he lived, was disastrous. "True humour is more common than those are who can see it,"[114] he once remarked, a wholly realistic expression. Yet men cannot be great humorists unless there is something worthy which their humour is defending.

It is with some hope that we turn to a consideration of comedy in France. There the nineteenth century offers, as a matter of fact, a host of comic writers but none that is worthy of mention with the single exception of Balzac. And here Balzac's name is introduced for a few books only, chief among them the lusty and uproarious *Contes Drolatiques*. Through its pages we feel that the French were a natural people, that they did not cultivate the intellectual function of abstraction to any high degree, but that they were, in a way that surely animals are not, aware of the possibilities of the sensible life: commonsense reasoning and the enjoyment of the senses. They were keenly alive to the values of an actual existence here and now, and could not allow themselves to be devoted too strongly to any remote goal.

But if this kind of philosophy has its eventual drawbacks, it also has immediate compensations. The peasant brutalities notwithstanding (and these were plenty, as Zola has shown us), we get the distinct impression that the Frenchman of the nineteenth century laughed a great deal. Not for nothing did Paris become the celebrated capital of Europe. The comic operas of Offenbach and others, the vivid style of life, which Proust has recorded so well, the cabarets and night life, and *la vie gaie* in general, were to be found nowhere else. France indeed has

[114] *Note-Books* (New York, 1926, Dutton), p. 165.

always afforded the temporary relief which enables Englishmen to go on being Englishmen. But in the nineteenth century all of Europe looked to France for the style and enjoyment which makes ordinary existence bearable.

There is much to be learned from a study of Russian comedy. Gogol, the greatest of Russian comic writers, based his work chiefly upon the abuses of the official class. Both *The Government Inspector* and *Dead Souls* are political satires in which the casting of human types manages to rise above the special subject-matter selected for ridicule. Gogol has been called the Russian Dickens, although his criticism of government is more far-reaching. Goncharov, another Russian comic writer, has given us what was regarded as the typical Russian character of the period. In *Oblomov* (first published in 1858) the protagonist of that name is a petty landowner who is the epitome of lassitude. He is too lazy to get out of bed, too inert to dress himself, too vacillating and weak-willed to render any important decisions affecting his own life and career. Russians and others agreed that Goncharov had put his finger upon the true Russian character. Now that the Revolution has got everybody in the country dashing madly about constructing an industrial system in the shortest possible time, the conception of the Russian is one of the greatest energy and enterprise. We may well ask whether there is such a thing as national character.

In Germany, Goethe, who perhaps belongs with the eighteenth century, published the first part of *Faust* in 1808. *Faust*, like Dante's great poem, is a divine comedy. That is to say, it plays upon the eternal themes of God and the Devil and the struggle between them, which is more or less the drama of actuality itself. Mephistopheles from its Greek roots is a name which means "the-spirit-that-denies," and the character is that of an arch-comedian. Great comic epics sum up epochs. What Dante did for the Middle Ages, Goethe has done for the Renaissance. Each marks the end of a period, neatly disposing, by means of comic ridicule, of its myth. Can we imagine a character in Dante speaking of God as Mephistopheles does?

> From time to time I like the Old Man well,
> And I must keep from breaking with him.
> It is quite pretty when so great a man
> Will himself talk so humanly with the Devil.[115]

Goethe's poem exposes the Christian legend and thus prepares us for the scientific myth. It is not for nothing that alchemy plays so large a part in the poem.

Only one other German comedian of the nineteenth century is worthy of mention, and he happens to have chosen to live the greater part of his life in France. Heinrich Heine was escaping from a severe German effort to absorb the classic civilization and to swallow the Renaissance belatedly in a single gulp. The atmosphere did not admit of any laughter. Heine's travel accounts and his satirical lyrics reveal a spirit aware of much that was out of proportion; but its weakness was that it remained essentially literary—the same difficulty which prevents the English Beerbohm from being a great comedian. There is a romantic strain in Heine, a longing after lost orders, that tends to belittle all his efforts at comedy, though some are amusing enough.

We turn now for the first time to American comedy. The nineteenth century in American life was the account of a nation grown weary of building. It must have been a relief to have native comedians about; yet when we come to examine the fruits of their labours we are compelled to admit that it had a purely contemporary value. To turn the pages of an anthology of American humour[116] is to discover native types, a native dialect, and a native way of looking at things. But somehow none of it is permanently worth while. Artemus Ward understood something of the nature of comedy when he compared it with an uneven grindstone, but his deliberate misspellings are no longer very funny. The type of the Yankee and the fron-

---

[115] *Faust*, Part I, "Prologue in Heaven" (trans. mine).
[116] Walter Blair, ed., *Native American Humour* (1800–1900) (New York, 1937, American Book).

tiersman must have been amusing at one time, but they have disappeared, and nothing remains over and above these contemporary types to make the comedy itself worth saving.

We have reached the end of our survey of the history of comedy. From the point of view of a study of comedy, the nineteenth-century variety might be taken as very indicative. Its superficialities were the calm which came before the storm. Comedy is a very limited field, but were enough known and the presentation sufficiently logical, the history of the world could be presented faithfully from the point of view of any speciality. Comedy is a reflection of all that goes on, and high comedy selects significant trends in the development of a given period. The kind of sanctimonious regard in which the people of the nineteenth century held their customs and institutions is duly recorded in the comedy of the times. The attitude could not (and indeed did not) last. We shall in a later chapter discover what happened to it.

CHAPTER II

Some Classical Theories of Comedy

I. REALISTIC THEORY: PLATO

THE history of the theory of comedy properly begins with the philosophy of Plato. Earlier theories there must have been, but none are known. Although Plato established the implicit realism of the Greeks on a sound basis, and suggested a philosophical system on the broad assumption that being of any sort is an impossibility unless its independence of knowledge be accepted, he is not generally interpreted in that manner to-day. Rather has Plato's name among the moderns come to be identified with a subjective idealism, with the notion that all being as well as all intelligibility is mental. Platonism is called to the aid of the identification of philosophy with psychology, an error of which it is only partially guilty. The bias of most of Plato's writings lies rather in favour of the independent status of a set of possible ideas and values, which can enter into and affect this actual world anywhere and at any time, but which are themselves unaffected by such participation in actuality.

It is in terms of this realistic philosophy that we must approach Plato's theory of comedy; otherwise we might be misled. For Plato acknowledged the objective existence of the comic but was chiefly concerned with its effect upon the observer. That which is comic contains a contradiction; but it is with the conflicting sensations aroused by this contradiction that the observer is mainly concerned. Suppose that a terrible, and evidently inexorable, fate arises, from which there is no escape. To the observing subject this is tragic, and he fears for the safety of himself and his fellows. Suddenly, he realizes, the fate is not a fate after all, since it is not able to put its threat into effect, and so he rejoices over its impotence. Impotence masquerading as fate—this is the essential nature of comedy for Plato. We see this illustrated in comic characters on the stage, by the boastful man who is at heart a coward: Bacchus pretending to be Mars.[1]

Impotence masquerading as fate: a perfectly logical understanding of comedy, but at the same time one which never lets it be forgotten that comedy does have psychological effects. For to be amused by the power of fate when it turns out to be not a power at all but only the appearance of power is to undergo a certain emotional stress which has its end-product in laughter. Such a viewpoint in its conflict with realistic leanings was sure to produce an eventual disapproval of comedy. For to a thorough-going objectivist, as Plato at times was, anything whose sole claim to being is subjective is sure to be suspect.

We may note the outcome in another passage. Plato, in his Spinoza-like demand for the suppression of the passions as the only means toward "happiness and virtue," regarded the effect of comedy as something like a deception. "There are jests," he says, "which you would be ashamed to make yourself, and yet when you hear them in comedy, or in prose, you are greatly amused by them, and are not at all disgusted by their unseemliness. The case of pity is repeated: there is a principle in human nature which is disposed to raise a laugh, and this which you once restrained by reason, because you were afraid of being thought a buffoon, is now let out again; and having stimulated the risible faculty at the theatre, you are betrayed unconsciously to yourself into playing the comic poet at home."[2]

This is the lamentable Plato of the stern and puritanical later days. How well we have come to know him! Yet as always, we have only to take away that aspect in order to disclose lurking beneath some logical truths which are independent of

[1] Aristophanes, *The Frogs* (George Allen & Unwin).

[2] *Republic*, 10. 606.

75

morality. Throughout Plato's infrequent discussions of comedy, the psychologistic twist with its ascetic prejudices is seen warring with the genuinely objective theory of comedy which is presented in the description of impotence masquerading as fate.

There are few references to comedy in Plato, and all of them treat of it as the exposure of real impotence behind the appearance of power. The passage in the *Philebus*[3] is but a series of examples of this conception of comedy. We may cite the account of powerlessness taking the form of ignorance. "Those who are weak and unable to revenge themselves, when they are laughed at, may be truly called ridiculous. . . . Ignorance in the powerful is hateful and horrible, because hurtful to others both in reality and in fiction; but powerless ignorance may be reckoned, and in truth is, ridiculous." In his later works Plato pretended to an extremely low opinion of comedy, holding that it was fit only for slaves and strangers,[4] an opinion which seems to have been dictated more by political requirements than by anything else. For Plato gave great importance to the holding of power in its physical sense, an understandable prejudice since he elsewhere defined being itself as power. And since comedy was to be the revelation of impotence behind a pretended power, it was surely not to be discovered in the supreme leaders of the state, nor to be seriously treated by anyone except in the plainest jest and then only by inferior persons.

This rather crude interpretation of his own understanding of comedy is, fortunately, implicitly corrected in other dialogues of Plato. The *Symposium* itself is one grand comedy, comedy in the highest sense of the word, and there is nothing mean about it. Thus it replaces, by transcending, the explicit definition of comedy given by Plato in his later and less compromising works. That Plato could take comedy in good stead,

---

[3] *Philebus*, 48–50.
[4] *Laws*, 7. 816–17: "He should command slaves and hired strangers to imitate such things, but he should never take any serious interest in them himself." See also *Laws*, 11. 935–6; *Republic*, 3. 394.

is well illustrated in the *Apology*[5] where Socrates reminds his accusers of the satire which Aristophanes levelled against him in *The Clouds*; and again in the *Symposium*[6] itself, where Alcibiades speaks of Socrates in the very words used originally by Aristophanes, "in our streets, stalking and jetting like a brent-goose, and casting his eyes about askance."

In Plato's theory we see that comedy is never very far from tragedy, since the logical inexorability of fate which in tragedy has the power to make good its threat, in comedy is seen to be weak; yet by outward form at the beginning of any sequence of events they are both the same. So comedy becomes the avoidance of the terrible outcome of the events which were threatened in tragedy. Thus, as Plato says, "the true artist in tragedy was an artist in comedy also."[7] The difference between them relies merely on an exposure of the fact that power is not what at first it was supposed to be.

Plato's theory amounts in effect to the exposure of contradictions in actuality, and thus indirectly to the demand for a better state of affairs. Where tragedy deals with the substance of power, comedy is more concerned with contradictions revealed in the form of the absence of power. Thus tragedy is largely an affair of feeling, the feeling of the inexorable power of fate, while comedy is largely an intellectual affair, being concerned with the issue of logical contradictions. Plato is finally seen to be presenting a wholly objective and independent theory of comedy. Yet it is not with this theory but with the emotional effect of the recognition of the comic that Plato is preoccupied. He wants to note just what the effect of the observation of the comic is on the observer. This effect proves to be the arousal first of terrific fear, then of release, and finally of laughter at the needlessness of the fear. Or, for instance, if the object of comedy is a boastful man, we envy and admire him, and then when we realize that his boasts were in vain, we laugh at our own unfounded admiration and envy.

[5] *Apology*, 19. [6] *Symposium*, 221. [7] Op. cit., 223.

Plato was not unaware, however, that the situation could easily be reversed. The fool, the bumpkin, or the ignoramus, might at any time reveal suddenly to those who were laughing at him that his object was the logical pursuit of truth, goodness, and beauty. Alcibiades, in speaking of the virtues of Socrates beneath his rough and uncomely exterior, says, "his words are like the images of Silenus which open; they are ridiculous when you first hear them; he clothes himself in language that is like the skin of the wanton satyr—for his talk is of pack-asses and smiths and cobblers and curriers, and he is always repeating the same thing in the same words, so that any ignorant or inexperienced person might feel disposed to laugh at him; but he who opens the bust and sees what is within will find that they are the only words which have a meaning in them, and also the most divine, abounding in fair images of virtue, and of the widest comprehension."[8]

Comedy which is intellectual must be without relaxation, ever on the alert. For we can never be sure when contradictions will present themselves in actuality and when they will not. We have sloughed off the memory of Silenus as anything more than a fat, jovial, and drunken lout; but according to the Greek tradition he often fell asleep, and was at this time in the power oɪ mortals, and could become an inspired prophet when properly tended by the populace. It is here that prophecy becomes indistinguishable from comedy.

2. REALISTIC THEORY: ARISTOTLE

We need not dwell too long upon Aristotle's theory of comedy, since it does not differ sufficiently from Plato's to bring up any radically new points for discussion. The age-old belief that Aristotle's thought was based on a revolt against Plato is beginning to be abandoned, and the more correct notion that Aristotle was a Platonist who wished to categorize Platonism, while allowing himself the liberty of correcting

[8] *Symposium,* 221–2.

Some Classical Theories of Comedy

some of the Platonic excesses, is being substituted for it.[9] Thus in the case of comedy, Aristotle is not very far from Plato, but the former wished to remove the slur which the latter had placed on comedy by considering it fit only for slaves and strangers.

Accordingly, Aristotle transferred the ignominy from the comedians to the subject-matter of comedy itself. The laughable for Aristotle is a species of the base or the ugly. "Comedy is an *imitation* of persons of an inferior moral bent. . . . It consists in some blunder or ugliness that does not cause pain or disaster, an obvious example being the comic mask which is ugly and distorted but not painful."[10] This, as we can readily see by making a comparison, is merely a restatement of Plato's fate which is comic because it is unable to carry its threat into effect—the avoidance of tragedy. "Pleasure," says Aristotle, "belongs to comedy, where the deadliest of legendary foes, like Orestes and Aegisthus, become friends, and quit the stage without any one slaying or being slain."[11] The traditional death, so often celebrated by the tragic poets, offers in comedy the surprise of a harmless ending, which is pleasing yet sufficiently ridiculous to be amusing also.

Aristotle's understanding of the psychological effects of comedy is not the modern one. While modern critics tend to identify the effect of comedy (as laughter) with comedy itself, Aristotle shows in various passages that he must have implicitly understood the realistic distinction between the logical nature of comedy and its psychological effects. As Cooper observes, "that there is a comic, as well as a tragic, catharsis (i.e. emotional purgation) may probably be inferred,"[12] an inference depending mainly on a short passage in the *Politics*, 8. 7. Aristotle, however, must have been acquainted with the statement

---

[9] Werner Jaeger, *Aristotle* (Oxford, 1934, Clarendon Press).
[10] Aristotle, *Poetics*, 5.   [11] *Poetics*, 13.
[12] Lane Cooper, *An Aristotelian Theory of Comedy* (New York, 1922, Harcourt, Brace), p. 131. Throughout the chapter a deep indebtedness must be acknowledged to this invaluable source book on the classical history of the theory of comedy.

of Plato earlier cited,[13] which amounts in effect to a catharsis theory of comic reference. Elsewhere, however, Cooper says,[14] "the function in comedy of suspense, with a cheated expectation ending in a release of mental energy, is hinted at by a number of passages in Aristotle." Aristotle's interest in the psychological effect of comedy has in fact a very scientific ring. The scattered passages cited by Cooper[15] show an Aristotle who was very well aware of the laughter of infants[16] in various stages, and under varying conditions, such as that of tickling. He was also concerned with the arousal of laughter through tickling in adults,[17] as this differed with different sensitive areas of the body. In each case, Aristotle hazarded a guess as to the probable cause.

In other ways, Aristotle went much further in the understanding of comedy than did Plato. For instance, Aristotle understood the general nature of the comic art of the theatre, and stated that it applied to the general rather than to the particular,[18] that is to say he thought that the criticism implied in comedy went further than the immediate occasion of its invention. Moreover, despite the inferred comic catharsis, it seemed to Aristotle that the subject-matter of comedy is yet independent. Tragedy seemed to be exhausted of its purpose of purgation through pity and terror, while comedy remained an objective fact. For instance, Aristotle constantly refers to the plot of a comedy as the *logos*, and he elsewhere says, "If anyone says he had washed himself in vain because the sun was not eclipsed, he would be laughed at, since there is no causal connection between this and that."[19] Only a thoroughgoing empirical rationalism could speak, through the same investigator and speculator, of observations on the laughter

[13] See above, p. 75.   [14] Op. cit., p. 68.
[15] Lane Cooper, op. cit., pp. 162–5.
[16] Aristotle, *De Generatione Animalium*, 5. 1; *Historia Animalium*, 7. 10.
[17] *De Partibus Animalium*, 3. 10; *Problems*, 35. 6, 35. 8, 11. 13 and 11. 15.
[18] *Poetics*, 9.   [19] *Physica Auscultatio*, 2. 6.

of children and also of the necessity for causal connection in comedy.

Aristotle understood, too, in a way which Plato never expressed, the ideal nature of comedy. This followed logically from his understanding of the ideal nature of art. Aristotle quotes approvingly the dictum of Sophocles that the people and situations in his plays were not as actual people and situations are, for this was rather the manner of Euripides. For, said Sophocles, his own people and situations were not presented as they are but rather as they ought to be. Comedy, Aristotle pointed out, always deals with inferior people, with low personages,[20] presumably with their inferiorities pointed toward what ought to be and away from what is. For what other justification could there be for the insistence of comedy upon the shortcomings of humanity? Finally, the demonstration of the ideal nature of comedy is referred by Aristotle back to the problem of ethics. Just as the psychological justification of tragedy was laid to purgation through pity and terror, comedy was by analogy referred to purgation through pleasure.

But, as we have already seen, something of the purpose of comedy remained over after the pleasure was exhausted. Pleasure brings relaxation, but then pleasure is not the end of life, and we relax only in order to return to our serious tasks refreshed and more capable of shouldering them. "It appears to be foolish and utterly childish to take serious trouble and pains for the sake of amusement. But to amuse oneself with a view to being serious seems to be right, as Anacharsis says; for amusement is a kind of relaxation, and it is because we can not work for ever that we need relaxation. Relaxation, then, is not an end. We enjoy it as a means to activity; but it seems that the happy life is a life of virtue, and such a life is serious —it is not one of mere amusement."[21]

There is, so to speak, a logical structure of comedy, left over after the subtraction of its psychological effects, which contributes toward the serious aims of life, as hinted at here and

[20] *Poetics*, 2.   [21] *Nichomachean Ethics*, 10. 6.

there in Aristotle's analysis and adumbrated in the ethical notion which is left unexplained. We are told that comedy causes pleasure which in turn serves a serious purpose; and there is also another way in which comedy is put at the service of serious pursuits, but of this we are told nothing. Suffice to say here, however, that Aristotle well understood that the realism of comedy cannot by its very nature fail to be appropriately symbolical, and hence a call to improvement.

3. LATER GREEK COMMENTATORS: THE *TRACTATUS COISLINIANUS*, JAMBLICHUS AND PROCLUS

The next important work on the theory of comedy is the fragment which is known as the *Tractatus Coislinianus*.[22] This appears to be a Greek work, and scholars have dated it in the neighbourhood of the first century B.C. It is a condensed version of a theory of comedy, and evidently derives from Aristotle, although its author is unknown. On internal evidence, it is clearly an attempt to do for the theory of comedy what Aristotle's *Poetics* does for the theory of tragedy, and is presumably close to what Aristotle himself might have written on the subject.

The *Tractatus* takes for granted that comedy is an affair of the theatre, and does not attempt to concern itself with what may be described as informal comedy: casual humour accidentally appreciated. One branch of mimetic poetry is the dramatic form "directly presenting action." This branch is divided into comedy, tragedy, mimes and satyr-dramas. Thus comedy, like tragedy, is a subdivision of mimetic poetry.

Of course, assigning comedy to this place in a categorical system presupposes a theory of comedy. It has already been asserted by the classification that comedy is an imitation of action. But this does not as yet distinguish it from tragedy. It may be noted, however, that the imitation of action without any special emphasis would be neither comic nor tragic. No

[22] See Lane Cooper, op. cit., chap. iii.

actual situation can, as a matter of fact, be reproduced in its exact detail and complete vividity. Representative art often succeeds in being great art only because of the failure of its explicit programme. The attempt to reproduce in every detail some actual situation succeeds only in placing an emphasis on detail itself which the original situation did not make. For the original situation contained no such striving over exactness of detail, and moreover enjoyed a unity throughout its details which the imitation usually lacks. Francis Bacon once remarked that there could be no true art which did not have some strangeness in the proportions. It is this distortion which constitutes the criticism comedy always displays.

The *Tractatus* distinguishes between comedy and tragedy by noting that comedy is "an imitation of an action that is ludicrous and imperfect." The selection for imitation of only those actual occasions which are "ludicrous and imperfect" implies a highly critical canon of selection. Thus it recognizes the essentially critical nature of comedy. Were this criticism merely a negative affair meant to condemn actual customs and institutions for their imperfections and not affirmative of anything better, comedy would be, from one point of view at least, equivalent to abuse. But the *Tractatus* warns against any such limitation. "Comedy," it says, "differs from abuse, since abuse openly censures the bad qualities attaching, whereas comedy requires the so-called emphasis. . . ." Here the manuscript is unfinished. It is indeed unfortunate that we can never know what the "emphasis" was to be on; but we are safe in hazarding the guess that it was to be on something positive. However, the fact that it was an emphasis *other* than the censuring of bad qualities, is enough to support our point. Comedy, according to the *Tractatus*, is certainly a criticism of actuality and an affirmation of something else, which presumably is to be preferred to things as they are.

The Aristotelian approach is found almost intact in the psychological aspect of the *Tractatus*. The effect of comedy is that of purgation of the emotions through pleasure and laughter. This hedonistic theory is made to cover the entire psychological aspect, and the fact that the purging of the emotions, or catharsis, may be only one of the psychological effects of comedy is not recognized in this fragment of comic theory.

Like the great Greek comic dramatists, and indeed like the great dramatists of all time, the author of the *Tractatus* recognized that comedy is quicker than tragedy to break through the traditional rigid patterns prescribed for the exercise of the dramatic art. Thus it overthrows all fixed dramatic forms and flows easily into its own channels. What is true of the dramatic form is also true of the language employed. In contrast with tragedy, the purposes of comedy require no classic language of the stage. "The diction of comedy is the common, popular language. The comic poet must endow his personages with his own native idiom, but must endow an alien with the alien idiom." This warning must not be read as part of the "mimetic" programme. If comedy were entirely a mimetic affair, there would have been no need to distinguish it from abuse. But to be critical, comedy must be contemporary, and nothing is calculated to call attention to contemporaneity half so much as the use of the common idiom of the day.

The *Tractatus* has no great value in itself. It proposes nothing new for comedy which could not have been equally well deduced by others from the general theories set forth by Aristotle in the *Poetics* and elsewhere. Its importance lies rather in the lesson it teaches of the widespread acceptance of the implicit realistic point of view which the Greek mind brought to bear upon all abstract principles. The writings of Plato and Aristotle represent the highest reaches of an implicit realism which was prevalent for centuries afterwards. The divergence of our modern orientation from theirs can be observed in the way the theory of comedy has come to be regarded in so far as its psychological aspects are concerned. For the Greeks, laughter was the psychological *effect* of comedy. For the subjectively oriented modern, laughter is not the effect

Some Classical Theories of Comedy

of comedy but is constitutive of comedy itself. Laughter for the modern investigator *is* comedy; and so he seeks for an analysis of comedy in the physiologico-psychological mechanism. Of this approach, the anonymous author of the *Tractatus* was not guilty. But the *Tractatus* is to be numbered among the last of the realistic theories of comedy. Later, the psychological view grew rapidly in favour, and the realistic lesson was for the time lost.

The exaggerated realism of the neo-Platonic school which followed hard upon the decline of Athenian philosophy was slow to distort the theory of comedy initiated by the classic Greeks. Jamblichus of Chalcis, who is, somewhat doubtfully, given credit or having written the *De Mysteriis*, is led into several paragraphs of discussion of the theory of comedy by reference to the phallic consecrations which took place in the spring.[23] The phallus was representative of all productive generation, and, says Jamblichus, "the obscene language that is uttered indicates the privation of the beautiful in the world of matter."

While this statement reveals the implicit acceptance of a perfectly good theory of comedy, since it compares *what is* unfavourably with *what ought to be*, still the tendency to deprecate the whole world of matter is unquestionably present, and genuine comedy can never be willing to accept such a view. The religious element prefers to leave the world of matter in order to search for some world more beautiful. Its bias, fated to stifle comedy for some centuries, was already present. True comedy would criticize the absence of beauty in the "world of matter" only in order to call for more beauty in the "world of matter."

Jamblichus the religious had spoken; Jamblichus the philosopher recognized that the method of comedy is to emphasize the ugly in order to demand a change for something preferable. He said that "they pursue after the beautiful, since

[23] Lane Cooper, op. cit., pp. 82–3.

from the mention of ugly things they perceive the ugly; and although they avoid the doing of deeds that are ugly, they manifest their knowledge thereof through the words, and transfer their longing to the opposite of the ugly." Where was the opposite of the ugly to manifest itself: in this world, or the next? The classic Greeks wanted to make actuality more beautiful; the neo-Platonists had their doubts; and later the Christians definitely decided to leave the "world of matter" to the ugly, and to pursue the beautiful in the world to come. Hence in the history of the theory of comedy we are able to perceive the corruption of the Greek realistic philosophy at the hands of the exaggerated realism of the neo-Platonists, and, as we shall see later, also at the hands of the Christian Church.

In the very next paragraph, Jamblichus returns to the favourite theory of the psychological aspects, and sets forth some observations on the cathartic effect of comedy. This theory of the effect of comedy would seem to be argued by analogy from the catharsis theory of tragedy, as presented by Aristotle in the *Poetics*. "The forces of the human emotions in us, if entirely restrained, bestir themselves more vehemently; but if stirred into action gradually and within measure, they rejoice moderately and are satisfied; and, thus purified, they become obedient, and are checked without violence." Here, as with the *Tractatus Coislinianus*, it is only necessary to point out that while the emotional purge of comedy is undoubtedly a fact, it does not account for the whole of the psychological effects of comedy. The awareness of comedy goes deeper than those ebullient emotions which, ever ready for laughter, lie waiting at the surface of human reactions. Such emotions must of course be taken into account, but there are other reactions more subtle, protracted, and far more profound, which go unaccounted for in all theories of comedy through those of modern times.

Only one more neo-Platonist need detain us. Proclus was one of the last heads of the Academy at Athens. He advocated the catharsis theory for both comedy and tragedy, but whether or not he derived it from Aristotle is unknown. He may have obtained it from one of the Aristotelian commentators, since his mention is too brief to suggest that he developed it by himself. The rejection of both comedy and tragedy from the ideal state as envisaged by Plato in the *Republic* meets with Proclus' approval. He goes on to suggest that statesmen should devise better methods of securing emotional purgation, for comedy and tragedy may by intensifying emotions bring about the opposite effect from the one desired.

It is clear that neo-Platonism prepared the way for the solemnities of Christianity by picking up the prudish aspects of the classic Greek philosophers for especial approval. We have seen that whosoever looks down upon the material world of actuality will also tend to look down on comedy. The exaggerated realism of Christianity was prepared to leave the world of matter altogether, and hence comedy, too, for another world, which was to be actual elsewhere but certainly not here. It is significant that in this connection comedy and tragedy go together, and that Proclus in condemning the purgation theory of the emotions for placing too much emphasis upon the emotions themselves, condemns comedy and tragedy alike and does not attempt to distinguish between them. Those who would leave actuality in favour of the ideal rather than endeavour to render actuality itself a little more conformable with the ideal, are not comic but neither are they tragic. They are still pitiful, and by refusing to acknowledge the human predicament they fail to advance the human situation. The classic Greek recognition of the fact that comedy points to shortcomings of actuality which could be rectified in actuality is with Proclus almost entirely absent. Sentimental considerations aside, Justinian did little harm when he closed the Academy shortly after Proclus had ruled over it.

In Praise of Comedy

4. ROMAN COMMENTATORS: CICERO AND QUINTILIAN

The discussions of Roman scholars and thinkers who concerned themselves with theories discovered by the classic Greeks tended to emphasize the applications of those theories to daily affairs. The implications from Greek abstract theories to actual Roman customs, manners, and morals is what chiefly occupied the Romans. In few cases did they ever devote their attention to the development or elaboration of the theories. Cooper points out that the sources on the Greek theory of comedy which were available to the Romans were far more numerous than those which have been preserved for us.[24] Several works entitled *On the Laughable* have unfortunately since been lost, but must have influenced those Romans who thought about the practical effects of theories of comedy.

Cicero, whose references to comedy well illustrate the point that we have been making, had access to these works as well as to the teachings of post-classical Greek scholars who were in Rome at the time. That he had studied the Platonic and Aristotelian writings on the same subject is also evident. Since Cicero was an orator he was of course primarily interested in the relation of comedy to rhetoric, but the realism of his viewpoint is beyond suspicion. He began by dismissing the psychological aspects of comedy as these are contained in the nature and origins of laughter. He did not dismiss the subjective explanation, however, before stating that little or nothing was known about psychology—by him or anyone else.

What Cicero wanted to find out was the nature of the comic or the ridiculous. "The province," he says, "of the ridiculous lies within the limits of ugliness and a certain deformity; for those expressions are alone, or especially, ridiculous which disclose and represent some ugliness in a not unseemly fashion."[25] This is a realistic conception, since it establishes the objective nature of the comic subject-matter. Cicero proceeds, however, to bring the question immediately down to

[24] Lane Cooper, op. cit., p. 89.
[25] Cicero, *De Oratore*, 2. (58) 235 et seq.

his own professional interests. To what extent should the orator provoke laughter? Since the orator is addressing human beings, and for the most part his remarks are also concerned with them, it follows that "the subject of the ridiculous lies in the moral vices of men who are neither beloved nor miserable, nor deserving to be dragged to punishment for their crimes."[26]

Cicero said of comedy that it consisted in cheated expectations, thus anticipating later conceptions. We may call Cicero's notion an anticipation, since it is unlikely that either Hobbes or Kant was very familiar with Cicero's discussion, although it is quite possible. At any rate, it is an unfortunate understanding of comedy, for it throws the whole definition straight back upon the apprehension or appreciation of comedy and hence upon its psychological aspects, in a way that Hobbes or Kant may have intended, but that Cicero never meant. Cicero is speaking of the levels of comedy, and since he has no real interest in the theoretical side he must depend for his divisions upon practical distinctions, a method which was sure to lead him astray. Thus his speculations are fairly inconsequential, whereas his examples are excellent.

Cicero distinguished between wit and the ludicrous. It is worthy of note that he singled out Socrates in the *Dialogues of Plato* as the archetype of wit, and took him for his model in this respect to be followed in the practice of oratory. Wit, however, is not a trivial affair, to be contrasted with the heavy effect of the ludicrous. The difference is one which could be compared to the equally dangerous rapier and bludgeon. That wit concerned itself with positive reform was well understood by the Roman utilitarians; indeed they saw little else in it. Cicero says that "there is no kind of wit in which severe and serious things may not be derived from the subject."[27] Comedy is an indirect affirmation of a greater truth than the errors it criticizes, of a fuller value than the disvalues it ridicules, of

[26] Op. cit.

[27] Op. cit.

more logical manners than those whose outworn discord it notes; and the awareness of this did not escape Cicero. He says that "Comedy is an imitation of life, a mirror of custom, an image of truth."[28]

The Roman critic, Quintilian, also dismissed the psychological aspect of comedy in passing, and proceeded to the laughable itself. He did make one notable observation on the topic of laughter. While not trying to account for comedy but merely noting down its many forms, occasioned by many things from tickling to witty utterances, he points out that the impulse to laughter is a tyrannical one which most persons utterly lack the power to resist. "It bursts forth in people not seldom against their will, and forces expression not merely through voice and features, but shakes the whole body with its vigour."[29] As a consequence of this irresistible power, it "often changes the tendency of the greatest affairs."

Quintilian recognized that "everything is laughable which is obviously pretended." Comedy, for all that, is not a subjective affair. The notion that laughter is a response to the desire to laugh is a modern one, and owes its origin to the nominalistic understanding of psychological causes. Quintilian is at pains to point out that "those jokes are more choice and pointed which draw their force from external circumstances." But comedy does not reside entirely in words, although words themselves of course do describe "external circumstances" and are in no sense to be taken as subjective merely because they are uttered by a speaker or orator. For "the laughable is found in *things* and *words*." Quintilian preserves his respect for the γελοῖος, the laughable, as an objective affair which is stubborn and irreducible and which the human apprehension plays no part in creating.

Quintilian works on the moral note so far as is necessary in order to preserve the amenities of the privileged classes. They are to be saved from obscenity. But for the "humbler class of

[28] Cooper, op. cit., p. 91. [29] Op. cit., p. 93.

mankind" much more licence is allowed. The mistake of identifying gentility with prudish delicacy, and of allotting both to the tender mercies of the upper classes, is one which we shall meet with again in more recent times.[30]

5. COMEDY IN TRANSITION: TZETZES AND VICO

The discussion of comedy which has been preserved under the name of one John Tzetzes[31] is little worthy of notice, since it is no more than a repetition of what the Greeks left on the same topic. Tzetzes seems to have been familiar with the *Tractatus Coislinianus* and with the Greek dramatic comedies. On the purpose of comedy, however, and on the comparison of comedy with tragedy, Tzetzes in several passages is very clear.

"Tragedy," he says "differs from comedy in that tragedy has a story, and a report of deeds that are past, although it represents them as taking place in the present, but comedy embraces fictions of the affairs of everyday life; and in that the aim of tragedy is to move the hearers to lamentation, while the aim of comedy is to move them to laughter." The preference for past deeds on the part of tragedy is an old story, although dramatists more recent than those with whom Tzetzes was familiar have taken as their theme contemporary events and even hypothetical events projected into the future. But the comparison is valid nevertheless. It is questionable whether dramatic tragedies can ever be as tragic when they deal with present dilemmas as when they deal with those of the past which have had time to become encrusted with symbolic connotations.

Tzetzes' description of comedy in this regard is exceptionally good. Comedy deals with the "affairs of everyday life," since only the present can be amusing. For it is the present that can be altered with a view to achieving a better future. But, says Tzetzes, it is not merely the affairs of everyday life that preoccupy comedy; it is the "*fictions* of the affairs of everyday

[30] Cf. this chapter, section 9.   [31] Cooper, op. cit., pp. 86, 287–9.

life." This phrase would indicate a deep understanding of the demand which comedy makes for improvement toward the ideal. Indeed another passage confirms this point: "The comic poet, ridiculing in his comedies some plunderer and evil-doer and pestilent fellow, for the rest settles all into decorum. Thus tragedy dissolves life, while comedy founds it firmly."

To lay bare the fictions of the affairs of everyday life, with a view to founding that life more firmly, may be taken as an excellent brief account of what the comedian tries to accomplish and of what the purpose of comedy essentially is.

Although the Italian social philosopher, Giambattista Vico, did not appear until the very end of the seventeenth century, we must place him with Tzetzes as a definite transition figure. Vico was infected with all the influences which already in his day had begun to shape the modern cosmology: the empiricism of the scientists, the Cartesian dualism, the substitution of natural rights for theological law—in short, all the implications of the nominalistic postulate of the sole reality of physical particulars. Unlike the majority of his forward-looking contemporaries, Vico refused to throw overboard the valuable inheritance of the past, which he thought could be saved without those accretions of falsehood and disvalue acquired *en route* through the mediaeval centuries. Thus he wished to save religion without the Catholic Church, the realism of Plato without its confining restrictions, and the systematic demands of rationalism without any presupposed dogmatism.

The inferences to comedy of such an inclusive midway position in the development of world-philosophy should be of the utmost importance. The struggle between the contending forces evidently proved too great to allow for the endorsement of a theory of comedy. Social philosophy, especially where it bears strong moral considerations, did not, according to Vico, leave any place for humour. High seriousness was more in order. Accordingly, Vico looked down upon humour. It is frequently true that those who possess to a high degree the faculty for discovering the truth can see nothing ludicrous in things. But second-rate minds which see things only partially are inclined to recognize the ludicrous.

The attack on the comic is illuminating if not altogether justified. Men hold some things good and others evil, but God holds all things fair, said Heraclitus. But the ambition to see life steadily and as a whole requires a God's-eye view, which is enjoyed by no mortal. Man is condemned by virtue of his participation in actuality to a partial outlook on the world; the perspective predicament is his permanent condition. Thus the view which Vico recommends is never to be his, and the partial view which he must for ever take means also that the comic aspect of existence is his irrevocably. To rise above humour would mean to rise above partiality, and this as a human being he can never accomplish. In Vico's sense we are all second-rate minds.

Passing on to Vico's psychological interpretation of laughter, we find that he has given this also a sociological bearing, although fundamentally it is familiar enough in its strictly subjective aspect. Physiologically, laughter resides in the shock rendered to the nervous system when awareness, expecting the adequate and congruous, is suddenly presented with the inadequate and the incongruous. The fibrils of nerve and brain are shaken by disappointment, and laughter results.[32] This is the familiar surprise theory of expectation, couched as always in subjective-psychological terms. Vico, as a typically transition theorist, has added the old objective validity of the realist theory of comedy to the newer psychological theory. His theory in general, however, does not seem to have much objective validity; it is coloured by the subjective aspect, since comedy comes only to second-rate minds who do not see things as a whole.

Vico draws his sociological conclusions from this theory of comedy, much to the detriment of the comedian. Only wise

[32] H. P. Adams, *The Life and Writings of Giambattista Vico* (London, 1935, George Allen & Unwin), p. 179.

men see things as a whole, and consequently never occupy themselves with the ludicrous. On the other end of the scale, animals do not laugh, either, because they lack the faculty of comparison and cannot contrast what they expect with what they find. The man who laughs is a satyr or a faun, half-way between man and brute. The conscious humorist, says Vico, is a very low fellow who deliberately distorts things so as to arouse laughter in others.

The fact that animals, like sages, do not laugh, and the further fact that men who are half-way between animals and sages do laugh, evidently was a hint of the truth that Vico failed to exploit. It requires a certain explicit understanding of partiality, which brutes do not have, to apprehend humour. It requires a certain departure from high seriousness, which saints[33] rarely take, to apprehend humour. Between these extremes, however, lie the vast majority of mankind, who are enabled to apprehend the comedy of partiality in more or less degree.

6. NOMINALISTIC THEORY: HOBBES

By the sixteenth century, the date of our next comic theorist, the overthrow of realism had been completed. Realism was erroneously identified with the philosophy of the Catholic Church. Catholicism was realistic, but realism is not exclusively Catholic, and it is the latter point which the new empiricists failed to understand. Although science is also realistic, it took its start historically from a nominalistic revolt against the rigid and confining strictures of Church realism. Hence all realisms got a bad name, and the belief in the reality of universals fell into disrepute. Along with universals went logic

---

[33] That saints do not laugh merely means that comedy is something less than tragedy. "I could never believe in a God who did not know how to laugh," says Nietzsche. But to know how to laugh, and to consider the occasion proper for laughter, are two entirely different things. The trouble with Vico's sage is that he did not even know how to laugh.

and reason, so that logical investigation into the nature of comedy was no longer fashionable. The nominalistic emphasis on the sole reality of physical particulars threw all normative studies into the subjective category. As a consequence, comedy as an objective affair was no longer considered to exist. To survive at all, comedy had to be thought of as subjective and psychological. This is the condition in which we find it with our first modern student, Thomas Hobbes.

For Hobbes, man had not been natively gregarious and so experienced great difficulties of adjustment in endeavouring to become a member of society. Indeed the latter condition required constant correction and a vigilant attitude toward his fellow-men, lest they take advantage of the conventions of the social contract. With this primitivistic and unflattering view of the nature of man, Hobbes attempted to fit a theory of comedy. Let us first state this theory, and then examine it.

"There is a passion that hath *no name*; but the sign of it is that distortion of the countenance which we call *laughter*, which is always joy: but what joy, what we think, and wherein we triumph when we laugh, is not hitherto declared by any. That it consisteth in *wit*, or as they call it, in the *jest*, experience confuteth: for men laugh at mischances and indecencies, wherein there lieth no wit nor jest at all. And forasmuch as the same thing is no more ridiculous when it groweth stale or usual, whatsoever it be that moveth laughter, it must be *new* and *unexpected*. Men laugh often, especially such as are greedy of applause from everything they do well, at their *own* actions performed never so little beyond their own expectations; as also at their own jests: and in this case it is manifest, that the passion of laughter proceedeth from a *sudden conception* of some *ability* in himself that laugheth. Also men laugh at the infirmities of others, by comparison therewith their own abilities are set off and illustrated. Also men laugh at *jests*, the *wit* whereof always consisteth in the elegant *discovery* and conveying to our minds some *absurdity* of *nature*: and in this case also the passion of laughter proceedeth from the *sudden* imagination of our own odds and eminency: for what is else the recommending of ourselves to our own good opinion, by comparison with another man's infirmity or absurdity? For when a jest is broken upon ourselves, or friends of whose dishonour we participate, we never laugh thereat. I may therefore conclude, that the passion of laughter is nothing else but *sudden glory* arising from some sudden conception of some eminency in ourselves, by comparison with the infirmity of others, or with our own formerly: for men laugh at the follies of themselves past, when they come suddenly to remembrance, except they bring with them any present dishonour."[34]

It is at once evident that the psychological aspect of comedy, called laughter, is equivalent to the whole of comedy for Thomas Hobbes. In accordance with the implicit nominalism of his day, he could give comedy no objective status whatsoever. Nominalists in general, since they disbelieve in the reality of ideas, do not consider it necessary to refute the objective theory of comedy. It seldom occurs to them that such a theory is possible, and they accordingly go on to explain comedy entirely in terms of its subjective effect which is so obvious in laughter. Laughter is one of the "faculties, acts and passions of the soul of man" and it is nothing else. From this point of view, Hobbes first distinguished laughter from wit or jest, by taking it for granted that laughter is always aimed at incongruities which are not necessarily contained in the latter. Then he explained that laughter is not constant but may just be as something which is new and unexpected, a sudden realization, a surprise.

The next step in Hobbes's development of his theory was gradually to accord it some objective status, by showing that what we laugh at is some infirmity of others in comparison with some ability in ourselves—the feeling of superiority we should call it to-day. At this stage, Hobbes suddenly remembered the subjective aspect of laughter, and then tried to com-

[34] *The English Works of Thomas Hobbes* (London, 1839, John Bohn), vol. iv, pp. 45–6.

Some Classical Theories of Comedy

bine it in his theory: laughter is the sudden glory arising from a feeling of superiority over others. Laughter thus proved for him a psychological effect arising from an objective stimulation.

The expression "sudden glory" has become very well known. Yet there is some confusion about it in Hobbes's use. For he distinguished comedy (which he called laughter) from joy as well as from wit. If sudden glory is not the apprehension of joy, what is it? Subjectively, then, the sudden-glory description of laughter goes unexplained. The objective aspect is treated somewhat more suggestively. Elsewhere Hobbes explained that glory "has respect for the future" in the "quick ranging of mind."[35] Laughter is an intellectual affair, pointed toward the future: this begins to be orthodox theory which, despite its origins in Hobbes's social philosophy, swings round to the traditional conceptions of comedy. Despite Hobbes's view of the inherently anti-social nature of man, he recognized the softening effect of laughter. Men can laugh even at their own past infirmities, provided they bring no present dishonour; they can laugh at others without offence.

"It is no wonder that men take heinously to be laughed at or derided, that is, triumphed over. Laughter *without offence* must be at *absurdities* and infirmities *abstracted* from persons, and when all the company may laugh together: for laughing to one's self putteth all the rest into jealousy and examination of themselves. Besides, it is vain glory and an argument of little worth, to think the infirmity of another sufficient matter for his triumph."[36] At this point, the theory of Hobbes does not differ in any important respect from that of Aristotle. Hobbes's theory is a little milder, a little more subjectively expressed, than Aristotle's, but essentially they are the same.

In the *Leviathan* the position is more succinctly set forth, and laughter as pleasure is treated more slightly. Laughter at others becomes a matter of scorn, and nobility is judged by

---

[35] Op. cit., vol. iv, pp. 54–5.
[36] Op. cit., p. 47.

the extent to which laughter can be avoided rather than the reverse. "*Sudden glory*, is the passion which maketh those grimaces called LAUGHTER; and is caused either by some sudden act of their own, that pleaseth them; or by the apprehension of some deformed thing in another, by comparison whereof they suddenly applaud themselves. And it is incident most to them that are conscious of the fewest abilities in themselves; who are forced to keep themselves in their own favour, by observing the imperfections of other men. And therefore much laughter at the defects of others, is a sign of pusillanimity. For of great minds, one of the proper works is to help and free others from scorn; and compare themselves only with the most able."[37]

The subjective and psychological interpretation of comedy as laughter at the defects of others is sure, in any age when there still prevail some standards of morals and manners, to lead to the disapproval of comedy as levity. Assuredly Hobbes's conclusions follow hard upon his major premise: if laughter can be an attempt to raise self-esteem at the expense of the defects of others, then it must earn our disapproval. But the conclusion itself should have informed Hobbes that although his analysis was partly right something had nevertheless been omitted. Satire and ridicule are true forms of comedy, but they are not the only forms. Nor need even they be interpreted subjectively. For all subjective reaction which takes the form of laughter must be reaction to some external stimulus; it must be the subjective recognition of objective elements which are worthy of laughter; and it is these objective elements which we call objects of comedy.

Hobbes's failure was due to the fact that although he took these truths partly for granted in his theory of laughter, he never explicitly recognized the logic of the situation, and his

[37] Op. cit., vol. iii, p. 46. Locke's definition of comedy probably is, as Hazlitt maintains, taken without acknowledgment from Hobbes, and since they are much the same, there will be no need to give it separate consideration. Cf. the *Essay*, vol. i, p. 143, and *Leviathan*, p. 32.

shortcomings led eventually to his disapproval of laughter as levity, a sort of sudden glory, unjustified, of stolen fruits. The result was an insufficiently rounded theory of laughter itself.

7. GOTTSCHED AND SCHLEGEL

The next important figures we have to consider in the history of the theory of comedy are two German critics of the eighteenth century, Gottsched and Schlegel.

Gottsched was open to all the influences of subjective rationalism that were current about 1724.[38] The primary and secondary qualities and common sense of Locke, the false scepticism of Descartes, as exaggerated by Wolff, the windowless monads of Leibniz—all these notions were brought to bear on him, and led him, as it led all others of his day, to conclude correctly that reason was the final criterion of all theory and practice, and to conclude erroneously that reason was entirely a mental affair. Gottsched was a metaphysician who turned his attention to the analysis of comedy. Fortunately for the efficacy of reason, the invalid subjective interpretation leads to its employment just as much as does the truer objective view, and Gottsched along with others of his day returned reason to all topics which had grown foreign to exploration in rational terms. Comedy was one of these, at least in Germany.

From a knowledge of Gottsched's background and his metaphysical views, it would have been only natural to expect him to propound the usual subjective understanding of comedy: that which identifies it with laughter. Those critics in our day who think reason is entirely mental also think that comedy is entirely a matter of laughter. But the rationalism of eighteenth-century Germany did not err as far as that. Comedy, according to Gottsched, was not an "innate quality" but a "faculty for clear analysis, which could perceive and condemn anything

[38] For the facts concerning Gottsched and Schlegel I am indebted to Betsy Aikin-Sneath, *Comedy in Germany: in the First Half of the Eighteenth Century* (Oxford, 1936, Clarendon Press).

irrational and exaggerated in the behaviour of man."[39] Since reason is the only guide to truth, we only laugh at "that which seems absurd to our understanding."[40] Gottsched proceeded on the strict lines of his own day, according to which comedy consists in "the mental comparison of some eccentricity with a norm."[41]

Thus far, Gottsched's analysis of comedy is keen and incisive, and not very far from the truth. He understood very well that comedy is an affair involving the intellect, that it rests upon recognition of irrationals in behaviour, and that it assumes the existence of some kind of standard, in terms of which behaviour can be estimated. Such a conception, however, distorts the understanding of comedy, because it sets forth one narrow aspect as the whole truth. The subjective prejudice creeps in here unannounced; and the subject-matter of comedy becomes limited to "the behaviour of man." But can comedy be so limited? Do we not think that puppies are often funny? Do we not speak of the happy laughter of rivulets? Why does a theory, which does not attempt to hold comedy down to its subjective aspect (i.e., laughter), still confine it to the behaviour of man? If there is anything objective which is capable of arousing laughter, then it cannot be confined to human behaviour.

This is, in fact, just where Gottsched's theory did break down. Gottsched did not take the empirical point of view which was so commonly associated with the new rationalism. He did not expect his comic artists to draw their study of comic character from studies of living characters. This would have been the consistent objective view, but Gottsched did not adopt it. On the contrary, German metaphysics led him to maintain that comic characters were to be conceived *a priori*.[42] "Cosmology was replaced by the study of man and by constant preoccupation with every aspect of his behaviour,"[43] yet this

[39] Op. cit., p. 13.
[40] Op. cit., p. 13.
[41] Op. cit., p. 13.
[42] Op. cit., p. 21.
[43] Op. cit., p. 14.

study was not to be influenced by the observation of *actual* behaviour but rather by imagined conceptions of behaviour. By this criterion, character faults became paramount in dramatic comedies of the time, and plot was altogether overlooked as a source of comedy.[44] Thus the empirical rationalism of France and England which wanted its subjective thoughts corrected in accordance with accurate observations, was stopped at the German border where the rational still depended upon the intellectual affinity for truth.

Within Germany, the same class changes were taking place as were occurring throughout western Europe. The middle class with its increasing wealth and affluence was beginning to imitate the manners and customs of the landed gentry. Thus there was matter for ridicule both in the embarrassed position of the declining nobility, and in the crude gentility of the rising middle class. Was the indication of both absurdities the task of comedy? Gottsched thought not. "Whether Aristotle had meant social or ethical lowness, when he had said that comic characters were to be lowly in status, Gottsched always had rigid class distinctions in mind. He excluded the aristocracy from comedy partly for reasons of respect."[45] On the other hand, he thought comedy must never deal with the lowest classes for fear of losing its social standing; comedy was to be severely confined to the middle classes.

In a word, Gottsched supposed that the uses of comedy are to maintain the *status quo ante,* to preserve the rigidity of the existing order; and in one sense he was right. For comedy is capable of taking any standard as a norm and criticizing from its point of view. But can this possibly be high comedy? Can it ever be as high as comedy which criticizes *all* reigning orders in the light of the possibility of greater order? In the last analysis that comedian is sure to be the most sublime, sure to produce the most immortal comedies, who has, so to speak, no contemporary axe of his own to grind, and who

[44] Op. cit., p. 27.
[45] Op. cit., p. 18.

wishes to improve the reign of order by first destroying all reigning orders. Ethics being still in the helpless and groping condition of normative science, all social movements of any considerable scope are usually moral movements. And morality finds itself as easily compatible with the conservative as with the revolutionary principle, in a sense belonging to both. Nevertheless, comedy, which Gottsched correctly saw as a moral force, is not at its best when criticizing change in the light of a reigning order, but rather works more naturally when criticizing the reigning order to make way for change. Comedy is an adjunct of the revolutionary principle.

Gottsched made the mistake of endorsing comedy only as a conservative moral force. This error led him logically to commit others. All strong emotions, all serious faults, Gottsched assigned to tragedy. Comedy, he said, should be confined to petty and ridiculous faults and incongruous situations such as " 'Indifferent actions': absent-mindedness, quaint mannerisms, eccentric habits, or mechanical tricks of behaviour."[46] These to be sure are comic actions, but is comedy to be confined to them? The reason why Gottsched thought so is easy to find. Having limited comedy to the middle class, and taken the aristocracy as the norm "for reasons of respect," it was only natural that the only faults Gottsched could discover in this light were petty errors committed by the middle class in its efforts to ape the manners and customs of the aristocracy. A true subject for comedy indeed, but hardly to be described as the only one.

Gottsched saw that comedy depended upon the exposition of latent contradictions. Given this profundity of insight into the true nature of comedy, it is difficult to assign any but a class occasion for his blindness to the obvious fact that contradiction itself can emphatically not be confined to the efforts of a bourgeois class to imitate the fine manners of the nobility. A responsibility—a moral responsibility—to one's class affiliation, fitted in nicely with the fundamental subjectivism of

[46] Op. cit., p. 26.

Gottsched's conception, in the notion that only where there was conscious moral responsibility could there be comedy. A madman is not comic because he cannot be blamed for his madness, or so Gottsched thought; but obviously he was wrong. For if we blind ourselves to the humanitarian aspect of a given situation, as comedy knows so well how to blind us, even a madman can be very funny. Further evidence lies in the fact that it has been the custom of comedians from olden time to feign madness in order to take the meaning out of situations and thus to provoke laughter.

In his philosophical leanings as well as in his class affiliations, Gottsched was a member of declining loyalties. There was nothing forward-looking about him; the middle class, experimentation, and the search for the ideal, were all equally lost on him. For he knew his aristocracy to be the vantage class, his mind and its *a priori* to be the preferred method of investigation, and he already had his ideal in an absolute dogmatism. Thus, paradoxically, he clung to the interpretation of comedy as the close imitation of nature, and yet was "unshaken in his faith in the efficacy of rules: *Es kommt nur auf die Wissenschaft der Regeln an.*"[47] The old order fortified by such belated apologists was going down with all hands aboard and all colours flying.

Gottsched had an impressive following, among whom he liked to number J. E. Schlegel, the comic dramatist and critic. Gottsched, however, looked to the past, whereas Schlegel turned to the future, a difference which inevitably led to vast distinctions between their points of view. On the very question of the close imitation of nature they were at odds. Schlegel thought that "comedy must necessarily present an idealized version of reality and could never approximate too closely to life."[48] Comedy should pursue the ideal of things and events as they ought to be. For "the perception of order, the recog-

[47] Quoted in op. cit., p. 24.
[48] Op. cit., p. 33.

nition of the relation of one thing to another, is an invariable source of enjoyment."[49]

Schlegel further denied Gottsched's contentions concerning the moral effect of comedy. Its purpose was not to show people their own faults on the stage so that they would correct them, since audiences were not in the habit of identifying themselves with comic characters. Rather did they feel with the authors above the battle, considering themselves in a position to ridicule the faults of the comic characters in their absurd situations. The theatre, of course, was to have a moral effect, but not in the way in which Gottsched had conceived it. Comedy was not to make fun of the middle class for its droll antics when imitating the gentry; it was, on the contrary, to teach the middle class how to be gentle-folk with all the required manners and graces.

The lessons became transferred by Schlegel from the moral to the social side of the equation. He wished comedy to make its appeal to all classes, and thus saw it in broader terms than did Gottsched; nevertheless, like Gottsched, he was prejudiced in favour of his own class. The difference, however, was that Schlegel's class was the middle class. So in his plans for a national theatre for Denmark, he "appealed for support, not to the aristocracy, but to the middle classes."[50] The transition from Gottsched to Schlegel marked a forward movement in history; yet both are guilty of a narrow conception of comedy,[51]

---

[49] Op. cit., p. 31. Schlegel, despite his differences with Gottsched, was consistent in his point of view. As much cannot be said for his English contemporary, Coleridge, who, unmindful of the German school, was trying to follow Aristotle, only to end in some confusion. Coleridge maintained, for instance, that the laughable "belongs exclusively to the understanding" but "does not appertain to the reason"! Coleridge added little to Aristotle, at least so far as the theory of comedy is concerned.

[50] Op. cit., p. 35.

[51] Schiller, the poet, who was Schlegel's contemporary, knew that there must be a *spieltrieb*, or play-impulse, included in comedy, yet his discussion lacks the logical rigour which characterized the writings of both Gottsched and Schlegel.

Some Classical Theories of Comedy

confined for its medium to the theatre; for its subject-matter to the promotion of inconsequential causes; and for its appeal to members of a given class. Comedy itself, however, was destined for something more.

8. KANT, SPENCER, SCHOPENHAUER, HAZLITT

The philosophy of Kant is marked by a prolonged preoccupation with the subjective or psychological aspects of being. Kant wanted to investigate the limits of cognition; he succeeded in pushing his investigation so far that he almost found himself on the objective end of his subject-matter. Not the limits of reason itself but the extent of those fields to which reason is applicable became his study. Hence much of his philosophy is valid from the realistic point of view by the simple transference of emphasis from the status of knowledge as things known to the status of knowledge as things having a one-to-one correspondence with objective states of affairs.

What is true of Kant's philosophy in general is also true of his particular theory of the comic. The theory itself is of course subjectively stated. Laughter, Kant said, is "an affection arising from a strained expectation being suddenly reduced to nothing."[52] We are strained to expect a certain thing, and when we find that it is not there the result is laughter. Making large allowances for the limitations of this theory of laughter, we may grant that it enjoys a certain truth. But the validity it has is not that of a theory of comedy but of a theory of laughter. Thus it is wholly psychological and not objective and logical at all. As an account of laughter it leaves out many levels of investigation which are necessary to complete the subjective description. For instance, Kant says nothing of the physiological level, except in a loose, literary way.

Humour in Kant's hands fares no better than does laughter. It is not only subjective but self-conscious. "Humour is

[52] Kant's *Critique of Aesthetic Judgment*, trans. J. C. Meredith (Oxford, 1911, Clarendon Press), p. 199.

clearly allied to the gratification provoked by laughter. Humour . . . means a talent for being able to put oneself at will into a certain frame of mind in which everything is estimated on lines that go quite off the beaten track (a topsy-turvy view of things) and yet on lines that follow certain principles. . . ."[53] The view presented by humour becomes a topsy-turvy view only if the way things are now is taken to be the way they ought to be. And if it is a topsy-turvy view, how does it happen that, as Kant reluctantly admits, it furnishes an estimation of everything along "lines that follow certain principles"? The subjective and random elements of humour appear to be at odds with the rational elements, a conflict which Kant attempts to resolve by making the principles "rational in the case of such a mental temperament" as is able to put itself at will into the frame of mind which produces humour. But the effort to reduce everything concerning humour to the subjective category is a failure. There is still the topsy-turvy view *of things*, implying a *correct* view *of things*, and there are still the rational principles which the humorous view follows.

However, as the subjective correlate of an objective theory of comedy, Kant's account would do very well. In accordance with what we said above concerning the transfer of emphasis from the subjective to the objective, we may endeavour to complete Kant's analysis for him in a way which would be conformable with his stated theory. Most commentators on Kant's theory of laughter quote only the famous sentence describing laughter as a strained expectation being suddenly reduced to nothing. They ignore, because it does not suit their purposes to take into account, the preceding sentence. Since it suits our purpose, we may give it here. "Something absurd (something in which, therefore, the understanding can of itself find no delight) must be present in whatever is to raise a hearty convulsive laugh."[54] Thus Kant himself admits that there is something inherently absurd in the object which

[53] Op. cit., p. 203.
[54] Op. cit., p. 199.

is responsible for raising a hearty convulsive (subjective) laugh. Laughter, by this admission, becomes the subjective response to an objective stimulus, and the objective stimulus in turn must then be some kind of non-subjective comedy.

Furthermore, the suddenness of the "strained expectation" may be understood as necessary in order sharply to indicate a certain contrast. Needless to add, time by itself accounts for nothing. The transformation and its disappointment on finding "nothing" would indicate the shortcomings discovered in actuality. Certain actual things are found to be not at all what they were expected to be—a fact which causes laughter when it is apprehended. Actual things, which are never wholly logical and valuable, and hence never what they ought to be, when taken past their limits amount to—nothing. This "nothing" is what occasions the contradictions and the disvalues of ugliness and evil which comedy decries in the world. In other words, objectively stated, comedy resides in the contrast between what is and what ought to be. This realistic description of comedy is the only one which would be capable of yielding the subjective effects which Kant properly notes as the "sudden transformation of a strained expectation into nothing."

Whether or not Herbert Spencer derived his theory of comedy from Kant, it is sufficiently similar to require little independent discussion. For Kant, laughter is the result of an expectation which of a sudden ends in nothing. For Spencer laughter is the indication of an effort which suddenly encounters a void. Spencer carries his explanation from psychology into physiology. Nervous energy, which makes preparation for the reception of a big thing when a little thing follows, is relieved by laughter. This is what Spencer called "descending incongruity,"[55] since the reverse process, from little to big, produces not laughter but a sense of wonder. The ordinary channels are closed suddenly to the nervous energy which must

[55] Herbert Spencer, *Illustrations of Universal Progress* (New York, 1867, Appleton), chap. iv, "The Physiology of Laughter," p. 206.

therefore discharge itself in another direction. The result is "an efflux through the motor nerves to various classes of the muscles, producing the half-convulsive actions we term laughter."[56]

Spencer's physiological mechanism covers the same ground as does Kant's psychological theory, and also requires an objective contrast between what is and what ought to be. Indeed Spencer's theory is in effect exactly the same as Kant's. Yet neither undertakes to discover what are the objective conditions which the subjective apprehension recognizes by the reaction of laughter.

Arthur Schopenhauer was influenced considerably in his philosophy by Plato and Kant. In his work, which is of enormous importance to the history of the theory of comedy, he strove manfully to weld these two influences together into one significant and valid metaphysic. The result was a philosophy in which Platonic realism struggles to overcome the subjective elements of the Kantian position. Voluntaryism, as Schopenhauer sets it forth, is nothing more than what we to-day would call realistic value, since his "will" is independent not only of the human will but indeed of all subjective elements. Nevertheless, the Schopenhauerian writings divide neatly into a mental rationalism inherited from Kant, and a realistic metaphysics devised along Platonic lines.

In the theory of comedy, Schopenhauer allows these two influences to come back into play, and the result is another struggle, in which, despite the perfectly good realistic arguments, the mental interpretation of rationalism gets rather the best of it. But let us turn to Schopenhauer's own explanation of comedy. He says that the "very incongruity of sensuous and abstract knowledge, on account of which the latter always merely approximates to the former, as mosaic approximates to painting, is the cause of . . . laughter." And again, "The cause of laughter in every case is simply the sudden perception

[56] Op. cit., p. 204.

of the incongruity between a concept and the real objects which have been thought through it in some relation, and laughter itself is just the expression of this incongruity."[57]

As may readily be seen, Kant so far has won. It is the subjective recognition of the fact that subjective concepts are insufficient to cover subjective feelings, which Schopenhauer tells us is the cause of laughter. The objective occasions which set off this prolonged process of introspection are evidently accidental and unimportant. But this is to explain comedy entirely in terms of psychology. Modern physiological psychology has some facts which are not covered by this piece of philosophical dogmatism, and so it cannot any longer prove adequate. Does nitrous oxide cause a person to examine the deficiencies of his own concepts to explain his feelings? At least there seems no reason to believe so.

It is unfortunate that the subjective twist has prevented Schopenhauer from saying something true about the nature of comedy. For had he but kept his same analysis, only transferring it all out into the objective field, there would have been much of value in his theory. The failure in practice of all limitations: ideas, customs and institutions, etc., to account for everything in the abundant stream of actuality, is something nearer what comedy criticizes; and this latter theory is but Schopenhauer's theory objectified. Something of this is suggested by Schopenhauer's own analysis of the ludicrous in terms of strict logic. "It is," he tells us, "possible to trace everything ludicrous to a syllogism in the first figure, with an undisputed *major* and an unexpected *minor*, which to a certain extent is only sophistically valid, in consequence of which connection the conclusion partakes of the quality of the ludicrous."[58]

In the nineteenth century, the traditional logic became the "laws of thought," and instead of being an independent set of

[57] *The World as Will and Idea*, Haldane and Kemp trans. (London, no date, Kegan Paul), vol. i, p. 76.
[58] Op. cit., vol. ii, p. 271.

conditions which the mind, like everything else, had to obey or run into difficulties, the laws of logic became indistinguishable from other psychological conditions. Thus again Schopenhauer's happy predispositions were vitiated by psychologism.

In order further to make plain the contention that Schopenhauer's own understanding of comedy was hurt by the influence of psychology outside its own valid realm, we may examine one illustration of comedy which Schopenhauer gives. "Two young peasants had loaded their gun with coarse shot, which they wished to extract, in order to substitute fine, without losing the powder. So one of them put the mouth of the barrel in his hat, which he took between his legs, and said to the other: 'Now you pull the trigger slowly, slowly, slowly; then the shot will come first.' He starts from the conception, 'Prolonging the cause prolongs the effect.' "[59] The point here is that the "conception" happens to be a logical proposition. The anecdote is funny because we recognize—objectively—that the proposition is false and hence inadequate to deal with the actual situation. We anticipate that the peasants in applying a false proposition to an actual problem will run into disastrous actual contradictions.

Again, Schopenhauer says of Don Quixote that he "subsumes the realities he encounters under conceptions drawn from the romances of chivalry, from which they are very different."[60] Here again the same criticism may be applied. Schopenhauer certainly has hold of the true meaning of comedy, but in accordance with the error of his day insists on perverting its truth by reference to psychological categories. We are amused by Don Quixote in exactly the same way in which we are amused by the antics of a kitten overturning a plate of milk. And presumably we must admit that the comic elements are inherent in the situations whether or not anyone is present to recognize their effect and react to it in the form of laughter.

[59] Op. cit., vol. ii, p. 278.
[60] Op. cit., vol. ii, p. 278.

Some Classical Theories of Comedy

The ludicrous, and its effect of laughter, are obviously pleasurable affairs. No one has ever disputed this, and Schopenhauer taking the fact for granted attempts to give some kind of explanation of why it should be so. Since on this explanation turns the whole exposition of the falsity of the subjectivist position, we are constrained to quote it at some length. "In every suddenly appearing conflict between what is perceived and what is thought, what is perceived is always unquestionably right; for it is not subject to error at all, requires no confirmation from without, but answers for itself. Its conflict with what is thought springs ultimately from the fact that the latter, with its abstract conceptions, cannot get down to the infinite multifariousness and fine shades of difference of the concrete. . . . It must therefore be diverting to us to see this strict, untiring, troublesome governess, the reason, for once convicted of insufficiency. On this account then the mien or appearance of laughter is very closely related to that of joy."[61]

Schopenhauer's argument finally is driven into defending a variety of primitivism. The fact that human perceptions are continually confuting human conceptions is for him an occasion for some kind of primitive and secret exultation over the defeat of reason. Our animal natures have triumphed over our human power of reasoning, and that is what gives us pleasure. The same fact of course could be read the other way, by looking toward the future instead of toward the past. We could maintain with equal cogency that the confuting of limited conceptions by perceptions is not an exposé of the whole sorry business of conception but merely a call for the establishment of broader and more adequate conceptions in the future. But such is not Schopenhauer's moral. He prefers to take the anti-rationalist's position that we rejoice at every temporary defeat of reason, and that this is why comedy is pleasurable.

In his argument is made plain the further fact (which is far from anything he intended to show) that the philosophy

[61] Op. cit., vol. ii, pp. 279–280.

of subjective rationalism is not rationalism at all, but merely irrationalism in disguise. Mental reasoning must be understood to be a partial apprehension of the objective and independent existence of the world as a network of logical relations, and this is the only possible kind of true rationalism. Schopenhauer's arguments over the pleasurable nature of comedy defeat the mental rationalist position. For he started with comedy, or as he calls it, the ludicrous, as an intellectual affair wholly, but then the intellectual comedy succeeds in being pleasurable only through the recognition of the failure of reason. In other words, rational comedy yields pleasure through the recognition of its own irrational nature—which is an obvious contradiction. The explanation is invalid and confused because involved in mental rationalism.

It is not until we come to volume iii of Schopenhauer's definitive philosophy, that we find the Platonic and largely realistic doctrine of the will coming to the rescue of the earlier errors of subjectivism as set forth in the theory of the ludicrous. Comedy, despite its earlier betrayals and defections, joins hands with the realistically defined "will to live" and reasonably looks forward to a better future, one in which the errors and disvalues at which we have laughed shall have been corrected. Comedy finally proves to be "an incitement to the continued assertion of the will."[62] Furthermore, "it is true that comedy . . . must bring before our eyes suffering and adversity; but it presents it to us as passing, resolving itself into joy, in general mixed with success, victory, and hopes, which in the end preponderate . . . Thus it declares, in the result, that life as a whole is thoroughly good, and especially is always amusing."[63]

Finally, comedy as the call to action for the improvement of actuality in the future, is understood by Schopenhauer morally. "If once we contemplate this burlesque side of life somewhat seriously, as it shows itself in the naïve utterances and gestures

[62] Op. cit., vol. iii, p. 218.
[63] Op. cit., vol. iii, p. 218.

which trifling embarrassment, personal fear, momentary anger, secret envy, and many similar emotions force upon the forms of the real life that mirrors itself here, forms which deviate considerably from the type of beauty, then from this side also, thus in an unexpected manner, the reflective spectator may become convinced that the existence and action of such beings cannot itself be an end; that, on the contrary, they can only have attained to existence by an error, and that which so exhibits itself is something which had better not be."[64] The shreds of subjectivism remain in the examples of error which are given in this passage. It is difficult indeed to free Plato from Kant. Nevertheless, Schopenhauer made desperate efforts to do it, not wholly successful but armed with the right inductions, so that something of value in his theory of the ludicrous remains, and the last word on this topic is forward-looking.

We should not leave this period without mentioning one contemporary of Schopenhauer's, the English critic, William Hazlitt. Hazlitt wrote well, and since he went more by insight than by deduction from any given position, he wandered from good theories into bad ones and back again. Subjective impressions rather vitiated the interest in metaphysics which Coleridge had engendered in him. Hazlitt said that "Man is the only animal that laughs and weeps; for he is the only animal that is struck with the difference between what things are, and what they ought to be."[65] This statement is remarkably objective and valid; but then Hazlitt a few pages later falls back upon the old subjectivistic incongruity theory. The ludicrous depends upon a contradiction between the object and our expectations.[66] Our expectations aim at what we think ought to be; but what we think ought to be and what ought to

---

[64] Op. cit., vol. iii, pp. 218–219.
[65] William Hazlitt, *Lectures on the English Comic Writers* (New York, 1845, Wiley and Putnam), p. 1.
[66] Op. cit., p. 4.

be are not by any means necessarily the same. Hazlitt's subsequent discussion favours the subjective view almost exclusively. Good logical insight was finally overridden by the
implicit prejudices of the times.

9. MEREDITH AND THE GENTEEL TRADITION

George Meredith's life spans the greater part of the nineteenth century, and his viewpoint is typical of this period.
The dictates of good form rose above the necessity of first
principles; and though fundamentals were challenged by many
men, from such unconscionable revolutionaries as Karl Marx
to such conservative conformers as Alfred Russel Wallace,
the challenges went unheard. Meredith was a novelist, capable
and competent for his task. He was sensitive, fearless, and
sincere. He attacked those foibles of the moment which he
conceived it his duty to attack. But the economic level must
have been for him what experimental science was for Plato:
something ignoble and menial, a slave's occupation. Thus he
failed to touch anything very deep in the current of his times,
and played upon the superficial, and even unimportant,
weaknesses that he found before him, and thought that he was
himself something of a revolutionary in manners and morals.
And so perhaps he was. But critics are made of sterner stuff;
Meredith remains a good novelist, but only a delightful little
man to the critical intelligence.

The ideas on comedy inspired by this set of general notions
and ambitions are just what might be expected. Meredith
gives them to us in *An Essay on Comedy*.[67] The first require-
ment for true comedy, he says, is a staple society of cultivated
women as well as men, to serve both as the subject-matter of
comedy and its appreciation. The comedian cannot deal with
crudities and change, for "the semi-barbarism of merely giddy
communities, and feverish emotional periods, repel him;
and also a state of marked social inequality of the sexes; nor

[67] (New York, 1910, Scribner's.)

can he whose business is to address the mind be understood where there is not a moderate degree of marked intellectual activity."[68]

Unhappily for most people, they are to be excluded by Mr. Meredith from the enjoyment of comedy. If cultivated men and women are expected to furnish both "matter and an audience" for the comedian, the latter is perforce constrained to deal with the most limited of societies. For the number of cultivated persons in the world is far short of what we should like it to be. This is typical nineteenth-century thinking, as restricted and as uncompromisingly superficial as might be expected from a social order which regarded its own conventions as the final ones toward which all creation had moved.

Meredith recognized the essentially critical nature of comedy; he was aware of its objective nature as well. He also knew that the criticism of comedy is directed against what is current and contemporary. But how can contemporary criticism be kept within the confines of that circle which includes only cultivated men and women? Surely we cannot benefit from the criticism which comedy offers when such criticism is directed only at the top layer of a social order, and is moreover appreciated only by that same group. Comedy cannot penetrate deeply, or accomplish much, when the objects of its criticism also furnish the appreciation of the comedy. This is setting the arena for the pulling of punches.

It is to Meredith's credit at least that he saw the predicament and accepted it. The comic poet, he says, "is in the narrow field of the society he depicts; and he addresses the still narrower enclosure of men's intellects, with reference to the operation of the social world upon their characters."[69] The comedian, then, is that member of polite society who can most amuse it by lightly and wittily pointing out its foibles. We certainly could not deny the name of comedy to this branch, but we can and must deny that it is anything more

[68] Op. cit., p. 2.
[69] Op. cit., pp. 79–80.

than a branch. Comedy is not exhausted by this tame variety, though it is abetted by it. Lane Cooper observes that Meredith's theory "reminds one of the supposed preference of Aristotle for comic 'innuendo.' "[70]

Meredith has nothing but admiration for the comedies of Aristophanes, which were so powerful and so effective against the shortcomings of the Athenian society at every level. But over this outburst of praise for strength and fearlessness, Meredith's weakness eventually wins. "A political Aristophanes, taking advantage of his lyrical Bacchic licence, was found too much for political Athens."[71] "Aristophanes," says Meredith, "is not likely to be revived."[72] "Indeed," he adds, "I would not ask to have him revived," presumably since he might upset the existing social order. For this was against Meredith's intent. He only wished for the occasional visit of an Aristophanes, so that "the sharp light of such a spirit as his might be with us to strike now and then on public affairs, public themes, to make them spin along more briskly."[73]

The chief merit of Meredith as social reformer is his insistence upon equality between the sexes. He saw, rightly enough, that civilization and its progress is somehow intimately tied up with the raising of the status of women to full equality with men. This is a claim which to-day it were retrogressive to deny; indeed only the fascists deny it. But that it is closely related to the idea of comedy is hard to see. We may fully concur in Meredith's opinion that there "never will be civilization where comedy is not possible," but what we cannot concur in is his further opinion that both are entirely dependent upon "some degree of social equality of the sexes."[74] The relation which Meredith goes on to make in the simultaneous occurrence of sexual equality and high comedy is rather an evidence of the fact that an advanced stage of civilization is likely to offer both, but it does not make one dependent upon the other.

[70] Op. cit., p. 81.
[71] Op. cit., p. 64.
[72] Op. cit., p. 66.
[73] Op. cit., p. 64.
[74] Op. cit., p. 54.

Some Classical Theories of Comedy

On the credit side of Meredith's analysis of comedy, we may inscribe his recognition of the objectivity of comedy. The appreciation of the comic is aroused by objective occasions which are independent of the appreciating subject. He also dimly recognizes its inherently rational appeal, since he says it is intellectual, appealing to the mind, and aroused by the conventional life. Comic interpretation, he says, may be put upon "doubtful causes,"[75] and the true purpose of comedy is to awaken "thoughtful laughter."[76]

Meredith's understanding of comedy, so typical of the century in which he lived, is too narrow and limited. Comedy is something light and superficial; playing over the surface of contemporary society; too much in good taste to criticize or even mention any but the most unimportant foibles of the most important people; too delicate to offend the most sensitive tastes. By this canon, slapstick is excluded and so is divine comedy. For Meredith's formula for a cultivated life, sexual equality is essential, and the existence of a small but select and exquisite society. The French dramatic comedies of Molière are chosen as the best to be found. In Meredith's comic world there is nothing to disturb either the property or the fastidiousness of the owning and aristocratic classes. It is all urbane and settled. Comedy is nothing very profound; it is certainly not revolutionary. It does not and cannot call for any radical changes. Meredith sees comedy as objective, as intellectual, and as critical, but consisting of a criticism merely of superficial manners, graces and foibles, not of anything which could shake the self-assurance of the established order of society.

Perhaps a short digression will be permitted here, in order to attack the *genre* of writing which Meredith's essay on comedy so well represents. There is a type of what we may call critical appreciation which attempts to bridge the gap between fiction and rational prose. Far be it from any of us to restrict or in any

[75] Op. cit., p. 81.
[76] Op. cit., p. 82.

117

dogmatic way limit the scope and variety of literary work. Words are very complex affairs; the most abstract of them is still connotative, and the most emotional still has some exact communicable meaning. Yet is not the kind of rational writing, to which literary men are most subject, a mistaken contradiction? *Belles-lettres* of this sort attempt to describe in a rational manner the intrinsic vividity of appreciative feelings, and then to present this mixture as an argument whose cogency is expected to be convincing. There is no logic, however, in the attempt to describe feelings. The quality of feelings is indescribable, and cannot be conveyed rationally. The attempt to overcome this innate contradiction can never be construed as a rational argument in favour of anything. Meredith, for instance, offers us his impressions about comedy, without argument, without proof, in the hope that the elaborate style of his prose and the persuasiveness of his impressions will prove convincing. This, from a rational point of view, at least, is strictly illegitimate. The *genre* fails to be a meeting ground of the arts and human reasoning, and falls back into the novel. This is perhaps where it belongs.

10. Everett and Psychology

There is a significant similarity about all the theories of comedy, from those of Plato's day to the present time. Philosophers both large and small, thinkers profound and superficial, adherents of every stripe and of every interest, from theology to the theatre and from psychology to metaphysics, betray a very enormous measure of agreement about the nature of comedy. Such agreement, being far in excess of the agreement reached by the same men concerning other matters, over which, for the most part, they are at daggers' ends, must indicate something valid. This, to be sure, it does. For comedy is so intellectual a pursuit, yet withal such a common one, that its logical nature, exceeding perhaps the logical nature of any other study which is intelligible to a large number of persons, is hard to pervert. The rigorous logical structure of comedy demands attention; and he who would wish to show that it was not primarily an affair of logic would have to go pretty far afield to demonstrate his point. This latter detour, as we have seen, has hardly been attempted before the present day. And even in modern times, of course, the traditional views on comedy, in one or another emphasis, are kept alive.

Typical of the traditional viewpoint as held by moderns is that of C. C. Everett, in his work, *Poetry, Comedy, and Duty*.[77] Like all moderns, Everett fails to understand what the independent and objective existence of objects of knowledge means from the standpoint of the realistic philosophy. Accordingly, his innate common sense and good judgment inform him that comedy is something which can be known and appreciated but which is not created by such knowledge and appreciation, but his absorption of the modern atmosphere of ideas commits him to the view that comedy "is created in the mind of the beholder."[78] He had previously quoted with approval Bain's point that a certain sense of superiority is essential for any perception of the ludicrous, and that all humour involves others in degradation.[79] Humour of this sort was illustrated by the old lady who remarked that "It takes all sorts to make a world, and I thank God I am not one of them."[80]

Thus far, what Everett has said had already been said better by those before him. There is some basis, of course, for his argument. Comedy, psychologically, always does involve the assumption that the persons and situations which give rise to comedy are involved in the flux of actuality, whereas the observer takes a quasi *sub specie aeternitatis* attitude of being free from time and change and imperfection of all sorts. But this, to be sure, is a psychological way of putting the matter. And to assume, as Everett does in the passages already quoted, that the psychological effect of comedy on the observing sub-

---

[77] (Boston, 1890, Houghton Mifflin.)
[79] Op. cit., p. 161.
[78] Op. cit., p. 180.
[80] Op. cit., p. 161.

ject is all there is to comedy, is to stray from the plain logic of the situation. Indeed, Everett himself in other passages of his book gives good indication of the fact that he sometimes knew better. All Christian theology is touched with realism, and Everett's divinity training must have guided him better when he was being unaffected by the psychological logic of all nineteenth-century thinking.

Everett's own theory states that comedy is simply the recognition of incongruity. Perhaps the definition could be better emphasized as the *recognition* of incongruity. Immediately the admission is made that there is a recognition of objective elements, the subjective nature of comedy is repudiated. The subjective aspect proves to be the *recognition* of the objective aspect. This is fair enough. From here on, Everett's thesis develops into the standard one. "Incongruous elements" is a synonym for actual defects or contradictions. The recognition of actual contradictions has as its purpose the indirect demand for change and improvement. Comedy constitutes the refusal to admit that anything imperfect is final.

Everett well sees that comedy is concerned with reasoning, whereas tragedy is concerned with feeling. Put objectively, this means that comedy is concerned with logic, while tragedy is concerned with value. Everett's words are that comedy is occupied with form, and tragedy with reality. "By reality I mean the elements that enter into the relation,"[81] i.e. the content. "In the comic we are taken into the world of surfaces. The forms about us mean nothing. All is empty. We are wholly free from the substance and are refreshed."[82] This is a penetrating observation, and accounts well for the intellectual nature of comedy. But it is by no means sufficient.

Everett's was not a great mind. His importance in this book consists in the fact that his work constitutes an excellent illustration of how close to the uniform classical conceptions of comedy the mediocre thinker can come. The inability to

[81] Op. cit., p. 188.
[82] Op. cit., p. 196.

Some Classical Theories of Comedy

stray from the truth about comedy is due entirely to the rigorous logical nature of comedy itself, which is the most intellectual training that the common uneducated person ever receives. For comedy is the only intellectual pursuit appealing to all alike, irrespective of the wide variety of intellectual failings and attainments.

The logical structure of comedy is so evident in every composition, that the misunderstanding of its nature is rendered very difficult so long as logic itself is given homage as a discipline essential to analysis. Thus while the Greeks did not penetrate very far in their studies of comedy, they did not make any very erroneous statements either. We have seen this to be true throughout Hellenistic and Roman times, and even as late as Tzetzes in the eleventh century.

But with the overthrow of the philosophy of realism and the rise of nominalism as a dominant metaphysics in the later Middle Ages, the emphasis of all normative studies upon the subjective aspects of existence brought new difficulties into play in the study of the theory of comedy. So deeply was the subjective postulate of nominalism accepted, that the question of an objective basis for comedy was not even discussed by the various philosophers who dealt with the topic, and no need to refute it was ever felt. It simply was not envisaged as a possibility. Instead it was taken for granted that comedy must be altogether a psychological affair, and the only question at hand was the nature of that psychological reaction which is called laughter. Thus the logic of comedy was transformed into the psychology of laughter.

Deserting logic as a discipline and clinging to psychology as an empirical study in the hope of unearthing the nature of comedy, the modern student has been led farther astray than ever in his investigations in this field. True, some important and valuable discoveries of an empirical nature have been made. But failing to understand what, for instance, physics has always implicitly understood, that the investigation of every field requires the united and mutually complementary efforts of both empirical research and logical consistency, modern studies of the theory of comedy have lost as much ground as they have gained. The weakness is already evident in Everett, since he lived in a period whose influences forced him to succumb to the substitution of psychology for logic without giving him the advantage of empirical psychological findings, which, as we shall see in the next chapter, is what the early twentieth century offered in their place.

CHAPTER III

Criticism of Modern Theories of Comedy

THE account of modern theories of comedy is entirely devoted to the following of nominalistic presuppositions. The assumption of the sole reality of physical particulars allows hypotheses or principles no objective standing and forces the investigator to look for them in the mind. Thus the theorist of the comic is driven either to explore the implications of its psychological aspects or else to seek in vain for a way of escape from the psychologistic explanation. There are few exceptions. Comedy for the vast majority of modern thinkers reduces to the apprehension of comedy, which is thought to be the whole form of its being. The creation of comedy is assumed to take place in the very act of its apprehension. There is of course one good reason for being grateful to this turn of thought, for to it we owe our understanding of the psychology of comedy, an understanding which might not have been developed so quickly under any other presuppositions. But as to the question of whether comedy is exhausted by such an analysis, that is quite another matter. We shall have to remember that in our study of the history of comedy much was revealed by realistic Greek thinkers which is not taken into account by the psychological explanation.

1. THE SUBJECTIVE-METAPHYSICAL: BERGSON

Henri Bergson is the author of a famous explanation of comedy, but before we set it forth in his own words it is only fair to warn the reader that the explanation is not half so simple as we are led by the simplicity of its expression to suppose.

In Praise of Comedy

Comedy, Bergson informs us, depends upon the recognition of something mechanical encrusted on the living. "*Something mechanical encrusted on the living* will represent a cross at which we must halt, a central image from which the imagination branches off in different directions."[1]

This phrase, which is taken as the keynote of the little book on laughter, does not come to the reader without a warning. Indeed he has been cleverly prepared for it by being asked first to accept some frankly subjective axioms. The first of these is that "the comic does not exist outside the pale of what is strictly *human*."[2] This is an axiom which it would be hard to demonstrate. Note that Bergson does not say "laughter" but "the comic," which implies that human beings do not apprehend the comic in laughter but rather create it. We can prove that the comic exists within the human range at least to some extent, but to demonstrate that it does not exist at all outside the human range would appear to be little short of impossible. It is always conceivable that comedy exists in nature and is apprehended and appreciated by humans and other forms of living organism. There is at least one modern theory which holds laughter to be a primitive antagonism and aggression, an evolutionary holdover from the days when bared fangs served the same purpose; and if this be true then the bared fangs of our modern dogs and tigers are instances of a kind of rudimentary comedy. The theory is not here supported but is set forth merely to show that there is at least much room for doubt concerning Bergson's limitation of the comic to the human.

Another axiom which Bergson asks us to accept is that the laughable is always excited by any comparison between the human body and a machine. "The attitudes, gestures, and movements of the human body are laughable in exact proportion as that body reminds us of a mere machine."[3] This, of course,

[1] Henri Bergson, *Laughter*, trans. Brereton and Rothwell (New York, 1928, Macmillan), p. 37.

[2] Op. cit., p. 3. [3] Op. cit., p. 29.

124

is true, but whether it is a fundamental factor in the theory of laughter is another matter. We must beware of accepting obvious truths as more basic than others less obvious which are equally true and no less basic. For by this method it is possible to throw an emphasis wherever it is required and thus to make out a conclusive case for whatever theory is being demonstrated. We may be amused when the body reminds us of a machine, but we are no more amused by this than we are by many other analogies. The ground is obviously being laid for the major thesis, already noted, that laughter is caused by the recognition of *le méchanique placque sur le vivant*, the mechanical encrusted on the living.

In order to criticize this thesis it will be necessary to go back of Bergson's theory of comedy to certain aspects of the metaphysics upon which the theory rests. We must recall that according to his metaphysics time is the primary reality. Understanding the close association between time and change, those things are the most immersed in time, as Bergson would say, which change the most. Of the items which suffer change, it is notorious that on the whole living things change more rapidly than non-living things. As opposed to the tremendously changing force of living things, in which time is, so to speak, intensified, we have the timeless, the changeless, the dead, the mechanical, the automatic, and the lifeless. Bergson identifies the lifeless with the mechanical as its very essence. Now comedy, says Bergson, is the mistaking of the mechanical for the living, the assumption that living forms can be held as they are, just as though they were mechanical—*le méchanique placque sur le vivant*.

The recognition that the stream of time sweeps all before it, including all such temporary abstractions as the customs and institutions of a certain day, is what causes laughter. It is indeed unfortunate that the recognition of the reality of time, a situation overlooked so often and for such long periods in the world's philosophy, should have brought with it the unjustifiable emphasis upon the *superior* reality of time. Is it not possible indeed to correct an error without committing its opposite? However, Bergson's philosophy has been criticized better elsewhere: here comment must be restricted to his theory of comedy alone. For it is his avowed metaphysics which manifestly lead him astray from an intuitively apprehended correct position. Bergson is not writing about laughter but about comedy. His metaphysics, according to which all abstractions are attempts to hold something out as of permanent truth and worth, an attempt doomed to failure by the very nature of things, compels adherence to the doctrine that abstractions belong to the abstracting operator—in short, that all distinctions are mental, and arbitrary from the point of view of an equably flowing temporal process.

The distinction between the mechanical and the living, conceived as opposites differing in quality and in kind, will not bear examination. As we know from physiology and anatomy, the living organism has its mechanism; and as we know from mechanics and statics, every mechanism has its purpose in terms of which it is a mechanism. The living organism is a higher form than the physical machine, but the idea of mechanism applies at the higher levels as well as at the lower, and the lower organizations certainly have their purposes, however subordinate these may be. Reality does not reside exclusively either in the one or in the other. They are equally real; therefore the ascription of reality to either one is meaningless if it is intended as a distinction. Furthermore, there are mechanical systems which may be quite successfully encrusted on the living without any loss of life. Scientific truth is developed to the extent to which mathematical systems are employed and mathematical tautologies utilized as scientific language. Certain of such truths are, to be sure, saved from time, and among these some scientific truths learned about living systems.

It is from the inside out, by means of the inherently subjective point of view, that Bergson would explain comedy; but his theory is actually better than that. There is much evidence in his own work for this contention: including the fact that there would be on his grounds no distinction between comedy and tragedy. For instance, the three properties by which he would distinguish the living from the mechanical: repetition, inversion, and reciprocal interference of series,[4] would be equally applicable to tragedy and to "light comedy." All the faults of Bergson's theory of comedy, to sum up these brief remarks, are due to the fact that he has twisted an inherently objective theory around to a subjective point of view, in order to make it more conformable with his metaphysics.

It requires only a slight shift in terminology, a change in emphasis, to see the objective and logical validity of the theory of comedy as set forth by Bergson. First of all, it must be understood that we are talking about comedy and not about laughter. The fact that the mechanical cannot be encrusted on the living since the process of time cannot be arrested, is equivalent to the proposition that *what is* will have to change slowly if it is to change in terms of *what ought to be*. The criticism of the limited forms of actuality constitutes an indirect approval of the logical order with its unlimited forms. But of course actuality is submitted to criticism not for being actual but for not being more logical. We want to improve the forms of actuality in exemplification of the hierarchy of possible forms which is the logical order; but we do not want to dispense with form itself in favour of an unmitigated flux. Nor of course, on the other hand, do we want to dispense with the flux, for the flux is what enables us to secure improvement of the forms. Bergson's theory has logical validity in that it recognizes the service of comedy as pointing to the limitations of forms in the flux. But it is limited in that it does not recognize the inevitability of forms, the necessity for their improvement, and hence the recognition of the equal reality of both orders: of forms and the flux.

Comedy for Bergson is the imposition of the mechanical on the living—well, this is at least an objective theory, whatever way Bergson may have tried to contort it. The recognition of

4 Bergson, op. cit., p. 89.

127

the fact that finite forms are not final is the recognition of an objective situation. Bergson's language in this regard is revealing; by "mechanical," "rigid," "stereotyped," Bergson is referring to the limitations of actuality, the insufficient inclusiveness of all actual organizations. Thus he is correct in observing that there is an animus in all humour; and that it is directed against the limitations of actuality, or, as he would say, of time.

Bergson is keenly aware of the rational and abstractive nature of comedy. He sees that it is devoted to generality whereas other forms of art are more individual.[5] Tragedy, of course, generalizes through feeling, but its symbols are of an individual nature. Comedy, however, generalizes through generalizations, and makes no bones about it. It does not, moreover, pay the price for this honesty of being far removed from actuality. On the contrary, comedy besides enjoying a high degree of generality is a pretty close adherent of fact. "Comedy," as Bergson observes correctly (although, alas, he has a subjective reason for saying so), "is far more like real life than drama is."[6] Elsewhere he also observes the social connections, "you would hardly appreciate the comic if you felt yourself isolated from others."[7]

The instinctive feeling for the logical rather than the psychological, which is apparent in every word of Bergson's essay, is most evident in several fine passages, wherein he observes that any upsetting of the logical order is an event which constitutes an object of comedy. The means substituted for the end is comical, and so is any illogical arrangement. "Any incident is comic that calls our attention to the physical in a person, when it is the moral side that is concerned."[8] This is a clear enough statement, albeit too specifically worded, of the truth that any reference downward in the hierarchy of value is funny. When Huysmans' secretary visited Anatole France with a message from the newly reformed Catholic to repent

[5] Bergson, Op. cit., p. 163.   [6] Op. cit., p. 136.
[7] Op. cit., p. 5.   [8] Op. cit., p. 51.

before it was too late, France replied by advising Huysmans to have his urine examined.[9] Any inference that a psychological event may be exhaustively caused by a physiological one is always humorous, because of the inexorable logicality of value. Thus comedy points not to the overestimated worth of the higher values but rather to our ignorance of their logic. Bergson's theory of comedy allows for deductions which are more justifiable than they appear to be.

However valid and important Bergson's intuitions concerning the implications of true comedy may prove, we shall have to abandon the chief position because it is fundamentally untenable. The metaphysical basis on which all of Bergson's work rests, namely that time is, so to speak, the essence of the contract, that what fluxes is more real than what is saved from the flux, can apply with equal force to his own philosophy which he no doubt hopes to keep safe and inviolate from change. Finally, when Bergson speaks of the mechanical encrusted on the living, it is with human beings that he is mainly concerned. Any attempt of the clown to ape the movements of a machine is funny; comedy consists in the simulation by the human being of a lifeless form, Bergson says. Subtly, but none the less surely, the argument comes back to an unshakable subjectivism which invalidates the whole theory. Despite the objective pretensions of Bergson's work, it is laughter and not comedy that he is writing about, and furthermore he is not writing in subjective terms. Thus his theory, however suggestive it may be, lacks both the objective basis of a realistic theory and the exact scientific information of a psychological theory. It would appear that we have more to learn either from a candidly metaphysical objective theory or from a candidly psychological subjective theory than we have from Bergson's confusion of the two.

[9] Jean-Jacques Brousson, *Anatole France en Pantoufles*.

In Praise of Comedy

2. The Subjective-Metaphysical: Croce, Carritt

It is unfortunate that idealism, a term we owe to Plato, the father of realism (in the mediaeval sense of the term, namely the objective reality of ideas independent of the mind and of anything actual), should have become identified with the wholly subjective point of view. But such is the case; and Croce's idealism is a name for an undisguised subjectivism. Everything for Croce must be explained on the basis of a knowing mind and a creating individual; it is all from the inside outward. Here we have nominalism in its most intensely subjective form: the knower is the creator not only of his knowledge, but of all reality as well, so that a sharp cleavage appears between the mind and the brute physical world. Interaction between the mind and the external world presents a problem which such a theory leaves unexplained, although interactionism is always required. This is the case with Croce's own theory, as we shall see.

Croce sums up his theory of the comic in the following words. "The comic has been defined as the displeasure arising from the perception of a deformity immediately followed by a greater pleasure arising from the relaxation of our psychical forces, which were strained in anticipation of a perception whose importance was foreseen."[10] This theory of comedy, which, Croce insists, includes that of all his classical predecessors from Plato to Kant, is an example of the "relief" theory of comedy. According to the relief theory, comedy is psychological, and is due to the sudden relaxation afforded when something serious proves to be not as grave as was expected. Psychic forces (whatever these may be) which were pent up are now released and the result is laughter.[11]

The first glaring presupposition is, of course, that comedy is entirely a psychological affair, which is very far from being

[10] See the whole passage on comedy in B. Croce, *Aesthetic*, trans. Ainslee, pp. 148–51.
[11] Cf. above, e.g. Kant, Spencer, etc.

proved. It is not proved, because it is not even discussed; it is taken for granted in the statement of the position. What must be denied here is not the limited validity of the psychological relief theory but its attempt to stand for the whole of comedy. The relief theory could be true and still be true only within certain limits. The psychological aspect of comedy can be said to be the whole of comedy, as with Croce, or it can be said to be merely the subjective reaction to a comic situation which is independent of all apprehension, as is more likely to be the case. In all events, Croce's claims for the relief theory sweep through a wider territory than his arguments attempt to defend.

The second presupposition is that "the perception of a deformity" is possible, although it would call for interaction between a radically separated mind and external world. Croce admits that the comic is psychological, and then states that laughter is its "physiological equivalent." Then after defending the traditional parallels to his theory he slowly begins to abandon it himself. His reason is that the theory is too wide because it "enunciates characteristics which are applicable, not only to the comic, but to every spiritual [sic] process." Such definitions, he warns us, must not be "taken too seriously," else they will become themselves comic instances; and he suggests that the danger is just what "Jean Paul Richter said of all the definitions of the comic: namely, that their sole merit is to be themselves comic."

If Croce himself is not willing to defend the theory of the comic to which a few pages earlier he has subscribed, why should anyone else? To suggest that all theories of the comic are false is to state that comedy is unanalysable. But this means to challenge all rational analysis, and since we, like Croce, have by the very act of undertaking philosophical speculations, committed ourselves to the view that valid rational analysis is at least possible, there appears to be little more to be said. Suffice to add that the psychological relief theory has the extremely limited validity which must be accorded all similar common-sense observations concerning the psychological reactions to comic situations. When something objective appears to be funny, we laugh. Our reaction does not constitute an analysis but merely the starting-point for analysis.

Professor E. F. Carritt, a disciple of Croce's, has attempted to set forth[12] a theory of comedy which would be conformable with the aesthetics of the master. He departs from Croce, however, in that he does not cast any final doubt upon his own theory. Carritt begins by calling attention to an obvious fact which few of his predecessors have noted: namely, that the ludicrous is part of the theory of beauty and that comedy therefore is one of the subdivisions of aesthetics. There is no doubt that a comic situation is in a certain sense a beautiful situation.

Carritt's chief contribution (if indeed we may call it that) is his idealistic theory of the ludicrous. The ludicrous, we are told, is always referred to human standards;[13] it always involves something hostile or inferior to us.[14] Appreciation of the comic implies the exercise of "aesthetic activity."[15] We are suddenly confronted with the incongruous,[16] and "our dissatisfaction with what is ugly or aesthetically incongruous can give rise to an aesthetic satisfaction only by being expressed."[17]

That such a theory of the ludicrous is a fair deduction from orthodox Crocean idealism we need have no doubt. The finality of the human reference, the recognition that the non-human material or medium is stubborn and therefore in need of bending to human design, the subjective exercise of aesthetic activity, these are plainly idealistic implications. It is all a matter of exquisite personal and human judgment and sensibilities, and the world is allowed to exist, so to speak, merely as a field for the expression of the artistic human. Self-expression is the pivotal thought, and the theory of the ludicrous

---

[12] E. F. Carritt, "A Theory of the Ludicrous," in *The Hibbart Journal*, vol. xxi (1923), p. 552.

[13] Op. cit., p. 553.   [14] Op. cit., p. 554.   [15] Op. cit., p. 557.
[16] Op. cit., p. 560.   [17] Op. cit., p. 563.

winds itself about this phrase just as the whole of the Crocean metaphysics does. The ugly, says Carritt, upsets us because of its incongruity; and where we can do nothing to render it more beautiful, when we are powerless to change it as we should like, we laugh.

Professor Carritt has by this time evidently forgotten that he had previously posited the ludicrous as a specie of the beautiful, and that the ludicrous should somehow be beautiful, therefore, without having to be changed. But the incongruous at which we laugh turned out to be the ugly, and so there is an unresolved contradiction in the position. The theory reveals its subjectivism again in reducing the ludicrous (an objective term) to the "aesthetic satisfaction" of "being expressed," to laughter and the recognition of the comic. Professor Carritt speaks of "the comic aspect of real life,"[18] but maintains that this implies that human activity has been exercised upon it. The ludicrous consists in the appreciation of the comic aspect of real life, but the comic aspect of real life consists in the aesthetic satisfaction to be derived from the self-expression of dissatisfaction with the incongruous and the ugly, all of which is a variety of beauty. This is what we are asked to believe, and as set forth here it is merely a condensation of the position which Carritt thinks would be conformable with Croce's aesthetics. There is some doubt as to whether Carritt has successfully accounted for the ludicrous, but in all events the theory of comedy still remains to be explained.

3. The Subjective-Literary: Jankélévitch, Eastman, Leacock

No less subjectivistic than Carritt and no less influenced by contemporary psychologism is the little work on irony by Jankélévitch.[19] For him irony like art is the child of leisure, and irony differs from other artistic manifestations in being

[18] Op. cit., p. 557.
[19] Vladimir Jankélévitch, *L'Ironie* (Paris, 1936, Alcan).

the voice of conscience. The perpetrator of ironic humour is freer; he, more than the creative artist, is the appreciator.

The historic origins of the position can be traced back to Socrates. So-called "Socratic irony," we may recall, was usually employed in the dialogues to make fun of the subjective positions taken up by the Sophists. Its classic task was to establish and defend the realistic position. To see it used now as a synonym for conscience is irony indeed! But as we have noted already in Chapter II, the few references to comedy in the writings of Plato consider it to be impotence masquerading as the appearance of power. Plato was concerned with the nature of comedy and with its effect on the observer. Jankélévitch seizes the aspect of its effect upon the observer, and assumes that the creation of irony or humour takes place in someone's mind, an assumption unjustified by the references to comedy in Plato's writings. For the recognition of the fact that in a given situation impotence is masquerading as power does not depend upon any human creator but merely on the capacity of the observer to apprehend that aspect.

It is a fact that in the struggle of contradictory theories of reality we do not find truth opposed to error; the situation is not as simple as that. Rather do we find truth opposed to lesser truth, broader truths struggling with the error which lurks in the lesser truths. Thus there is certainly an element of truth in Jankélévitch's contention that irony is the voice of conscience. If conscience has any affinity whatsoever with the nature of things (and we may assume that it has, since nothing that exists can be said to be unrelated to other existing things, and all such things have something in common from which non-existence is excluded, namely their existence), then it may to a certain limited degree be true that conscience in its reference to the logical order is appealing away from things as they are and to things as they ought to be. But such an appeal, framed in subjective terms, can have little reference to other than the subject's own *ought*. It is a limited *truth* indeed, but one whose truth is too *limited*. Comedy in its broadest sense is the appeal away from things as they are and toward things as they ought to be; but this must be without exclusive reference to any one thing, such as a particular individual's personal conscience. There is a sense in which every actual individual mirrors everything else in the universe, as both Whitehead and Leibniz have very well shown, but there is also the additional sense in which the actual individual is only one among a number of other individuals whose name is legion; and it is this latter truth which no subjectivist theory of irony as the voice of conscience can satisfactorily take into account.

Comedians, both professional and amateur, find an irresistible temptation in the desire to give vent to speculations concerning the theory of their art. The tragedian rarely finds it necessary to explain to the world the nature of tragedy in general, but to the comedian the impulse to speculative theory is one he cannot resist. As Max Eastman has pointed out in many instances in his recent work,[20] almost every American comedian has at some time or other offered either an abstract suggestion or a complete theory of comedy. This phenomenon is not difficult to explain. Comedy, as Bergson and others have often shown, is an intellectual affair to some extent at least. The psychological reaction to comedy is of course emotional, just like the apprehension of tragedy. But in comedy, as many of the theories of comedy which have been set forth above indicate, logic lies, so to speak, nearer the surface than it does in tragedy, and the evidences of its inherently logical nature would be hard to overlook. Aristotle's fundamental logical laws, almost in their candid form, furnish the framework of the professional comedian's timeworn stock-in-trade. For instance, there is the use of the law of identity, as in Burns' and Allen's radio broadcast, when Gracie Allen says, "there's the band leader, for instance: we could let him be the band leader."

In this company of theorizing amateur comedians we must

[20] *Enjoyment of Laughter* (New York, 1936, Simon & Schuster).

include Max Eastman himself, since by the composition of his book, which is half joke-book and half popularized theory, he has chosen his own category. Mr. Eastman's theory is timidly set forth, and for the most part lacks development, although it certainly does not go in want of illustration. We are told that "things can be funny only when we are in fun" and that "when we are in fun . . . disagreeable things . . . tend to acquire a pleasant emotional flavour and provoke a laugh"[21] and that " 'being in fun' is a condition most natural to childhood" which "grown-up people retain in varying degrees."[22] We may grant the last statement, since it is true not only of laughter but of other human emotions, such as fear, grief, hunger, and many others. As to the first part of the thesis, it has a certain amount of validity too, but the trouble with it is that it was not worth saying; it is not a very profound analysis.

Eastman's theory is not profound because it is merely a re-statement of the "play" theory without the excuse of any fresh analysis. Ludovici stated that humour consists in aggression, somewhat concealed, and Freud has advanced the same hypothesis. Eastman adopts the opposite view, that humour is not concealed aggression but rather playfulness. No one will disagree with the comic aspects of play; the only question is whether play exhausts comedy or constitutes its essence. Playfulness is a subjective category, and therefore there is always the possibility that play might constitute a reaction as well as an initiated action. The analysis would certainly have to go further than Eastman has carried it in order to be defended at all. For the most part he is under the impression that a wealth illustration carries the proof of a theory, which it assuredly does not. It does no more than allow the theory. The proof rests upon grounds which Eastman has not succeeded in presenting.

We have been previously told by many philosophers from Hobbes and Kant to the present time that the viewpoint of

[21] See also p. 8 on this point: "It is the unpleasant in general which, when taken playfully, is enjoyed as funny."
[22] Op. cit., p. 3.

comedy is not to take tragedy seriously; that we can laugh at danger because it has, so to speak, had its teeth pulled. We were told so first by Plato and Aristotle. Eastman's theory is not new because he has merely couched an accepted truth in the language of what Santayana has called "literary psychology"; he has endeavoured not to do any pioneer thinking but rather to present a piece of painless knowledge. For this reason its worth as a contribution to theory is minimal. Eastman is chiefly to be thanked for the many useful examples of different kinds of comedy which he has collected in his volume.

Like Eastman, Leacock is a comedian, but unlike Eastman he is a very good comedian. True, he never ventures very deeply in the criticisms of his own times which furnish the subject-matter of his comic writings, but he is a good comedian nevertheless, since what he has to say is often extremely funny and what he criticizes is often deserving of criticism. Since the key to the understanding of the shortcomings of his theory of comedy are contained in his own comic writings, we may say another word about them. Leacock ventures to criticize the customs and institutions of the actual world in which he lives, but his criticisms in this direction are always at the most superficial level. He objects to the minor pretensions of the middle class, whose actions and observances no longer represent true beliefs, but at heart Leacock does not want to change anything very fundamental. This shortcoming, added to the fact that he is living in a swiftly changing world, throws him back upon himself and stalemates most of his comedy. Since change is abhorrent to him, he has come to regard things-as-they-are as more or less equal to things as they-ought-to-be, and any drastic social change as an attempt to transform the current scene into one of things as they ought not to be.

Hence the old realistic distinction between things as they are and things as they ought to be receives a curiously twisted interpretation in Leacock's hands. "The Romans liked to see a chariot and its occupant smashed in the circus; we prefer to see a clown fall off a trapeze. Our clown, poor creature, is the living symbol of our redeemed humanity, uplifted from cruelty to make-believe. Humour thus grew to turn on a contrast between the thing as it is, or ought to be, and the thing smashed out of shape and as it ought not to be."[23] This is certainly a curious conclusion to emerge with from so eloquent a passage. Things in this world are as they ought to be, and to change them is to render them as they ought not to be! Would that it were so.

Later Leacock sums up his theory and defines humour as "the contemplation and interpretation of our life" which finds its basis in the "incongruity of life itself,"[24] and in a later work he has declared that humour "may be defined as the kindly contemplation of the incongruities of life and the artistic expression thereof."[25] Although much too broad a statement, there is evidence here that something of the truth about humour is peeping out. The kindly contemplation of the crucified clown is at least a symbolically true picture of the rôle of the comedian. But is it not clear that Mr. Leacock is in love with the old order of things for what was good about it, and therefore wants to see it preserved? This is not in itself a crime, surely, provided that the cost is not too great. But neither is it the traditional intent of comedy, which is always willing to see the old order perish for what was limited about it, with a view to preserving the possibility of greater order.

4. THE SUBJECTIVE-LITERARY: MENON, SEWARD, GREGORY

The influence of the psychologists upon those who to-day speculate on the nature of comedy and humour is immense. A glance at a bookshelf containing works on humour reveals this tendency through the titles alone: Gregory's *The Nature of Laughter*, Bergson's *Laughter*, Menon's *A Theory of Laughter*. It is clear that for the modern speculator, comedy and humour

[23] Stephen Leacock, *Humour: Its Theory and Technique* (Toronto, 1935, Dodd, Mead), p. 11.
[24] Op. cit., p. 15.
[25] *Humour and Humanity* (New York, 1938, Holt), p. 1.

may be reduced entirely to their effects upon the appreciator. The question asked nowadays is not what is the essence of the comic situation but rather what is it that makes us laugh, what is the essence of laughter. We may single out one of these works for examination as typical of the trend, and for this purpose Menon's will be the most satisfactory, for in it more than in any other is the surrender to professional psychology utter and complete.

Menon begins with the candid appeal to the instinct psychology of McDougall, the most old-fashioned and subjective of the contemporary psychologies.[26] McDougall himself is unwilling to allow the explanation of laughter to rest upon the shoulders of psychology but pushes it farther down to the "scientific" level of physiology. Laughter, it seems, has to do with the liberation of energy, and for confirmation Menon quotes another physiologist, Baillie. The case is now clear; without asking whether this understanding of laughter differentiates laughter from anything else in the actual world (since according to thermodynamics all activity has to do with the liberation of energy, which is constantly seeking lower levels of availability), Menon draws his first conclusion. The liberation of energy in the case of laughter certainly takes place inside the human body; hence "we are then justified in seeking for the cause in the person himself who laughs and not in the situation."[27] "The cause of laughter is more intimately connected with ourselves, the subject, than with the object, and laughter has to be explained subjectively rather than objectively."[28]

So at least there is an object. It doesn't really count, because, as we have seen, laughter is caused by events in the somatic organism; but the object has, even in Menon's theory, a curious way of creeping back into the argument more or less uninvited.

Menon arrives at his psychological conclusions from the

[26] V. K. Krishna Menon, *A Theory of Laughter* (London, 1931, George Allen & Unwin), pp. 14–15.

[27] Op. cit., p. 17.   [28] Op. cit., p. 18.

physiological premises and a further argument. These premises are as follows: "(1) Laughter is a demobilization of forces; (2) these forces are psycho-physical, instinctive; (3) in some elementary form it (laughter) is common to all animals; and (4) its biological value lies in providing an outlet for unused energy, and in providing the alternative to repression and its attendant complications." Let us examine these in their numerical order.

(1) With regard to the point that laughter is a demobilization of forces, we may say that it has already been discussed. It is merely the formulation of physiological findings in convenient form for psychological application. With the proviso that the statement is so broad as to serve no useful definition, we may accept it. (2) We may accept too, within limits, the condition that these forces are psycho-physical. For an event within an organism, what else could they be? But that they are instinctive assumes that all drives toward goals originate from within the subject; and this is far from having been conclusively shown by McDougall or anyone else. The term instinct is merely a postulated entity to cover an ignorance of cause. It does not have the scientific sanctity which its hallowed use in psychology would suggest, and it is not nearly so explanatory as are other more recent psychologies. (3) Laughter in some elementary form is common to all animals. This is a likely point, although far from having been demonstrated. The saving item is the phrase, "in some elementary form." If laughter is common also to the lower animals, as well it may be, we still might not recognize it when we see it, since elementary forms of familiar elements have a way of being qualitatively very different from more advanced forms. (4) Is there any distinction of an important nature between the biological value of providing an outlet for unused energy, and laughter as the demobilization of forces, except the fact that the investigation is carried on at the biological rather than at the psychological level? Once again, does not almost any activity in which an animal engages provide an outlet for unused energy?

Criticism of Modern Theories of Comedy

Thus we see that starting with the theoretical foundations of physiology and psychology Menon has arrived at a completely subjective view of humour, namely that it consists in laughter, and that laughter has a physiological explanation. We may assume that for Menon at least this argument will prove conclusive. After stating his theory of laughter, Menon compares his theory with other theories, and it is here that he begins to weaken a little. Finally, when he seeks in the empirical field for actual examples of comedy and laughter, his position shifts almost entirely. Actual events have a way of proving stumbling-blocks to theories whose original formulation did not attempt to take them into account. Menon's explanation of laughter finds heavy going when confronted with actual instances of comedy and laughter drawn from the great comedians of literature.

In discussing the nature of humour preparatory to considering the definitions put forward by Goethe and Samuel Johnson, Menon falls back upon the old incongruity theory. " 'Humour' thus implies an incongruity of perceptions. Our first perception is from one point of view and the second from a different point of view. Considered so, humour may be taken as involving a change of standpoints or attitudes."[29] It would have been possible to state the incongruity theory in terms more consistent with Menon's subjective interpretation of comedy and laughter. There was no need to go this far. Indeed Menon has stated the incongruity theory in terms of a perspective on the objective, and thus nearly robbed the original theory of all its subjective validity. Certainly a considerable shift has taken place. The objective has not only been introduced as an important factor, despite what has previously been said as to its unimportance, but has been given a central place in the situation. It is merely by a comparison between the perspectives on the object that the incongruous appears, and thus laughter as well as humour must hang upon perspectives on the subject.

But let us read further. Menon finally comes to a discussion

[29] Op. cit., p. 41.

of Bergson's theory of laughter. Bergson might be described as a sly subjectivist; which is to say that although his theory is couched in objective terms, it is fundamentally subjective, being in the last analysis a variety of nominalism in that it asserts the flux to be alone real and ultimate. The result of this on Menon's struggle with his own theory is illuminating. With the aid of the incongruity theory, Menon has finally been driven to maintain that "humour is the result of incongruous perceptions of an object made possible from our knowledge of its nature and its relations to other objects."[30] This is a *dénouement* indeed. The subjective theory with which Menon started is now in full retreat. The whole business now hangs on the relations which the object has with other objects, plus our knowledge of its *nature*. Menon himself is aware of the betrayal, and his dismay is conscientiously displayed on the next page, where the subjective theory is brought back in, as a tag phrase hung onto the new formulation of the definition of humour. "We may, from the intellectual point of view, say that humour is a sense of the incongruous suggested by an object in its nature and relation to other things as known to us."

Menon's theory of laughter, of comedy or of humour, is not sufficiently original or sufficiently important to deserve so protracted a discussion. There are other and more authoritative statements of the subjectivist position. But Menon's case is typical. He begins with the now orthodox subjective theory, but when he comes to examine other theories and, even more important, when he is faced with specific examples of humour chosen from the great humorists of literature, he is gradually forced out of his subjectivist shell and into the light of day where broader facts which are recognized by society, and which are obviously stubborn and exist whether they are so recognized or not, give the lie to any but an objectivist theory of humour. In all justice it should be urged in defence of Menon that he was logical enough to understand that when facts contradict a theory the theory must at least be modified, and the existence

[30] Op. cit., p. 68.

of an object of comedy is a fact so elemental and irreducible that there is no other way but to recognize it.

Another variety of the subjective theory of comedy is that which endeavours to found itself upon the spirit of play. Such a one is that of Seward, and it is somewhat more involved than the play theory of Eastman's which we have already examined. The theory comes to light in his explanation of the psychological origins of the ludicrous. "The process as a whole may be thought of as one of building up, of enriching the meaning of the playful spirit, of adding to its resources for pleasure.

"And now when the spirit is thus prepared, we stumble across some incongruous spectacle that brings us vivid associations, direct or indirect, with this stored-up sense of playfulness. The playful mood is thus reinvited, and it dominates our feeling as we regard the incongruous spectacle. This feeling, this emotional attitude accompanying observation, is not the recollected pleasure of any definite experience, but a vaguer sense that there is matter here inviting a playful attitude. Though this attitude was cultivated in an active pursuit of playful pleasure, it has now become essentially passive, contemplation steeped in pleased emotional consciousness. The charm of the subjective mood has transferred itself to the objective spectacle. The original active mood was felt as a mood of fun; the spectacle that awakens the mood is now felt to be funny. In that transference our sense of the ludicrous is born."[31]

There is so much comment to be made on this theory that it is hard to decide where to begin; but perhaps the less said the better. The sense of play is taken as basic and given. We feel in a playful mood, and then we run across "some incongruous spectacle," which presumably is also given. We have already seen other writers hanging their entire theory of

[31] Samuel S. Seward, Jr., *The Paradox of the Ludicrous* (California, 1930, Stanford University Press), p. 27.

comedy upon a postulated incongruity. But there is a surprise in store, a surprise that we can not refuse to call novel; for Professor Seward has his own little incongruity theory. Our mood is said to be one of fun, because when playful in spirit we ran, or rather stumbled, across some incongruous spectacle. This event caused us to transfer the fun to the incongruous spectacle, which is now felt to be funny. This is the new incongruity, that somehow we found funny things when we felt funny—and it was this transference which caused our sense of the ludicrous to be born. And, O yes, we must not forget, either, that after the transfer had been made, it turned out that it was the spectacle after all that awakened the mood of fun. The title of Professor Seward's book would seem to indicate that the perpetration of such compounded contradictions was intentional; but at least we can give him the benefit of the doubt.

Metaphysical postulates cannot be dismissed, since they are not dependent upon our consciousness of them. Anything, any action, is in a sense a proposition whose metaphysical status is susceptible of analysis. Thus although the explicit importance of metaphysics has gone out of fashion as a theory, this development in no wise operates to dismiss its functioning as a fact. Postulates are still postulates, and in some ways more powerful when we are not aware of them than when we are. For example, never once does J. C. Gregory[32] stop to consider that the very title of his book commits him to a certain point of view. This view is of course the inevitably modern one of subjectivity: comedy is a matter of laughter, and laughter results from certain physiological or psychological events that take place within the body. The external stimulus which arouses laughter is regarded as a sort of necessary evil: it has to be mentioned but it really has little to do with the case. What counts is the analysis of psychic events which give rise to the physiological manifestation of laughter.

[32] *The Nature of Laughter* (New York, 1924, Harcourt, Brace).

Criticism of Modern Theories of Comedy

Gregory's book is a mine of quotations: he is aware of the many varieties of humour, and he realizes that the effort to get them all included under a single definition is no small task. His solution to this problem may be stated in his own words.

"The 'happy convulsion' of laughter occurs in a situation of relief. It collapses the laugher into a stationary exerciser of his own body who is convulsively withdrawn from intervention in the active affairs of life. It marks the sudden relaxation of unrequired effort, and its repetitive series of respiratory explosions or tremulation of body, more vigorously or more quietly, rehearses an original situation in which a call upon effort is sharply called off. The original, more physical situation of the laugher is too plainly exposed in the motions of his body to be mistaken. As a spring firmly pressed against an obstacle vibrates when the obstacle is withdrawn, so the body shakes to and fro, with gasps in its breathing, in tremulous laughter, when its effort suddenly relaxes into relief. A quick interruption of activity that precipitates into relief is the essential characteristic of laughter as it is revealed in its characteristic bodily expression. Laughter is a *diversion*—a pleasant expenditure upon the body of energy released from other activities."[33]

There is nothing strictly wrong with any statement of Gregory's analysis of laughter. The analysis has been made almost entirely at the level of common sense, and his sins are rather sins of omission. The mechanism is what we might have been able to conclude for ourselves while watching someone engaged in hearty laughter, provided only that we had been given the key of the notion of "relief." Elsewhere Gregory says that "laughter may be interjected whenever and wherever a call upon effort is suddenly called off into relief."[34] This is the classic "relief" theory; the rest is merely common observation. It is neither abstractive nor highly penetrating. The language is that of textbook psychology shading off into physiology, but

[33] Op. cit., pp. 203–204.
[34] Op. cit., p. 207.

not at any very precise scientific level. It would be an admission of defeat to state that such an amazingly superficial analysis was all that could be made of the subject of humour.

Throughout his work Gregory has quoted Freud and others whose analyses, while remaining strictly psychological, are more highly abstractive than any which Gregory himself has succeeded in making. And there are still other quoted definitions and explanations of humour which offer evidence that the ambitious programme of Gregory, shared by all those who have ventured to speculate on the same topic, has failed of its avowed purpose to include all the aspects of humour under a single explanatory definition. This purpose, however, is defeated chiefly because Gregory has chosen arbitrarily to assume a subjective metaphysics, one which takes for granted in a rough way that the world external to the somatic organism is incidental only to what happens within the organism. Thus the objective nature of comedy, corresponding to the subjective nature of laughter, is omitted altogether in a sweeping exclusion which is not even self-aware. Mr. Gregory is plainly not conscious of the fact that there can even be such an aspect as the objective meaning of comedy. Its omission is a blind omission.

Nevertheless, to account for such objective meaning is a necessity for any comprehensive explanation of the topic of comedy, and we do not avoid the obligation to render a solution by ignorance of the existence of the problem. The "incongruity" theory, which many have vainly attempted to render in subjective terms, the recognition of the incongruity of things, is a necessary part of humour and demands explanation and a place in any inclusive system of humour, comedy and laughter. The derogation of what-is in favour of what-ought-to-be, which certainly gives rise to comedy, must be discussed and explained. The critical aspect of comedy, which depends upon the objectivity of its field of consideration, cannot be taken into account when the whole explanation is rendered in terms of laughter. The latter certainly has its very important place, but this place is not a central one. Laughter is a reaction to an objective situation, a mechanism set off by an event itself inherently comic. We must learn what characteristics this kind of situation has before we can say anything in a conclusive way about the nature of comedy and its manifestation in laughter.

5. THE PSYCHOANALYTIC: FREUD

The release of nervous energy, following a disappointed expectation, was the explanation of laughter given by Herbert Spencer, and the German Lipps enlarged upon this suggestion in his theory of "psychic damming." The occasion of the comic, said Lipps, is the exposure of pettiness under the imposing front of seeming grandeur.[35] In understanding both Lipps and his follower Freud it is necessary to bear in mind that Lipps was a Kantian, which means that he accepted the view that the world is divided between an unknowable external world and a knowable internal or subjective world. It follows from this that all reliable and important knowledge must belong to psychology, since all that we are reasonably capable of knowing is ourselves.

Freud admits at the outset that he is a disciple of Lipps and that he is taking his start in the theory of wit from Lipps' own theory. Consequently he swallows without any examination all the presuppositions that are implicit in Lipps' account. The major of these is the Kantian postulate. Now the Kantian postulate is by no means something to accept blindly and unchallenged. The entire modern school of realist philosophers has doubted that we are confined to concepts of our own making. The arguments are too numerous to list here, but suffice to say that the central Kantian position is one that has been successfully doubted and in part discredited by more recent thinkers. The difficulty is that of founding an ontological hypothesis upon an epistemological investigation. The problem of whether knowledge is possible and also the additional problem of just what the status of knowledge is, seem to have

[35] Lipps, *Komik und Humor*.

very little to do with the altogether different problem of what
it is that we know.

At the outset Freud loyally advertises Lipps' committal
of wit to an irrevocable subjectivity when he states that wit is
"essentially the subjective side of the comic, i.e. it is that part
of the comic which we ourselves create, which colours our
conduct as such."[36] It is clear that Freud is fully aware he is
following Lipps in treating of wit as the subjective aspect of
the comic. As we shall later see, the comic, too, turns out to
be subjective, thus invalidating the claim that wit is the "subjective side" of the comic by putting the comic also on the
subjective side. However, it is from the hint given by Lipps
with his psychic expenditure that Freud eventually comes to
his theory of the relief and aggression mechanism operating
to release unconscious psychic forces and thus produce pleasure.

There is probably no significance in the fact that wit, which
is ordinarily regarded as a rather trivial form of comedy or
humour, is taken by Freud as the topic for investigation.
However, since it is given Freud's and Lipps' own peculiar
definition as the subjective aspect of the comic, we must turn
next to Freud's description and definition of wit.

"The process of condensation with substitutive formation
is demonstrable in all witticisms,"[37] we are informed. In the
question of the analysis of wit, "condensation remains the
chief category."[38] This is "word-wit,"[39] or wit resulting from
plays on the means of expression of ideas. But there is also
"thought-wit," or plays on the ideas themselves. Freud insists
on identifying the latter with the dream-formation. Thus
"witty character" must be sought for in "the form of expression,"[40] since the "character of wit depends upon the mode
of expression."[41] Here we are on treacherous ground so far
as logic is concerned. Some wit evidently has to do with the

---

[36] Sigmund Freud, *Wit and Its Relation to the Unconscious* (London,
no date, Kegan Paul), p. 4.

[37] Op. cit., p. 32.   [38] Op. cit., p. 50.   [39] Op. cit., p. 125.
[40] Op. cit., p. 17.   [41] Op. cit., p. 135.

manner in which wit is expressed, while other wit has to do with that which is expressed, with the *content* of expression. The whole business, both means and end, being wit, the distinction is made rather superfluous. For what Freud is saying is that wit can be divided into two varieties according to whether it is concerned with its own means or with its own end. But since it must always have a means and an end, else it could not be expressed or there would be nothing to express, the division itself seems wholly unjustifiable.

There is of course a special meaning in all this. Freud apparently is trying to say that wit is often concerned with language as an end, with making fun of language (plays on words, for instance), while at other times its butt is different (something material, for instance). Also, wit employs language as a means sometimes (as in spoken or written jokes), while at other times physical motions may be the means employed (as in funny gestures). These two sets of means and ends are badly confused in the Freudian analysis. The distinction is really very simple, but by means of an elaborate and technical vocabulary it is made to appear difficult and profound. "Word-wit" and "thought-wit" taken together cover a bit of muddled thinking.

"Wit serves to acquire pleasure";[42] that is its function. "When we do not use our psychic apparatus for the fulfilment of one of our indispensable gratifications, we let it work for our pleasure, and we seek to derive pleasure from its own activity."[43] "Wit . . . is an activity whose purpose is to derive pleasure—be it intellectual or otherwise—from the psychic processes."[44] But how is this purpose served; how does wit function to procure pleasure? "Wit affords us the means of surmounting restrictions and of opening up otherwise inacessible pleasure sources."[45] "The main character of wit-making is to set free pleasure by removing inhibitions."[46]

---

[42] Op. cit., p. 287.
[43] Op. cit.., p. 136.
[44] Op. cit., p. 137.   [45] Op. cit., p. 150.   [46] Op. cit., p. 206.

In Praise of Comedy

Let us analyse these various propositions. We find immediately that they divide into two: namely, method and aim. The aim of wit is asserted to be pleasure. That wit does afford pleasure is a statement that none will attempt to deny. It is pleasant to laugh; otherwise, in most cases at least, we would not do it. In fact, the close connection between all forms of wit, comedy and humour, and joy is well known. Joy and pleasure have always been identified with one or another of the varieties of comedy. There is nothing to quarrel with in this innocent observation; but underneath it there lies a very broad and questionable premise. This premise is our old subjective adversary, namely, the proposition that wit has no other than a narrowly subjective purpose. Wit affords pleasure well enough; the only question at issue is whether this is merely a secondary aim or the sole aim.

Of course the way in which Freud has defined wit, namely, as the subjective side of the comic, renders this assertion a truism. If wit is subjective, then its aim is likely to be subjective also. But it would be strange indeed if all comedy (and Freud has chosen wit as the most important form of the comic) had no other aim than to afford subjective pleasure. The subject is an organization existing at a number of levels: the physical, the physiological, the psychological, and even the social, and none of these levels of organization are wholly explicable except in terms of reaction with the remainder of the world. The subject, in other words, is part of an external world, which is required for the total explanation of any of its activities. Now Freud makes wit a subjective occurrence having none but a subjective aim. The external world is not called in at all to account for an event which takes place within the subject for the subject's own benefit. It is more likely, then, that the affording of pleasure is a secondary and incidental benefit to be derived from the comic in its subjective manifestation as wit. This leaves the question of the primary aim as yet unaccounted for. That the primary aim is implied but not explicitly set forth by certain passages in Freud's treatise will be presently shown.

The second point to be considered in the case of wit has to do with the method employed. The statement that wit sets pleasure free by removing inhibitions involves the whole structure of the Freudian psychology. There certainly must be some truth in it. But in order to determine just what the limits of this truth are, a whole volume devoted to the analysis of psychoanalysis would be required. Psychoanalysis can be accepted only with certain reservations. [47] At the level of analysis investigated by Freud, the situation is probably more complicated than he imagines. His theory is difficult of empirical verification. The subjective orientation here produces further difficulties, since the inhibitions removed very likely are also those of all objective appreciators who may have been placed already in a situation where they were able to apprehend instances of wit.

Freud himself is confronted with the problem of accounting for what appear to be obvious instances of objective comedy. Why are things other than human beings funny? Freud is determined to hold on to his subjective theory at all costs, so he meets this new objection by fiat. "Even animals and inanimate objects become comical as the result of a widely used method of personification." [48] By objectifying the subject while keeping him a subject, the trick is turned. Here Freud switches over to a new master. Lipps is temporarily abandoned for Bergson, whose subjective theory we have already discussed. Freud says, "We laugh because we compare the motions in others with those which we ourselves should produce if we were in their place." [49] "We laugh when we admit to ourselves

---

[47] See my critical essay, "The Logic of Psychoanalysis," in the *International Journal of Individual Psychology*, for the fourth quarter, 1936, p. 55. The essay gives an indication of some of the logical fallacies of Freudian psychology; it does not attempt to set forth the valid aspects.

[48] Freud, *Wit and Its Relation to the Unconscious*, p. 302.

[49] Op. cit., p. 306.

that had we been placed in the same situation we should have done the same thing."[50]

There are two definite world-views differing with respect to the 'way in which the subject is assumed to be situated in the world. The first assumes that the subject is part of an external world in whose welfare he has an interest, and thus his own welfare is of the nature of an incidental benefit to be derived from the welfare of this external world. Society is a larger part of this external world than the subject taken alone. Therefore by serving society and the whole of the external world, the subject can gain the incidental benefit of his own advantage.

The second view assumes that the subject is a force arrayed against a hostile world which is indifferent to his welfare, but in which he must pursue his own advantage regardless of the effect of such action upon the rest of the world. Society on this view is merely a collection of such self-seeking subjects, and can be benefited only by the successful pursuance by each subject of his own welfare and advantage.

Freud adopts for his psychology the second view. Hence any pleasure which the subject takes in the objects of an external world must somehow be justified subjectively by Bergson's theory of personification. The point is that it would be just as easy, and less of a distortion, to take the common-sense objective view, which simply observes that some objective things are funny because we do not find them as we have come to know they ought to be. Although sympathy is ingredient to any understanding of the world, a cat with a can tied to its tail does not remind us of how we would feel in a similar situation, since we have no tails; it simply reminds us that cans tied to the tails of cats are out of place. The incongruous substitution of what is for what ought to be is funny. We compare the actual not with ourselves but with an objective norm, which we have come through our experience with actuality to know.

[50] Op. cit., p. 316.

Criticism of Modern Theories of Comedy

The obstinate insistence upon the absolute subjectivity of wit is bound to reach a climax in some reduction to absurdity. This reduction Freud himself has accomplished for us. "The subjective conditions of wit," he says, "are frequently fulfilled in the case of neurotic persons."[51] In popular parlance it is commonly observed that comedians are nuts; but this is very far from saying that they are neurotic. That some neurotics are witty may be a necessary condition to fit Freud's theory, but it certainly has no relation to the facts. There are certainly many neurotic persons who are not funny at all but quite tragic. Such a statement as Freud's is only understandable when we remember that Freudian psychology is abnormal psychology. In physical science, any event which departs from a rule refutes the rule, since empirical laws admit of no exception. But in Freudian psychology we have the strange situation of rules only observable in their departures. It is no more neurotic to observe that things are not as they ought to be than it is to laugh. Laughter has always been construed as a manifestation of well-being rather than of neurosis.

The spectre of the subjective determination continues to oppress us with its indifference to error. Let us consider the relation of wit to the comic. It will be recalled that Freud adopted Lipps' definition of wit as the "subjective side of the comic," which definition by implication forces the comic to be something non-subjective whose subjective side wit is. Let us see, then, just how objective is the comic. To begin with, Bergson's subjective definition of the comic is formally adopted.[52] Freud has also stated in comparing wit and the comic, that "Wit is made, while the comical is found; it is found first of all in persons, and only later by transference may be seen also in objects, situations, and the like."[53] Again, "the comic situation is largely based on embarrassment."[54] Alas, this is not very objective. It starts as subjective and can

[51] Op. cit., p. 285.
[52] Op. cit., pp. 337–338.
[53] Op. cit., p. 289.

[54] Op. cit., p. 367.

153

become objective only by transference. Such a transference is of course a personification. "Wit is, so to speak, the contribution to the comic from the sphere of the unconscious."[55] For some reason or other, the conscious is strictly taboo in Freudian psychology. But where else can we place the comic? It is not objective; and it is not unconscious; there is no other place for it on these assumptions but consciousness. Now consciousness is subjective, albeit not in the depths of the unconscious. Therefore the comic is subjective and resides in consciousness. It must be the conscious recognition of wit, as the latter rises up from the unconscious.

In an effort to clear up the relation of wit to the comic Freud resorts to genetic psychology, and seeks an explanation in childish comedy. The laughter of the child is not an expression of superiority but of "pure pleasure."[56] "The comic is actually always on the side of the infantile."[57] That the origins of adult conditions should be found in children in a primitive state is not to be denied; but it is not very enlightening either. We do not demonstrate what a thing is by showing what it was. An oak is a tree and not a big acorn. Why is the comic on the side of the infantile any more than the tragic is? Is the comic any more the "regaining of lost infantile laughing" than starvation is the regaining of lost infantile hunger, or bathing the regaining of lost infantile cleanliness? The argument is indeed absurd. Everything is explained by Freud as being either infantile or abnormal. What, pray, are the normal and the adult in themselves? They must have at least an equal validity with their defections.

Although wit is the chief item of Freud's analysis, he explains the comic in an attempt to demark it from wit, and later on he performs the same service for humour. Freud's penchant for subjectivity leads him to distinguish each new term from the others by fresh assertions of its special subjective

[55] Op. cit., p. 336.
[56] Op. cit., p. 363.
[57] Op. cit., p. 365.

nature. Thus humour, we are told, is a psychological process, or, at first, that this process furnishes the necessary conditions. "If we are in a situation which tempts us to liberate painful affects according to our habits, and motives then urge us to suppress these affects *statu nascendi*, we have the conditions for humour."[58] The conditions for humour, then, consist in a psychological process, but this would not necessarily make humour subjective. The subjective mechanics might give rise still to a social and communicated humour. But no, Freud has protected himself against this contingency by defining humour as inherently non-social. "Humour is the most self-sufficient of the forms of the comic; its process consummating itself in one single person and the participation of another adds nothing new to it."[59]

What obvious nonsense all this is! Freud has here taken the fact that it is possible, as we say, for a man to enjoy a quiet little joke all by himself, and elevated it to a new variety of humour essentially different from both wit and comedy. There is no justification for such a distinction. Wit was unconscious, the comic conscious, and now humour is differentiated from these by being made personal rather than social! Psychologically speaking, all forms of the comic, including wit and humour, are appreciated more when rendered social. The impulse of everyone with a new joke is to communicate it to someone else and thus to enjoy it all over again.

Freud continually confuses genesis with logical status, the origin of jokes with their appreciation. The very example with which, on the same page, he illustrates the non-social nature of humour could be an example of the reverse. The confusion is made even more pointed when Freud tells us that Don Quixote "is purely a comic figure," but "a figure who possesses no humour."[60] The fact that Don Quixote is unable to enjoy his own predicament as comic has nothing to do with the case.

---

[58] Op. cit., p. 371.
[59] Op. cit., p. 372.
[60] Op. cit., p. 377 n.

For we are interested not in what Don Quixote may or may not think but with an objectively comic situation. We are concerned solely with the objective situation and not with the psychological responses of the characters involved. Modern psychologism has laid its dead hand over all modern thinking, so that it appears to be almost impossible to regard with a detached view anything that happens in the world.[61]

The summary which is found on the last page of Freud's book sets forth his conclusions with regard to wit, the comic and humour. "It has seemed to us that the pleasure of wit originates from *an economy of expenditure in inhibition,* of the comic from *an economy of expenditure in thought,* and of humour from *an economy of expenditure of feeling.*"[62] Are these three to be taken as existing on the same level of analysis? Thought, feeling, and *action* would not be wrong, but is "inhibition" the only activity of the psychic life? Is thought entirely divorced from wit, feeling from the comic, inhibition (or action) from feeling? We cannot believe so. The conclusions emerge neatly enough, but like many such conclusions their simplification is also a falsification. Dogmatic definitions, in conformity with a previously accepted fundamental psychological view, have been forced to yield deductions, and these deductions have been confined in conclusions which are not justified by the facts.

The psychoanalytic theory of wit, comedy, and humour is actually not half so faulty as Freud would have us believe. It

[61] At least one disciple of Freud and Adler has attempted to describe comedy objectively. Erwin Wexberg holds that comedy consists in the overcoming of tragedy. This is an objective and common-sense re-statement of the classic danger theory where the threat proves impotent and the reaction is relief from fear. But stated in Wexberg's form the theory is a truism: if all is divided between comedy and tragedy, then comedy can only occur upon the elimination, or "overcoming" of tragedy. Certainly a sense of tragedy lurks behind the apprehension of comedy always, but this is psychological. Logically, comedy and tragedy are closely related, as contraries always are. Both comedy and tragedy deal with high, metaphysical matters. But they are after all contraries and not contradictories, and hence the absolute opposition is not required.

[62] Op. cit.., p. 384. (Italics Freud's.)

can be demonstrated that his insight is better than his doctrine. As a consequence the final work which is offered cannot be accepted literally; however, it does furnish wonderfully acute suggestions as to the true nature of the psychological aspects of comedy. It is possible to reverse these suggestions and to discover something about the objective nature of comedy from Freud's own work. Freud, in common with many modern thinkers, unquestioningly raises the epistemological distinction to the ontological level; that is, he poses the problem of knowledge and the subject-object relation as final for being. There is no good reason to accept this. We do not have to maintain that the subjective view of wit is basic in order to present the subjective view. We might argue with equal cogency that what is true of the subjective view represents the subjective aspect of a fundamentally objective affair.

In one place[63] Freud says that "wit-making is inseparably connected with the desire to impart it." This would make wit social and thus objective, the intersubjective argument being untenable here because of Freud's contention that we do not laugh at our own humour but at the objective humour of others (i.e. objective in language or actions). In several places, the argument is of such a nature that the objective parallel to the subjective presentation is implicit and almost obvious, all that is needed being a shift in terminology. The "unmasking of the psychic automatism"[64] could be turned into the "observation of the shortcomings of actuality." Again, Freud says that "Every one who allows the truth to escape his lips in an unguarded moment is really pleased to have rid himself of this thought."[65] We might change this type of "tendency-wit" into an objective statement by asserting the tendency of the wit rather than of the psychological person. We might say simply that the truth has a tendency to seek expression.

The force of an objective logic is felt inadvertently in several parts of Freud's argument. When he tries to prove that naïve

[63] Op. cit., p. 220.
[64] Op. cit.., p. 327.   [65] Op. cit., p. 156.

humour must be the result of conscious intention, he unexpectedly demonstrates that humour is objective at basis by showing that the humorist is trying to draw a valid conclusion from premises.[66] The tendency of humour to expose analytic levels underlying purposive actions and language is essentially a logical affair, as for example the statement that "the sphere of the sexual or obscene offers the richest opportunities for gaining comic pleasure beside the pleasurable sexual stimulation, as it exposes the person's dependence on his physical needs (degradation) or it can uncover behind the spiritual love the physical demands of the same (unmasking)."[67] Thus comedy serves as a critical destructive force which is certainly objective. The subjective furnishes the occasion for wit, not its logical cause. This is clear in Freud's definition of its purpose. He says that "the purpose of obtaining pleasure must be recognized as a sufficient motive of the wit-work."[68] A motive is an occasion, not a logical cause, since many other motives could give rise to the same effect. There is always a closer, non-temporal connection between a logical cause and effect.

In many other significant passages Freud catches the logical and critical nature of wit and the comic in general. For example, he recognizes the extreme contemporaneity of wit;[69] he recognizes, too, that it constitutes at times a reaction against tyranny;[70] and finally he lists the varieties of ways in which wit can furnish the criticism of current customs and institutions,[71] thus demonstrating its revolutionary nature. These suggestions indicate an insight into the true meaning of comedy which is not defeated by a dogmatic adherence to the analysis of a postulated but largely mythical psychic mechanism.

[66] Op. cit., p. 293.
[67] Op. cit., p. 360.   [68] Op. cit., p. 214.
[69] Op. cit., pp. 185 ff., "The Factor of Actuality."
[70] Op. cit., pp. 192 ff., "Reproduction of Old Liberties."
[71] Op. cit., p. 204.

Criticism of Modern Theories of Comedy

6. THE PHYSIOLOGICAL: DUMAS, BECHTEREV, CRILE

It is possible for all schools to agree that laughter, if not comedy itself, is a psychological phenomenon. The only point of disagreement (and it is admittedly a large one) is whether laughter and comedy are one and the same or whether laughter is the subjective reaction to an objective comedy. Laughter is an event which takes place at a number of levels. Certainly there is the psychological occurrence of laughter, which has, for instance, been described as a psychological release of pent-up emotion. But there is also a lower level at which laughter can be examined, and this is not properly psychological at all but physiological. Among those who have studied the physiological mechanism of laughter, we may cite Dumas, Crile, and Bechterev as typical.

Dumas, the French psychologist, has given considerable attention to the emotions, particularly of laughing and crying.[72] He distinguishes the problem of the physiological mechanism from the other problems of laughter, as for instance the psychological question of the distinction between the laughter of joy and the laughter of comedy. He finds that the fifteen facial muscles used in smiling, the respiratory muscles, the vocal mechanism, and in a falling-off series other muscles throughout the body, are all active in the process of laughing. But the question which neither Dumas nor any other speculator on the physiology of laughter has been able to answer is, "given the feeling that a certain thing *is* funny, why should we express that feeling by working the muscles of the face"?[73] Dumas, in despair of finding any new solutions by means of physiological investigations, is forced to fall back upon a familiar theory, namely, that laughter is a release of energy occasioned by some sudden contrast. He says that when there

---

[72] Georges Dumas, *Traité de psychologie* (Paris, 1923, Alcan), vol. i.
[73] Carney Landis, "The Expressions of Emotion," in Carl Murchison, editor, *The Foundations of Experimental Psychology* (Worcester, 1929, Clark Univ. Press), p. 499.

is a sudden contrast or contradiction, especially when the contrast is a descent from the greater to the less, the nervous energy stored up in the first case finds an unexpected outlet through laughter.

This is not much help. A child could perceive for himself that laughter involves the muscles; and it must also be true of laughter that energy is released, since it is true of every other event in the world. The question of levels is suggestive but not sufficiently developed, and raises many questions, and then other unanswered questions arise. Why does laughter weaken the muscles and render the laugher physically helpless? Why do we "laugh until it hurts"? Finally, the real question concerning physiological laughter, namely, the way in which the feeling of "funny" gets communicated to the facial muscles is, as Landis points out, as yet unanswered by anyone.

Bechterev, the Russian physiologist, is more concerned with reflexology, the study of conditioned reflexes, than he is with the investigation of laughter *per se*. He is bent on emphasizing the relation of laughter to certain centres of the brain, and he finds that those reflex centres associated with laughing "can show symptoms of excitation through the mere absence of inhibition from the cerebral cortex." In other words, without the inhibitory action of the cerebral centre, laughter tends to be more easily excited and unrestrained. Little if anything is proved by this observation. In the first place, Bechterev notes that exactly the same is true of crying, and any theory which cannot offer a distinction at the physiological level between laughing and crying is not of much use as a theory. What interests the student of comedy is to discover the meaning of controlled laughter. What do we have when, under the properly functioning control of the cerebral cortex, joy continues to be unconfined?

Dr. George Crile offers a variety of the familiar surplus-energy or letting-off-steam theory of laughter.[74] He tells us

[74] George W. Crile, *Man an Adaptive Mechanism.*

that "every one of the causes of laughter, when analysed, resolves itself into a stimulation to motor activity of some kind." Laughter follows when stimulated motor activity is checked suddenly and the energy has no other way of escape. Once more it must be observed that the characterization of laughter as a form of energy is not sufficiently specific, since it leaves this activity in the same category with a host of other activities from which it fails to be distinguished. As for the theory that laughter is a release of pent-up energy, which Crile too is offering, this is comparable to the "relief" theory of Gregory and others. Only in Dr. Crile's case, the theory claims the authority of scientific physiology when it too is taken from the level of gross common sense. We ask from a scientific explanation not only the complete explication of *what* happens but also of *how* it happens, and we want the account to be couched in terms of a mechanism of some sort. What the physiologists of Crile's stamp give us is merely a purposive explanation of the kind with which psychology has already made us familiar.

Physiology has little to offer as yet in the way of the analysis of laughter, although there is much to be hoped from a later and more thoroughgoing development of our knowledge of this level. The point to be borne in mind always, however, in connection with the physiological explanation is that it can never exhaust its subject. Laughter is psychological as well as physiological, and will always be constituted of more than the innervation of certain facial muscles. The inference, intentional or otherwise, always seems to be that laughter is accounted for when we understand the physiological processes which accompany it. Nothing could be farther from the truth, as any physiologist familiar with the limitations of his field would be the first to testify.

7. THE LOGICAL: ZUVER, GRAVES

We shall not have been fair to our topic unless we have reviewed the brief and unsuccessful efforts at the explanation of comedy ventured on by those non-professionals who are not consciously trying to escape from the nominalistic web which catches all the professionals but whose explanations take other forms and assume entirely different premises. Into this strange and motley company fall both Dudley Zuver and the poet and novelist, Robert Graves.

We may consider first the position of Dudley Zuver. It is odd indeed to find comedy keeping company with the Church. The prophets have always been more or less serious, and their followers, with the excess of zeal which we may always expect from followers, have been even more so. Yet it has occurred to one man at least to consider comedy and religion in a single connection. Zuver states his position as follows.

"My thesis . . . is that there exists a . . . gulf . . . between the two worlds, both of which man inhabits. . . . The ideal fails of embodiment, yet the real cannot be permitted a final or decisive word. In our intercourse with our environment we listen to two voices which are discordant and seldom speak in unison."[75] "The Church will prosper not through diminishing its requirements upon its members, nor in punishing them too severely for their delinquencies, but in showing mercy and kindness. Mercy is the flexible connective between the ideal and the real; it is a proper manifestation of the comic spirit. God, too, has a sense of humour; has He not been revealed unto us as full of compassion, long-suffering, and merciful?"[76]

The contemporary world has witnessed the almost total acceptance of the philosophy of nominalism, that actual particulars alone are real, a philosophy which divides the world between real persons and real things. The world of flux, we are told, is alone real, and nothing possible of potential has any important standing. On this account, there are no essences or possibilities in other than a verbal sense. The philosophical opponent of nominalism, the doctrine of realism, holds, on

[75] Dudley Zuver, *Salvation by Laughter* (New York, 1933, Harper), p. 33.
[76] Op. cit., p. 35.

the contrary, that there is a logical possibility which is wider than the actual world but which includes it and is equally real with it. Realism divides the world into the logical and the actual (or the essential and the existential, or the ideal and the real). Extreme realism holds that the realm of essence is alone real, and denies reality to this actual world, but we can afford here to neglect extreme realism and consider merely moderate realism.

In the triumph of nominalism in the modern world, realism survives in the official doctrine of the Catholic Church. Its survival in this form alone is unfortunate. Since the Church is realistic in its theology, philosophers and laymen equally have been misled into supposing that there is something characteristically theological about realism. But although the Church is realistic, this is not true, because realism is not necessarily ecclesiastical. Nevertheless, we must be grateful to those theologians and speculators who keep us in mind of the true aspect of realism by sustaining, at least in part, its philosophical position. Thus Zuver holds, as he says, for a gulf between the ideal and the real. He understands that the actual life of any individual is the struggle to achieve, in more or less degree, something of what that individual recognizes ought to be, while having to compromise because of the limitations of actuality by accepting, at least to some extent, what is.

Since the world is a long way from being what any speculator thinks it ought to be, the individual is involved in the necessity of having to a predominant extent to accept things as they are. This acceptance is not easy, and requires some mediating factor. This mediating factor is the sense of humour. This is the subjective aspect of a theory which we shall examine more fully in a later chapter on its objective side.[77] Zuver was clearly on his way to a very interesting theory of comedy, one which held the possibility of approaching closer to the truth than do any of its contemporaries. It is pertinent to inquire, therefore, what interfered? What premises, what interests intruded

[77] Chapter IV, Section 3.

themselves upon a logical chain of reasoning which was bidding fair to develop such interesting consequences? Something evidently stopped Zuver in his tracks, for he says that his thesis "is capable of little development beyond continual restatement and manifold illustration."[78]

The only clue to the difficulty is contained in Zuver's preoccupation with the Church and its welfare, but this seems to offer all the answer required. Comedy, as the mediator between the ideal and the real, between the logical order and actuality, is given a psychological twist because of Zuver's interest in the Church's rôle. The Church, he says, can only prosper through the exercise of mercy; which is not only the flexible connective between the ideal and the real, but also a manifestation of the comic spirit. Having swallowed this without a murmur (although there is plainly no reason to do so, since mercy as a mediating factor was introduced without any warning and employed without any further explanation) Zuver is now prepared to go to any length. Indeed he does so when he states that God must have a sense of humour because He is merciful.

The position ends in complete absurdity. God has a sense of humour, and since this is the faculty which mediates between the ideal and the real, God must be doing the mediating. Then why is a sense of humour required in humans at all? The answer is that on these grounds it is not. By employing good realistic premises, Zuver was doing very well with the development of his theory of humour, until he suddenly remembered his Church connections. Then perfectly good logical reasoning was turned aside, and, in an effort to be of service to the Church, he assigned to mercy the part originally played by humour. As a result, the quality of mercy got pretty badly strained, and the whole question of humour had to be referred back to God, who not only has a sense of humour but everything else, and who consequently cannot afford to play any favourites by making finite distinctions of partiality.

[78] Zuver, op cit., p. 33.

In all fairness, it should be said that Zuver does not set all this forth as a complete theory of humour, since he says that mercy is "a proper manifestation of the comic spirit." He is not trying to define comedy, but merely to exhibit one of its important functions. This he might very well have done, save for the sudden intrusion of faith into a logical chain of reasoning. The moral, of course, is that if realism is to be saved at all for what is valid in it, and important deductions sought, its long theological and institutional associations must be forgotten. They do not count in the last analysis, because truth remains truth whosoever utters it, and error remains error.

In an amusing little book, devoted more to examples than to theories of humour, Robert Graves ventures upon several suggestions as to its nature. From the fact that Graves himself is something of a comedian, and also from the type of comedian that he is, we should be led to expect some variety of the "foolishness" explanation of humour. This is in fact just exactly what Graves appears to be preparing the ground for early in his book. There he states that "Humour, it must be said at once, is first of all a personal matter, losing its virtue by diffusion."[79] In other words, there is something peculiarly individual and specific about objects of humour, which becomes crude and loses its force when generalized. Graves cites as an example the fact that jokes about Scotsmen and Fishermen and Marriage tend to be trite and dull because they have become diffused. There is and must be something unique and highly specific about every work of art, and an example of humour is a work of art to the extent to which comedy is a part of aesthetics. But Graves seems to be confusing the object of humour with its meaning. Every example of humour arises from some actual and specific object, and is to this extent highly concentrated and not "diffused," but the *meaning* of

[79] Robert Graves, *Mrs. Fisher or The Future of Humour* (London, 1928, Kegan Paul), p. 9.

such an example of humour is general, to some extent at least, or it would have no meaning at all.

Later Graves offers a serious definition of humour, when he says that "humour is the faculty of seeing apparently incongruous elements as a part of a scheme for supra-logical necessity. Humour is not of the Gods who have . . . only the most rudimentary sense of the ridiculous, but of the Fates and of this Necessity, who is, according to the Greek theologian at least, above all the Gods."[80]

We may omit the term "faculty" from this quotation, since it does nothing but place the whole situation in the subjective category, and thus render it modern and to some extent false. Humour certainly cannot be the "faculty" for seeing what Mr. Graves says it sees, but is that sight itself. The postulation of a mental faculty which chooses from a wide environment only the elements which are humorous is as silly as the theory concerning those "red" areas in the brain which are excited when red is seen. But there is no need to press the point, since it is clear Graves did not emphasize this aspect of his definition. What he did emphasize was the rôle played by logical necessity in the reconciliation of incongruous elements under a single scheme. Graves sees the ridiculous as a lower form of humour, and humour as a form of the endorsement of logic.

There is the inclination here toward a realistic theory of humour, similar to that put forward by Zuver. It is not a far cry from the understanding that humour is the mediator between the ideal and the real, between the logical order and actuality, between things as they ought to be and things as they are, to the understanding that incongruous elements form part of a scheme for supra-logical necessity. The same essentially realistic, logical and non-psychological conception underlies both definitions and gives them justification. It is in this direction, perhaps, that a sound definition of comedy or humour is to be sought. This is not to say, of course, that the

[80] Op. cit., p. 55.

psychological accounting of humour is without validity. Nothing could be farther from the truth. Certainly there is a psychological aspect, but the point is merely that this aspect alone is incapable of constituting humour. The psychological aspect of humour is, as illustrated by the various theories which we have been examining, a matter of laughter, since that is the form which the reaction of the individual takes to comic situations. But certainly there is something which occasions the laughter, something in the nature of a generalized comical situation; and this must be logical in its nature. We have seen in an earlier chapter that the logical view of comedy is the one with which theorists originally started. It failed to be broadly developed; nevertheless it was the Greek theory of comedy and humour. And we shall see in the next chapter that the truth of such a theory, somewhat more detailed in development, is what lends meaning to comedy.

CHAPTER IV

The Meaning of Comedy

1. APOLOGY

ONE critic reviewing a work on the theory of laughter observed rather disappointedly that "evidently theories of laughter are no laughing matter." There is much to be said on the important point concerning the logic of comedy which this expression of chagrin unintentionally exposes. For there could hardly be displayed a greater confusion of categories than in the mixing of theories of comedy with comedy itself. Comedy belongs to the realm of intrinsic value, but the *examination* of comedy is part of logic. The analysis of comedy can no more be funny than the analysis of water can be wet. It is a familiar valid proposition that in the analysis of a thing we immediately abstract the properties of that thing as a whole. Since the logic of comedy is part of aesthetics, an aesthetics of comedy which proved amusing would be a false aesthetics, just as a vaudeville comedian who chose to expound to his audience the Bergsonian theory of laughter would be a bad comedian.

The error of confusing value with the analysis of value is a prevalent one. It argues from the fact that by analyzing a thing we rob it *pro tem* of its content of value, to the conclusion that analysis is inimical to value. The premise is true enough; but the conclusion does not follow. The question may well be asked, why do we rob things of their contents? Surely not in order to demonstrate that instead of human beings we are dry professors whose business it is to take the joy out of life! The process of analysis deprives a field of investigation of all contents, in order to discover the abstract conditions which make contents possible, always with the aim in view of returning with richer contents. Physics does not hesitate to analyse its field of investigation, to tear away values in its search for structural conditions; yet how powerful an instrument of control is physics! The analysis of the conditions of motion, conducted in the horse-and-buggy days, never moved themselves, but have made the incredible speeds of to-day possible. There is nothing in the vivid content of existence except value, and analysis invariably deprives us of that value. But it does so in a given field only in order eventually to increase the amount of value in that field.

The argument that definition defeats its own purpose, since the essences which are to be defined escape in the very process of definition, is a common one. G. K. Chesterton, in an article which seeks to define humour,[1] affords us a typical instance of this misunderstanding. He feels obliged to begin his discussion of humour with an apology for the purpose of his article, observing that "it would commonly be regarded as a deficiency in humour to search for a definition of humour." The familiar fear of the destructive effect of analysis rests upon a lack of understanding of the aim of the analytic process. Why should the search for a definition of humour have anything to do with what is commonly called having a sense of humour? Is the physicalness of a physical object destroyed by the measurement of its weight, mass, density and dimensions? Is the colour of yellow light any less yellow because it has been found to have a wave length of 5.89×10^{-5} cm? Analysis reveals the logical elements of structure; it does not, and is not intended to, reveal the effective content of value or essence. It defines systems, but never tells us anything about that which is systematized. We may here reaffirm the Platonic doctrine that everything which comes into being is subject to the technique of measurement, and add that nothing having being, however fragile, however subtle, is ever destroyed thereby. This is as true of comedy as of any other kind of being.

The question may be asked, why if the analysis of comedy is not a humorous affair should it ever be undertaken? If

[1] *Encyclopædia Britannica*, fourteenth edition.

theories of laughter are indeed "no laughing matter," why should they be set up at all? Most persons at one time or another wish to be amused, and we know that the examination of comedy in the high-handed and dull fashion of the logicians and metaphysicians does not contribute to their amusement. Surely, it will be concluded that all explanations of why comedy is funny do "take the joy out of life." This objection has some weight in part, for the analysers do seem to be destroyers as well. But as a whole the argument cannot be sustained. We take the joy out of life temporarily in order to put more joy back into it. Whitehead has answered this argument when he showed that we employ the utmost abstractions in order to control concrete fact. For it is only by attempting fully to understand those most general principles which condition all activity that we can hope to direct somewhat the development of the actual course of events. Now, what happens in the analysis of comedy is merely one illustration of the wider process. We abstract from what is concretely comic to the principles which make comedy possible, and this enables us to return with a greater appreciation of the concretely comic. This is far from being the only purpose of analysis, but it is sufficient at this point to answer the question of why we analyse. In the analysis of comedy, as in the analysis of anything else, we abstract from the intrinsic vividity of actual situations to their logical relatedness in order to understand, and therefore also to increase our appreciation of, the intrinsic vividity.

The relation between the appreciation of contents and the analysis of structure is the same as that between feeling and reasoning. Let us discuss this relation for a moment. Feeling and reasoning are related in a way that is not fully understood; but there have been found suggestions which lead toward its understanding. We know first of all that both feeling and reasoning are reactions to external stimuli. Even in the case of what are described by psychologists as centrally-aroused emotions, that is, emotions having their point of origin within the human organism, these are in a sense reactions to something which is objective from the point of view of the core of awareness. Furthermore, this much at least is certain: that feeling and reasoning are not absolutely opposed, as they have been thought to be in the past. Those who act from impulse do not realize how much their impulses, and therefore their actions, are conditioned by rational training. To a definite extent, the feelings of those persons who have become familiar with some deductive background do not remain the same as the feelings of those who have not. This is true at least for the actions called for by the scope of the deductive background. One who has been trained in the humanities cannot have the same reactions as one who has not been so trained.

Enemies of rationalism have long contended that this is not so, since to scratch deep enough in any man, educated or uneducated, is to find the savage. Civilization is only skin deep, thay tell us, and not far under the surface lie those primitive instincts or urges which can be occasioned to play their ignoble part upon the slightest provocation. This is true enough, yet it does not constitute a refutation of rationalism. For what the enemies of rationalism are challenging is not the efficacy of reason but merely the extent of its permeation. The resistance of man to reason is almost as extraordinary a spectacle as the lengths to which it sometimes is able to carry him. The end of the rationalist influence has been mistakenly thought to lie in learning. The acceptance of ideas does not end with learning but only begins with it. The order of the acceptance of ideas goes from acquaintance to learning, to conscious belief, to unconscious belief. The extent to which a person may have his feelings conditioned by his reasoning is measured by the extent or depth to which reasoning has gone with him.

Another argument for the opposition of feeling and reasoning is constructed on the ground that scientific advances are attained by means of intuitional insight and not by deductive reasoning. This objection considers only the psychological aspects of the problem; it neglects to take into consideration the systematic background of induction. The scientist no doubt proceeds largely by intuitions, but his scientific insight is made possible by the fact that he has taken pains to acquaint himself with the deductive field of science. For certainly the artist as well as the scientist has intuitions, yet the artist does not have them in science nor the scientist in art. Intuitions or inductions depend upon a deductive background, which has been arrived at by means of inductions, *ad seriatim*. We may be sure that the layers of feeling and reasoning which rest one upon the other are somehow connected and mutually influential. Thus with regard to comedy, a thorough understanding cannot fail to lead to a heightened sensitivity and hence to an increasing appreciation of the comic elements discovered by others, which in turn will lead to further understanding and further appreciation.

It is a commonplace that understanding leads to appreciation. Those who are slow to grasp the meaning of a witty proposition (and all of us are guilty of this at some time or other) laugh only after they have had it explained to them. Rational comprehension is the condition of intrinsic enjoyment. Deliberate denial of the comprehension may result in the indefinite postponement of the contingent enjoyment. Thus it is finally in the interests of comedy itself that we are led to the analysis of comedy.

2. The Aesthetic Background

Comedy, like tragedy, is included under the study of aesthetics, that branch of philosophy which treats of the logic of the beautiful. Aesthetics in turn rests upon certain metaphysical assumptions which render it possible. No study is ever very far removed from first principles, and the relation of comedy to metaphysics has only one intermediate step. Thus if we turn aside for a moment to examine the metaphysical basis of aesthetics, it is only because by so doing we may hope to emerge with a better comprehension of what is involved in comedy.

The Meaning of Comedy

The subject and the object of knowledge do not exhaust the world. The observer and that which he observes are not definitive for all being. John Doe and the scene he surveys are parts of a whole which has other parts. The subject does not create his world which contains much he would not create, including contradictions and disvalues. Few persons would wish to be held responsible as sole authors for the difficulties in which most of us sooner or later become involved. Rather is the subject a perspective on the world, and, in this connection, nothing taken by itself.

But neither can the object of knowledge exist by itself. For objects are not final entities but only historical identities. The truistic formulation of the proposition that nothing finite is infinite has long obscured its importance. The analysis of any object reveals it to be a sort of *locus* for the assemblage of qualities which it does not own. There is nothing innately green about a leaf, nothing inherently sweet about sugar; greenness and sweetness are, so to speak, borrowed for occasions. We may conclude, then, that if neither subject nor object is ultimate, the status of being must be such as to render it independent of the knowledge relation.

Since the subject, his knowledge of the object and the object itself, are all actual things, the knowledge relation can occur only in the flux of actuality. But many things have being which yet cannot be said to have *actual* being. The unicorn, the "light that never was on sea or land," the actions which we shall perform to-morrow, the economic problems of future societies, these are things which have being, though not in any vivid sense, and which may anywhere and at any time enter into actuality. They are *possible* things, and as such enjoy a logical being. But a possible thing is not a nothing, else nothing would be possible. Thus being must be considered to consist of two orders: the logical and the historical. We may now consider them separately.

The logical order is the order of possibility; it is fixed and unchanging, and contains the conditions of actuality. It is an unlimited, dense and undivided hierarchy of universals and values such that from any point the view down yields universals and the view up yields values. It is ideal, and enters absolutely into actuality only as the truths of logic and mathematics, and as the intrinsic vividity of feeling. In short, it is a realm not of perfect things but of possible things. In the logical order there are not only no broken vases but there are no vases at all; only the possibility of vase. Only an undistinguished logical relatedness and an unrealized affectability.

The historical order, on the other hand, is the order of actuality, or that which affects or is affected. It is of necessity imperfect, ever-changing and incomplete, but seeks to become perfect, fixed and complete, and thus endeavours to transcend its self-contained limits. Half chaos, half cosmos, it is the experienced confusion of restricted truths and partial values, of contradictions and false evaluations. It consists of fragments of the logical order out of order. Yet it contains the seeds of that order striving to reassert itself. Thus the historical order is characterized by motion, by all varieties of action, and indeed by all the distortions of felt vividity. It is a sub-division of possibility, but more limited and less inclusive; a fluxing and half-blind dialectic approximation toward a perfect exemplification of the ideal conditions of the logical order.

Since we live in actuality but conduct our lives according to the ideal of logical perfection, the relation of the logical order to the order of actuality assumes paramount significance. Perhaps the best way in which to approach the analysis of this relation is to examine particular items of actuality, or actuals, with the purpose of discovering the extent of their logicality. Now, another name for the logical relatedness of an actual is its organization. By organization is meant the systematic scheme of internal and external relations; or, in other words, the gathering of subsidiary functions under a single necessary function. Every actual is to some extent an organization. A horse is an organization, but so also is a tree, a shoe, a rainbow.

The Meaning of Comedy

Every necessary function is the form which employs subsidiary functions as the material.

The difference between the organizations of actuals varies according to quantitative scales of reference. Corresponding to the internal relations of a given organization is the complexity of its organization. Corresponding to the external relations of a given organization is the extent of its organization. The degree of organization of an actual can be calculated exactly by means of these two co-ordinates. Thus they are definitely empirical fields of investigation, and should some day be submitted to the operations of empirical sciences. Meanwhile, however, they are better known as normative studies, and recognizable by their ancient philosophical categories. On the latter classification, external relations of extent become the measure of goodness. Goodness can only be understood through the relation of an organization to a higher organization. This particular topic constitutes the analysis of the logic of the feeling for the good, which is the task of ethics. We shall not be primarily concerned with it here.

On the last classification, internal relations of complexity become the measure of beauty. Beauty can only be understood through the relation of parts of an organization to the whole organization. This topic constitutes the analysis of the feeling for the beautiful, which is the task of aesthetics. The extent to which subsidiary functions serve the necessary function in an organization is the measure of its beauty. Thus the goodness of subsidiaries for the necessary constitutes the beauty of an organization. Thus. the beautiful can be understood simply as the interior relations of organization. Harmony, economy, and justice are ways of describing the beautiful. Harmony is recognized in the perfect functioning of an organization, made possible through the perfect serving of the necessary function by its subsidiaries. In human relations this is exemplified by the justice contained in the balance between obligation and privilege. Economy lies in the use of neither more nor less subsidiaries than those required exactly to express the necessary function. Parts of an organization which have no functional usefulness are in that organization ugly. On the other hand, organizations which are not adequately expressed for lack of subsidiary functions are also awkward and ugly.

Aesthetics, then, is the study of that aspect of value which is felt as the beautiful, and which analyses into the degree of the perfection of organizations in actuality. It is chiefly this branch of value theory with which we shall be occupied in the study of comedy.

Now, the beautiful, or the perfection of actual organizations, may itself be subdivided into two aspects. These aspects involve the given perspective of the individual observer, or in other words his perspective predicament. These aspects are not in any wise to be understood as subjective, since they do not depend upon the awareness of the knowing subject but upon his predicament. The perspective predicament itself is nothing subjective; it does not involve the conscious awareness of the knowing subject but is a frame of reference which the subject of knowledge may or may not take up. The aspects which are available from the perspective predicament may be roughly termed the positive and the negative.

From the perspective predicament, an actual organization may be accepted positively, as the inevitable compromise which has to be made, as the best possible approach which can be obtained to the ideal of organization, under the given circumstances contained in the current conditions of actuality. Such an acceptance establishes the meaning of tragedy. Tragedy always affirms and never denies. Thus tragedy is the recognition of what value there is in actuality, and the ignoration of its limitations.

But there is another choice possible. An actual organization may be rejected negatively, as an insufficient compromise under *any* given conditions of actuality—those of current circumstances or any other. Such a rejection establishes the meaning of comedy. Thus comedy tends to ignore the values of actuality, and points chiefly to its limitations. Comedy always denies and never affirms. This is done with the aim of decreasing the limitations and increasing the positive content.

But before we venture further into a comparison of comedy with tragedy, it will be well to analyse in some detail the meaning of comedy.

3. WHAT IS COMEDY?

Our analysis of the aesthetic background has revealed that comedy is a unique field of investigation. That which is comic is also beautiful; it is an intrinsic value, and as such comparable only to other intrinsic values. As intrinsic it cannot be explained away or reduced. There are no words to describe logically the intrinsic aspect of any value—it just *is*. All that logic can hope to do is to effect an analysis. Now, the logical analysis of any value has for its ideal the eventual reduction to measurement. The kind of laughing mirrors found at Coney Island, which distort the reflected image according to a symmetrical pattern, illustrate the mathematical analysis of comedy. Such analysis, leading toward measurement, is candidly analysis and not a presentation or even a description of the intrinsic quality of the comic. This quality, like all others, defies exhaustive description. It is the *content* of that of which analytic definition reveals the *form*, and this is as near as we can hope to approach rationally. Of course it would be possible to tell a joke and thus to convey something of the experience of the feeling of comedy, but then we would lose the generality of meaning. By means of definition and analysis we gain generality—at the expense of intrinsic quality.

How can a technique be devised for the determination of how much of the value of comedy is involved in every instance of comedy? At present we seem to be very far away from the discovery of such a technique. The aim of this work is only to make a start toward the achievement of such an ambition. Certainly the very first step toward the mathematical formulation of any field of investigation is the logical analysis of that field. Such a logical analysis must consist in the tentative segregation of the field itself and in the exploratory attempt at definitions. It is this task to which we must address ourselves.

Comedy is one kind of exemplification of the proposition that nothing actual is wholly logical. Expressed as the truism that nothing finite is infinite, that nothing limited is ideal, this truth appears to be self-evident. Yet such is not the case. Self-evidence is an *a priori* judgment, and has often been disproved in practice. It is a notorious historical observation that customs and institutions never enjoy more than a comparatively brief life; and yet while they are the accepted fashion they come to be regarded as brute givens, as irreducible facts, which may be depended upon with perfect security. One of Ibsen's characters poses the final objection to a completed action with the remark that "people don't do such things."

All finite categories, the theories and practices of actuality, are always compromises. They are the best possible settlements which can be made in the effort to achieve perfection, given the limitations of the historical order of events. Thus the categories of actuality are always what they have to be and seldom what they ought to be. It is the task of comedy to make this plain. Thus comedy ridicules new customs, new institutions, for being insufficiently inclusive; but even more effectively makes fun of old ones which have outlived their usefulness and have come to stand in the way of further progress. A constant reminder of the existence of the logical order as the perfect goal of actuality, comedy continually insists upon the limitations of all experience, and points to the narrowness of the field of all actuality as that only which can be experienced. The business of comedy is to dramatize and thus make more vivid and immediate the fact that contradictions in actuality must prove insupportable. It thus admonishes against the easy acceptance of interim limitations and calls for the persistent advance toward the logical order and the final elimination of limitations.

Comedy, then, *consists in the indirect affirmation of the ideal logical order by means of the derogation of the limited orders of actuality.* There are of course many and diverse applications of this principle. It may for example be achieved (1) by means of direct ridicule of the categories of actuality (such as are found in current customs and institutions), or it may be achieved (2) by confusing the categories of actuality as an indication of their ultimate unimportance, and as a warning against taking them too seriously. Comedians from Aristophanes to Chaplin, from Daumier to the Marx Brothers, have been occupied with the illustration of these approaches. The first is the method employed by Ring Lardner; the second, that employed by Gertrude Stein. A good example of (1) is the satire in Hemingway's *Torrents of Spring*[2] on the contemporary outlook of the literary generation. "Do come home, Scripps, dear," Diana, the girl in the beanery, says to her man, Scripps. "There's a new *Mercury* with a wonderful editorial in it by Mencken about chiropractors." Would that do it? she wondered. Scripps looked away. "No, I don't give a damn about Mencken any more," he replied.

A good example of (2) is contained in one of T. E. Lawrence's replies to the proof-reader's queries concerning the *Seven Pillars of Wisdom.* To an objection that his translation of Arabic names was full of inconsistencies, Lawrence replied, "There are some 'scientific systems' of transliteration, helpful to people who know enough Arabic not to need helping, but a wash-out for the world. *I spell my names anyhow, to show what rot the systems are.*"[3]

The first method is that of ridicule. It pretends to take actuality seriously—too seriously; and by so doing shows that what we have always taken with some seriousness is not worthy of respect at all. In other words, it overestimates that which it intends to lower in estimation. The other method is exactly the reverse: to underestimate that which it intends to raise in

[2] P. 131.
[3] *Seven Pillars of Widsom*, p. 25. (Italics mine.) See in this connection the whole of Lawrence's answers to the proof-reader as excellent examples of true comedy.

estimation. But in both cases, actuality is taken just as it is as the basis for comedy. The second method is not that of ridicule but of confusion. Comedy is always illustrative of the principle enunciated by Charles S. Peirce, that chance begets order.[4] It is indeed a principle upon which instinctively the great comedians depend. They shuffle cards representing the known actual relations and values indiscriminately, with a view to showing that by so doing some significant elements of order will be brought to light, elements of order which perhaps would never have been made to appear in any other way. Lawrence "spelled his names anyhow" not only "to show what rot the systems are" but also to show that even in this manner some system of transliteration would be developed.

Students of comedy are fond of pointing out the element of surprise which enters into every comic instance. Something is expected and does not happen; the result—comedy. A man sits down but the chair has been snatched away and he falls on the floor. As crude as this is, it is true comedy. But the attempt to hold comedy down to the failure of expectation follows from wrong interpretation of what is involved. First of all, comedy does consist in the absence of something which is expected, but it can also consist in the presence of something where nothing is expected. Always, however, the situation must illustrate the absence of what ought to be, if it is to reveal comedy. The unexpected indication of the absence of perfection (the *ought*) constitutes the comic situation.

Corresponding to the unexpected something and the unexpected nothing in the above analysis are the types of humour known as understatement and exaggeration. Understatement shows vividly the absence of something which is expected. It does not directly ridicule current estimations in order to show their limitations, but achieves the same end by other means. The beautifully simple means employed consists in the failure to take current estimations seriously on just those occasions

[4] Charles S. Peirce, *Chance, Love and Logic* (London, 1923, Kegan Paul), essay on "The Doctrine of Chances."

when they are most expected to be taken seriously. Charles Butterworth, the screen comedian, is a master of this kind of comedy. When on one occasion he was shown a very elaborate statue, so large that all of it could not be included in the camera's focus, he observed approvingly, "Very artistic." Again, when introduced to a woman who wore orchids and ermine, Butterworth said, "O, all in white."

Exaggeration shows the presence of something where nothing is expected. Exaggeration is commoner than understatement because it is so much easier to effect. Exaggeration ridicules current estimations by pushing the emphases to their apogees. Exaggeration takes the evaluations of the day, so to speak, at their word, and accepts them as almost the whole truth. The features which the cartoonist singles out for attention are made to stand for the whole face. Charlie Chaplin's shoes, the cascade of knives which flow from Harpo Marx's pockets, the grammatical errors of Lardner's people—the list is practically endless. Both understatement and exaggeration point the moral that by exceeding the ordinary limits of actual things and events, the arbitrary and non-final nature of these limits can be demonstrated. Thus comedy is an antidote to error. It is a restorer of proportions, and signals a return from extreme adherence to actual programmes, in so far as these programmes are found to be faulty. Thus indirectly comedy voices the demand for more logical programs.

Needless to say, this kind of ridicule does service to the ideal, to the truth of an unlimited community, an ideal society, by jesting at things which in the limited community, the current society, have come to be taken too seriously. Customs and institutions, by virtue of their own weight, have a way of coming to be regarded as ultimates in themselves. But the comedians soon correct this error in estimation, by actually demonstrating the forgotten limitations of all actuals. In this sense the clown, the king's jester, and the film comedian serve an important function. This function is to correct overevaluation, by exhibiting current evaluations in the light of their shortcomings.

In Praise of Comedy

The corrosive effect of humour eats away the solemnity of accepted evaluation, and thus calls for a revaluation of values.

Inasmuch as comedy deals chiefly with current evaluations, its specific points bear always upon the contemporary world. The butt of its jibes may be shortcomings which have enjoyed a long and rather persistent history, or they may be merely evanescent and fashionable assumptions which are doomed anyhow to have a short career. In either case they are usually highly contemporaneous. For example, the desire of insignificant men to appear important, as when Bacchus puts on the lion's skin and club of Hercules, in Aristophanes' *The Frogs*, illustrates foibles which can easily be shown to have been a weakness of human nature throughout historical time, and which still holds true of members of our own society.

Yet there are many contemporary allusions in the same play, some of which are now identified as having been aimed at known historical figures of Aristophanes' day, while others are permanently unidentifiable. When actual things and events have vanished, comedies which criticized them begin to date. *The Frogs* is valuable to the extent to which its criticisms remain applicable. Despite this saving element of atemporality, in the main it is true that classic comedies require extensive footnotes giving historical references, in order to render particular satires intelligible.

Thus the contemporaneity of comedy is one of its essential features. Sherwood Anderson is speaking for all comedians when he exclaims, "I want to take a bite out of the now." Comedy epitomizes the height of the times, the *zeitgeist*. Hanging upon the vivid immediacy of actuality, it touches the unique particularly embodied in the passing forms of the moment. A criticism of the contradictions involved in actuality, it must inevitably be concerned with the most ephemeral of actuals. Since its standpoint is always the logical order, it deals critically with the fashions of specific places—because they are not ubiquitous, and with those of specific times—because they are not eternal.

The Meaning of Comedy

We have seen that some comedies criticize customs and institutions which are no longer viable, while others go deeper to those which are still effective. Following upon this distinction, it is possible to divide comedies into the romantic and the classical varieties. Romantic comedy deals with that which was actual but is now remote; classical comedy deals with that which is always true and therefore perennially actual. Needless to add, the division is not an absolute one, and most instances of comedy contain elements taken from both varieties. Yet the division is important. We can perhaps best make it clear by further comparison between the classical and the romantic. Classical comedy is comedy that tends toward an absolutistic logical view. The classic aspect of comedy reveals the intrinsicness of value for its own sake. In classical comedy, the ideal of the rigorous logical order of values is unqualifiedly demanded by the criticism of actuality. No sympathy is felt for the extenuating circumstances which render that goal difficult of attainment. This uncompromising demand is the criterion of what is classical. It manifests a severity of outlook which marks particularly great comedy, and tends to be of permanent worth.

Nothing, however, is ever completely classic, and there is found throughout all comedy, even to the loftiest, a strain of sympathy for the uniqueness of actuality, a nostalgia for the lost particularity of actual things and events, especially when these belong to the past. The mournful regret that remembered events cannot be recaptured in all their frightful but fluid vividity is the hall-mark of the romantic. The romantic tends to relax a little from the uncompromising demand for the logical ideal of value, and to identify its interests somewhat with the irrevocable uniqueness of elements flowing by in the historical order. *Trivia*, by Logan Pearsall Smith, is replete with romantic comedy, though touched here and there with classic insight. " 'I have always felt (he says) that it was more interesting, after all, to belong to one's own epoch: to share its dated and unique vision, that flying glimpse of the great

183

panorama, which no subsequent generation can ever really recapture. To be Elizabethan in the Age of Elizabeth; romantic at the height of the Romantic Movement—.' But it was no good: so I took a large pear and ate it in silence."[5]

The romantic consists in a partial identification of interests with lost or perishable unique actuals. Since these must soon belong to the past, romanticism implies that perfection lies, or should lie, in the past rather than in the future. Thus romanticism is a form of primitivism. Romantic comedy points out that although passing actuals should have been better than they were, they were better than what has taken their place. The classic, on the other hand, like all true rationalisms, is directed toward the future; since what can happen is a wider category than what does happen and classic comedy criticizes actuality in order that possible things and events in the future might be more perfect. Thus romantic comedy is shot with nostalgic regret that certain actuals (i.e. specified ones in the past or present) cannot be made better than they were or are, while classic comedy takes the same observations of certain actuals but concludes from these observations that *all* actuals should be better than they are. Where romantic comedy is concerned with a segment of actuality, classic comedy is concerned with all actuality.

4. THE LOGIC OF ART

We have already noted that comedy is properly part of the study of aesthetics. But it will be observed that this would restrict comedy to works of art, and that this cannot be done, since comic elements are contained in much that lies outside the arbitrary aesthetic field. As we have already defined and further explained comedy, there is a comic aspect inherent in every actual thing and event. A short digression will be needed, therefore, in order to show just what is the artistic element in all its field of investigation with which comedy deals. This can

[5] *More Trivia*, p. 92.

best be done by exhibiting the logical structure which works of art share with other systems.

Every piece of knowledge, whether it be a thing or an event, a tangible object or an abstract system, possesses a formal structure. This formal structure consists in a set of primitive propositions or postulates which are arbitrarily set up, in a chain of deductions which are rigorously drawn from them, and in a necessary conclusion. This is not the way in which the structure has been constructed historically, but is the logical form which it has by virtue of what it is. Perhaps the most familiar example of formal structure is the system of Euclidean geometry. Here the number of postulates are simple and few, the deductions rigorous and the conclusions demanded. As a result, the system enjoys a remarkable generality of application.

This kind of analysis is a common one throughout the realm of abstract systems, such as those of mathematics and theoretical science. But what is not equally well known is that the same analysis can be made of events; nevertheless it is true for them also. Every event possesses some formal structure. An event may be abstracted from its context in the stream of actuality and considered as a self-contained system, having its own postulates, deductions and necessary conclusion. The mere fact that the postulates may be implicit rather than explicit, and the deductive actions following perhaps a matter of instinctive or even automatic reaction, does not alter the fundamental formal validity of the structure. A man who chooses to go to the movies, a lost dog which manages to find its way home, and a river which winds its way to the sea, are equally good examples of the principle that all actions are purposive, and as such must be served by mechanisms which are analysable into strictly logical systems.

What is true of abstract systems and events, with regard to their formal structures, is also true of works of art. For works of art also have their formal structures, though these are perhaps not so candidly expressed. Indeed it is the very difficulty presented by the problem of abstracting the formal structures of works of art which has led critics to suppose that no such thing exists. Nevertheless, it remains true that without their formal structures nothing actual could be. Works of art are sometimes admitted to have organization of a sort; but what such organization could consist of without formal structure cannot be imagined.

As a matter of fact, a close inspection of any work of art will bear out the truth of this contention. In some art mediums the form is more apparent than in others. For instance, the "theme and variations" scheme of most musical scores has a logical form which lies fairly obviously at the surface, and may be easily discerned by most appreciators. Indeed it is well known that any thorough musical appreciation must be grounded in an understanding of the form of the composition. The theme, or themes, announce the postulates, and the variations illustrate the deductions which are drawn from them. In the novel much the same holds true. The characters and situations as the reader finds them at the outset are here the postulates; the actions and interactions of the characters are the deductions drawn; and the climax presents the necessary conclusions toward which everything else has moved. What is true of music and fiction is true of every other kind of work of art; the effectiveness is always closely identified with a rigorous logical scheme, which is present even if never presented as such.

In abstract logical disciplines, all claims for the *a priori* and self-evident truth of postulates have been abandoned. In their place there has been substituted what is known as the postulational method. This amounts to nothing more than a recognition of the arbitrary selection and objective existence of postulates, which must rest not upon their self-evident truth but upon the fruitfulness of deductions made from them (i.e. the generality of their possible range of application) together with the self-consistency of the system of deductions itself.[6] Now, what does this mean in terms of works of art? It means simply that the sub-

[6] The later Greeks called the plot of a comedy the "hypothesis."

jective claims of intuition and the "creative" claims of the artist must be somewhat abated in favour of the deductive aspect. Induction and the artistic process are not to be abandoned, since there is no other method known for the discovery of works of art, but the fact is to be recognized that such inductive processes rest upon the prior assumption of a logical scheme in terms of which the inductions are made. Postulates are chosen by the artist by means of induction; necessary conclusions are drawn from them by means of deduction. Thus although the insight of the creative mind is an indispensable tool in the production of works of art, it yet remains true that the process, as well as the final product of the system itself, is strictly logical.

In this connection, it may be remarked parenthetically that the "genius" of the artist lies largely in the choosing of premises. Once they have been chosen, he may exercise his ingenuity in determining where the proper deductions can be drawn.[7] In a highly organized work of art (i.e. one which is technically perfect), all possible deductions are drawn. For here aesthetic economy has demanded that the postulates be kept few and simple, and therefore the number of possible deductions severely limited. The best of Bach's fugues are illustrations of this latter type of works of art.

The criticisms which comedy makes of all actual things and events is aimed specifically at their formal structures. Formal structure is alone responsible for the paucity of actual value; and it is this lack with which comedy expresses dissatisfaction. But warning must be issued against a grave danger which lurks in the fact. It is a mistake to suppose that ridicule levelled at the limitations of any actual system is being directed at the idea of system itself. To make fun of some man dressed for an afternoon wedding is not to make fun of formalism in dress, but might indeed be a plea for stricter attention to appropriate propor-

[7] It must be emphasized that although the artist is seldom, if ever, explicitly aware of the logic in which he is involved, this is not to detract from his contribution, which is considerable, but merely to call attention to the fact that the end-product of the artistic process is entirely independent of the artist.

tions in formal dress. To deride our government's short-comings is not to deride the necessity for some sort of government but is rather a demand for better government. Theories and practices are criticized not because they are theories and practices, which in one form or another must always have their place, but because they fail to be sufficiently wide and inclusive. Comedy, we must remember, upsets the categories of actuality only with the purpose of affirming the logical order. The literal nonsense of Gertrude Stein calls for the establishment of wider conventions in prose than those which her own prose came to destroy.

In short, it is not the content (i.e., the value) which is being criticized in comedy but the limitations put upon that value. Criticism of formal structure means criticism of the fact that the content contained by formal structure is not un-limited content.

5. PSYCHOLOGICAL ASPECTS

We have learned in a previous chapter that comedy as a logical affair must be distinguished from its psychological effects. Comedy cannot be explained in terms of its psychological aspects, but rather the reverse. Laughter is not its own explanation. We laugh because we have apprehended something external which is funny: the comic elements in a situation. The laughter is the result of the apprehension of these elements, but is certainly not the elements themselves. Laughter can be studied as a psychological reaction; but such a study, important as it is from a psychological point of view, can never yield a theory of comedy. At best it can yield a theory of the psychological effects of comedy.

The logical consideration of comedy which we have been setting forth above appears to place emphasis upon its negative aspects. Comedy of course is not only negative but also positive, since it consists of certain definite kinds of value. But the affirmative aspect is brought forward more definitely when we consider comedy from a psychological point of view. Laughter is sometimes the reaction to insuperable obstacles in the way of a goal, by which means the observer is thus reconciled to defeat. Life is not so bad after all, when we can laugh at disaster. For there are many contradictions and disvalues inherent in the human predicament itself which we can never hope to surmount: these arise from the fact that every individual is an actual affair, and in this sense necessarily limited and partially involved in difficulties and conflict. Changes may occur to correct some contradictions and to alter some disvalues, but cannot do so for all in the case of any actual thing. It is the final difficulty of human life which comedy accepts because it cannot change, and in this psychological sense we may see clearly the vistas of affirmative value inherent in comedy.

Due to its task of affirming the logical order only by means of the derogation of the limited orders of actuality, comedy, then, is perforce mostly preoccupied with limitations, with what is homely and familiar and vivid. And having to deal with these things, it is compelled psychologically to accept them. Thus psychologically comedy is not felt as criticism but as an acceptance, an acceptance of the comic aspects of actuality. Much of comedy as experienced is a mere recognition of the absurdity of the actual and is not necessarily a criticism in the sense of a violation of it.[8]

Comedians are always betraying an understanding, which is more often implicit than explicit, of the distinction between the logical nature of things and the psychological guise under which that nature is apprehended. Mark Twain once remarked that "Wagner's music is not as bad as it sounds." That this is true, any student of harmonics can affirm. For the value of musical composition is not to be estimated in terms of its psychological acceptance. We can estimate in terms of psychological acceptance—only psychological acceptance. The logical

[8] I have to thank Francis S. Haserot for calling my attention to this point.

value is psychologically acceptable or it is not. But certainly we cannot make logical nature causally dependent upon psychological acceptance. Wagner's music was just as good when it was first written, when nobody, not even professional musicians, liked the way it sounded, as it is now. But its psychological appreciation has changed considerably.

Of course, it must be admitted at the outset that psychological conditions do play a large part in the reaction to comic situations, or rather in the recognition of comic elements, for all situations have their comic elements. But the field of investigation of the psychology of comedy is not comedy itself, but the apprehension of and the reaction to comedy. It is well known that we tend to laugh more easily when we are feeling our best than when we are not. But this state of general well-being is not responsible for comedy and does not create it. The sense of being perfectly organized, the irradiation of perfect function, is the state of greater receptivity to comedy and makes for the easier discovery of comic elements, but is not itself comedy.

The fact that we are readier to appreciate the comic elements of situations when we are feeling fit then when we are feeling depressed lends additional support to our logical analysis of the nature of comedy. When we are weary or depressed, we are so to speak tied down physically and physiologically to the historical order, and we experience difficulty in rising above it sufficiently to be able to contemplate its shortcomings as ridiculous affairs. But when we are feeling extremely healthy, we can to a greater extent detach ourselves from the immediacy of actuality and contemplate its shortcomings as though we were in no wise affected by them. For comedy requires at least the pretended assumption of a *sub specie aeternitatis* attitude, and this is an extremely difficult one to assume, especially when we have a headache or are worried about desperate personal problems of the imminent future.

Another important psychological consideration is the fact that emotional and intellectual reactions vary enormously from individual to individual. The reaction of no one individual can possibly be a safe guide to the estimation of the worth of the external stimulus. Some persons laugh more easily than others, and past a certain point there is definite evidence of the existence of what is termed pathological laughter. The possession of low thresholds of emotion (emotional instability), on the part of persons who tend to laugh or cry too easily, is evidence of the fact that the psychology of laughter has its own peculiar field of inquiry. But on the other hand, if comedy were entirely an individual and psychological affair, what the French psychologist, G. Dumas, points out would not be true, namely, that we tend to laugh more freely when in a crowd than when alone.

What, then, is comedy from the psychological point of view? Why do we laugh? We expect, with a certain thing or event, to be tied down to actuality. We get instead, suddenly and unexpectedly, something or some event more logical. By this surprise we are lifted up and given over to a conception more valuable and more logical; and we laugh. Laughter is the result of the sudden recognition of the wide difference between what is and what ought to be. Psychologically, comedy consists in the recognition of the insuperable defects of actuality. That which we cannot react to is felt emotionally as inhibited action. The defects of actuality are unbearable to the feeling subject, and so an escape into the logical order is demanded. This escape consists in the recognition of the limitations of actuality, of the ridiculous and ludicrous aspect of existence.

Laughter is disarming and a positive good. It is in the very act of laughing that we become reconciled to the unimportance of limitations, and realize that we can surmount them. Indeed, to be able to laugh at the errors and evils of actuality is already in a sense to have surmounted them, and this is why we can laugh with impunity even at insurmountable obstacles. Laughter is thus a release of a sort from the limitations of the human lot, a recognition of the fact that obstacles in the path of improvement are not impossible obstacles, a recognition which itself to some extent renders them not impossible.[9] We have said that well-being is responsible for the apprehension of comedy; but comedy subjectively is also sometimes responsible for the state of well-being. In so far as one recognizes and appreciates the comedy in a situation, one is cognizant of its limitations and therefore close to the perfection of being—and therefore well.

How often have we heard it said by some person who has been confronted with a horrible but unavoidable situation that he had either to laugh or to cry, and that he had deliberately chosen to laugh? Tragic figures give rise to comedy through the effects of their actions. Comedy is never felt when the psychological subject accepts things and events as they are and for whatever value they contain. The tragic acceptance of positive situations surmounts the recognition of their shortcomings through ignoration. But comedy is continual rebellion and a refusal, even when faced with the inability to change conditions, to accept the compromises meted out by actuality. It is a continual cry for the perfection of the logical order which is ever possible.

Such is the nature of psychological comedy. Yet for all that, comedy is not created by its appreciators nor even in the act of appreciation itself. The fact that, as far as we know, human beings are the only ones to appreciate comedy does not make comedy a human affair; it makes only the *appreciation* of comedy by human beings human. Comedy is always *there* in the objective world and available for appreciation by whatever form of being is able to offer the necessary organization so that the proper perspective on the comic can be assumed and comedy itself apprehended accordingly. The appreciation of comedy has its purpose, but is susceptible to analysis into a psychological mechanism. To be able to assume the proper perspective for the apprehension of comedy we must possess as a prerequisite the necessary degree of organization. The

[9] In this sense, the catharsis theory of Aristotle has a limited validity; laughter is a kind of emotional purgation.

situation is exactly analogous to the radio waves which are always in the air but which are apprehended only by instruments sensitive enough for the task.

It can readily be understood that the foregoing explanation offers only the briefest hint of what is contained in the predicament which results from being unable to view the whole of existence under all its aspects and of being confined to the apprehension of but one aspect at a time. The psychological subject is only a part of actuality. Thus he stands in a certain relation to actuality, namely the relation of part to whole. He always views the world from a certain perspective on the world. But perspectives vary from individual to individual, and with each individual from moment to moment. Thus the perspective is independent of the psychological subject, and exists as a possibility whether the subject exists or no. But the psychological subject is under the necessity of viewing the world from some perspective or other, and thus may be said to be always in the perspective predicament. Perspective aspects on comedy are broader than psychological aspects and moreover are themselves non-psychological. It is to perspective aspects that we must turn, then, if we would understand more clearly the relation of the psychological subject to the field of investigation which is comedy.

6. Perspective Aspects

The perspective predicament is the situation in which every actual finds itself, of having to view the whole of existence from the position of a part. Now, the view of the part on the whole is necessarily a distortion, since it must be partisan and limited, and unable to view the whole as a whole. Only another whole could view the whole as a whole. But to view the whole from a part is to catch only certain aspects of it at a time and never the whole. Thus it is necessary for the actual to change its perspectives or have them changed from time to time, in order that it may apprehend a number of aspects, and thus be able to integrate them toward an approximation of the whole. The fact cannot be emphasized too strongly, however, that the whole is never dependent upon the part but exists *as a whole* totally independent of it. The same is true of the perspectives which come between part and whole, between, that is, the actual individual and the world in which he lives. Perspectives are independent of individuals; and, although they may be taken up at any time by individuals, they exist, regardless of this fact, as logical possibilities.

The theory of the perspective predicament may now be applied to comedy. Every actual situation wears its comic aspect. This aspect is sometimes appreciated, sometimes not. But it exists and is therefore available for appreciation none the less. "Humour is a kind of disappointment. If you expect to drive a tack in the carpet and drive your thumb instead, that is funny. You may not be able to see the point, but it is there, and if someone is looking on, he will see it and perhaps hope to show it to you, and if he too is disappointed, that will not make the situation any less intrinsically amusing."[10] Whether the intrinsic aspect of comedy is appreciated or not depends upon the perspective from which the subject is observing. In order fully to appreciate the instrinic nature of the comedy found in actual situations, it is necessary to be, or to be susceptible of being placed in, some perspective from which comic aspects are thrown into prominence. We do not say that objects of comedy are always funny to all men under all circumstances, nor that they are funny relative to certain men under certain circumstances. We only say that objects of comedy are absolutely funny relative to a given frame of reference, or perspective, which men may, but do not have to, assume. It is not being in a certain subjective creative mood but in a certain perspective, which is neither created nor owned by any person or group of persons, which enables the subject to apprehend and to appreciate the comedy inherent in actual situations.

[10] Max Eastman, *The Enjoyment of Laughter*, p. 7.

The Meaning of Comedy

There are an infinite number of perspectives. These differ over a wide range, and their differences depend in part upon the level of organization at which they are found. The hierarchy of empirical fields and of the sciences which study them are graded according to an upward increase in organization, as follows: the physical, the chemical, the physiological, the psychological, and the sociological. Every human individual exists in some sense at all these levels. He has a physical being, in terms of which his body is a mass having weight, density and dimensions. He has a chemical being, in terms of which the material of his body can be analysed into compounds of elements. He has a physiological being, in terms of which his organism consists of a flexor-reflex system of great complexity. He has a psychological being, in terms of which his organism is governed by higher centres which determine its search for the apprehension of independent values. And finally, he has a social being, in terms of which as a whole, including all levels, the individual is an atomic unit of society.

Innumerable perspectives are found at each of the levels. Happenings at these levels are determinative of the assumption of certain perspectives by individuals, and thus of the apprehension and appreciation of comedy. Thus the fact that the comic elements of actual situations are apprehended and appreciated, or not, is dependent upon the perspectives which exist at every level, and in which the individual may be placed or removed. We may give some examples.

Many simple and obvious instances of comedy may be said to be examples of physical perspectives on comedy. To slip and fall on a banana peel, or, quoting an example from Eastman, to hammer a thumb instead of a tack, are good examples.

The chemical perspective on comedy is best illustrated by the action of nitrous oxide, which is capable of producing laughter in any individual in whom it is introduced. Nitrous oxide interferes with the normal oxidative reactions of the central nervous system by limiting the oxygen supply. It appears from recent work[11] that anaesthetics of this type interfere specifically with the carbohydrate metabolism.[12]

Physiological perspectives of the lower level of physiological organization is illustrated by the reflex action of tickling, which varies enormously from individual to individual, but which is usually capable of causing reflex laughter. Of perspectives on comedy at the higher level of physiology, we have the compulsory laughter which accompanies certain diseases, such as multiple sclerosis and arteriosclerosis of the brain. Compulsory laughter of the sort is supposed to result from the release of mechanisms in the lower part of the brain, the basal ganglia, and particularly the thalamus, although this is still not conclusively proved.

Perspectives on comedy at the psychological level are highly complex, and little is known about them. However, we may make certain general observations. At the lower level of psychology, we may observe certain release mechanisms or reflex actions at work, of a nature to remind us of the upper physiological level. Certain persons exhibit instability, for instance; they have low thresholds of emotional excitation. Given the slightest hint as to the nature of the expected reaction to a situation, they are able to produce it in exaggerated form. They can laugh uproariously or weep copious tears easily and almost at will. This abnormal low threshold must be distinguished, however, from the perspective of what we may term normal low threshold, which is something quite different. The normal low threshold is a perspective in which no one is able to remain for very long. It is found with superabundance of health and animal spirits, with an awareness of well-being. The normal low threshold is found in children, and in old persons. Childish laughter and the cackle of old age need not be abnormal symptoms at all, but merely expressions of healthy perspectives.

[11] E.g. by Quastel in England.

[12] This, however, does not rule out the possibility of interference with the metabolism of other substances, such as protein decomposition products (amino acids), fats, and sterols. The problem is still wide open.

The Meaning of Comedy

Also at the psychological level there exist perspectives on comedy with high thresholds. These are apt to be the result of illness, personal disappointment, pain, and so on.

The increase in age is highly influential in the matter of the choosing of perspectives on comedy. This is particularly true at the sociological level. Our tendency to take the customs and institutions of actuality at their face value is in inverse proportion to our age. Children are accustomed to laugh at everything adult, and young people make the most fervent revolutionaries. Indeed for most persons it is only upon reaching the fully adult state that actual social conditions tend to become accepted as brute given facts, insusceptible of change or alteration.

At the level of the social perspectives on comedy, we learn that those individuals are wanting in something who apprehend only the comic or only the tragic aspects of existence. Those who appreciate only the comic aspect of every actual situation with which they are confronted are literally superficial. For they fail to take into account the empirical fact of their own actual existence as an item in the historical order of actuality. They are not so much preoccupied with the logical order of things-as-they-ought-to-be as they are ignorant of facts-as-they-are. On the other hand, those who appreciate only the tragic aspect of actual situations are equally ignorant of fact, since they assume in their positive endorsement of facts-as-they-are that what they are endorsing is the logical order of things-as-they-ought-to-be. But improvement only comes with change, and with the recognition of errors and disvalues which delimit the positive elements in existence. We must be warned of the gross stupidity of unrelieved solemnity.

The true comedian is one who is always cognizant of the logic of events. He reacts not only negatively away from tragedy[13] but also positively toward the logical order of the ideal. It should be emphasized again, however, that all these are perspectives from which certain aspects of existence are

[13] In Wexberg's sense. See above, p. 156.

seen as paramount; it is not a subjective or a necessarily conscious affair.

7. COMEDY AND TRAGEDY

There is nothing which does not have its tragic as well as its comic aspect. Comedy and tragedy are both members of the same class of objects, and are known to bear some close relation to each other. It will aid, therefore, in the understanding of comedy to contrast it with tragedy, for points of difference, and to compare them, for points of similarity. In order to make clear what we are talking about, it will be best to begin with definitions. We have already defined comedy as the indirect affirmation of the logical order by means of the derogation of the limited orders of actuality. What is required is a definition of tragedy which can be set over against this definition of comedy. Tragedy, then, is the direct affirmation of the formal logical order by means of the approval of the positive content of actuality. Tragedy is satisfied to endorse the threads of the logical order as these are found running through the historical order of actuality. Haserot calls our attention to the fact that tragedy is found also in the "frustration of that which . . . merits to survive."[14] Tragedy affirms the infinite value of the world through the endorsement of the remorseless logic of events.

This blind faith in the triumph of the logical order over the contradictions and evils of actuality is not defeated by the observation that in any limited time the logic of events may be accomplishing more harm than good. According to Dorothy Norman, Alfred Stieglitz has related an anecdote which illustrates very well this aspect of tragedy. "When someone asks him what he understands by the word 'justice,' Stieglitz replies, 'There are two families, equally fine. They go to a hillside, and there they build their farms. Their houses are equally well built; their situations on the hillside are equally

[14] Francis S. Haserot, *Essays on the Logic of Being*, p. 443.

advantageous; their work is equally well done. One day there is a storm which destroys the farm of one of them, leaving the farm of the other standing intact. That is my understanding of the word justice.' "[15]

Among the best examples of tragedy are the Greek dramas of Sophocles and Aeschylus. In the *Oedipus Rex* of Sophocles, the hero unintentionally sets off a chain of circumstances, of which he is himself the unhappy victim. Unwittingly, he establishes a postulate for action, and is himself enmeshed and crushed in the deductions which follow. He kills his father in order to become the husband of his mother, and then banishes himself from his own kingdom—all without his own conscious knowledge or consent. This play is a true illustration of the dramatist's recognition of the inexorable march of the logic of events, of the logical order as it operates through the medium of history.

There are many points on which comedy and tragedy may be contrasted, points which will serve to explain them both in a more thorough manner. Comedy is an intellectual affair, and deals chiefly with logic. Tragedy is an emotional affair, and deals chiefly with value. Horace Walpole once said that "life is a comedy to the man who thinks and a tragedy to the man who feels." Comedy is negative; it is a criticism of limitations and an unwillingness to accept them. Tragedy is positive; it is an uncritical acceptance of the positive content of that which is delimited. Since comedy deals with the limitations of actual situations and tragedy with their positive content, comedy must ridicule and tragedy must endorse. Comedy affirms the direction toward infinite value by insisting upon the absurdly final claims of finite things and events. Tragedy strives to serve this same purpose but through a somewhat different method. For tragedy also affirms the direction toward infinite value, but it does so by indicating that no matter how limited the value of finite things and events may be, such

---

[15] Dorothy Norman, "An American Place," in *America and Alfred Stieglitz*, p. 150.

In Praise of Comedy

value is still a real part of infinite value. Logic being after all only the formal limitation of value which is the positive stuff of existence, tragedy which affirms that positive stuff is greater than comedy which can affirm it only indirectly by denying its limitations.

Comedy is by its very nature a more revolutionary affair than tragedy. Through the glasses of tragedy, the positive aspect of actuality always yields a glimpse of infinite value. Thus tragedy leads to a state of contentment with the actual world just as it is found. According to tragedy, whatever in this finite world would be substituted for the actuality we experience would still have to be actual and therefore to some extent limited. It would have to be finite to be available for experience, and would not be the infinite value toward which we are always working. Moreover, the historical order of actuality, wherever and whenever it is sampled, yields a positive content however small which must be a fragmentary part of actuality. Thus, tragedy seems to say, since any segment of actuality is bound to be a fragmentary part of infinite value, why change one for another? Far better to stress the fact that whatever small fragment of value we have, it is as much value (though not as much *of* value) as any other fragment. Why then be dissatisfied?

Comedy, however, is occupied with the termini of things and events: their formal limitations, as opposed to tragedy which is occupied with their positive stuff or content. If it is only the limitations of actuality which prevent actuality from containing infinite value, those limitations should not be suffered. To justify the demand for their elimination it is only necessary to point out that they are effective limitations. Comedy leads to dissatisfaction and the overthrow of all reigning theories and practices in favour of those less limited. It thus works against current customs and institutions; hence its inherently revolutionary nature. Actuality may contain value, so comedy seems to argue, but it is capable of containing more of value; and it is necessary to dissolve those things and events which have some value in order to procure others which have a greater amount.

The Meaning of Comedy

Far better to stress the fact that however much value any actual situation may have, it is prevented from having more only by its limitations. Why then be satisfied? In periods of social change, we may expect to see the rôle of comedy assume an increasing importance, although, to be sure, both the comic and the tragic aspects of being are always and eternally omnipresent.

It has been pointed out by Bergson and others that comedy bears a closer resemblance to "real life" than does tragedy. This is true, and it is very obvious why it should be so. The contradictions and disvalues of actuality wear a greater vividity than do truths and values. In our daily occupations, we are confronted more frequently with the intense aspects of existence than we are with the diffused aspects. Error, ugliness, and evil, are, after all, colourful. Truth and value, as found for example in the systems of mathematics and the feelings of ecstasy, are wonderful; but they are likewise rare. Everyday life knows much more of the partial and extremely limited side of existence, and it is only a truism to say that this side is more familiar. Fortunately for the progress of humanity, familiarity is no index to value; what we are for ever condemned to pursue are just those fleeting glimpses of infinite value which come to us so seldom. But it is comedy which wears the common dress.

Comedy, then, criticizes the finite for not being infinite. It witnesses the limitations of actuality, just as tragedy witnesses the fragmentary exemplifications of the logical order. Tragedy affirms continuity by showing how it exists in every actual thing and event. Tragedy shows the worth of every actual, down to the most ephemeral, and so is always close to the permanent value of the worshipful. Comedy comes to the same affirmation, but inversely and by indirection, just as one might affirm beauty by criticizing the ugly. Comedy catches the principle of unity in every finite thing; tragedy attends to the principle of infinity.

It should be remembered that our contrast of comedy with tragedy tends toward a misleading oversimplification, as all analysis of necessity must. There are subtle relations between comedy and tragedy which reveal them to have more in common than do the rough comparisons we have had to make. Comedy compared with tragedy is after all only another method of becoming reconciled to the inevitably incomplete nature of finite existence. Both comedy and tragedy taken together are exhaustive functions of a certain grade of value-apprehension. Above them, as we shall see, lies their mutual fusing in divine comedy. Below there is only the bare recognition of factual existence in the temporal succession of awareness. For instance, the involuntary functioning of certain of the physiological processes is this mere awareness. But there is hardly a sentient individual whose average behaviour does not at some time encompass the experience of comedy however crude and elementary. Thus at its simplest comedy is universal and akin to tragedy. Often indeed the connection between comedy and tragedy is so close as to render them hardly distinguishable.

An excellent example of comedy in this sense is afforded by the episode of Alice and the Cheshire-Cat, in Carroll's *Alice in Wonderland*.[16] Alice had been nursing a baby, when suddenly, much to her dismay, it turns into a pig. She puts it down and it trots off into the woods. Alice walks through the forest, "getting well used to queer things happening," when with no warning the Cheshire-Cat re-appears exactly where it had been before. In the midst of this series of marvels, the Cat's conversation assumes the most casual, conversational tone.

" 'By-the-by, what became of the baby?' said the Cat. 'I'd nearly forgotten to ask.'

" 'It turned into a pig,' Alice answered very quietly, just as if the Cat had come back in a natural way.

" 'I thought it would,' said the Cat, and vanished again."

Here, too, comedy turns upon the logical order of events, but what events! Through the exposition of their connectivity, limitations are unexpectedly exposed and the comic aspect brought into predominant relief. Or the connectivity is

[16] Chapter VI.

emphasized as one of continuous value, and the tragic aspect triumphs. There is comedy in actual situations whose limitations have been laid bare. There is tragedy in the inexorable march of actual situations, because what value is contained in them will not be denied. We may see the actual situation as comedy or as tragedy; for in fact it is both. Comedy and tragedy emerge from the same ontological problem: the relation of the logical to the historical order.

8. KINDS OF COMEDY

There is only one kind of comedy, namely, that which we have said consists in the indirect affirmation of the ideal logical order by means of the derogation of the limited orders of actuality. Nevertheless, differences in comedy do appear upon examination; of what do they consist? If there is fundamentally only one kind of comedy, differences in kind must prove to be differences in degree. Yet the examples of comedy with which we are daily confronted present an almost bewildering variety. It is this qualitative variety which must be accounted for. A careful sorting shows that the differences can be reduced to three general classifications. Examples of comedy vary with regard to (1) the vehicle of presentation employed, (2) the nature of the object of derogation, and (3) the intensive and extensive degree of the comedy itself.

(1) Many are the vehicles which comedy employs. All the arts serve at one time or another as conveyers of comedy. There are funny pictures, funny sculpture, funny literature, funny dancing, etc. In the theatre of stage and cinema the range of comedy runs from classic comedies to the crude slapstick of vaudeville, and includes masque, pageantry, burlesque, and so on. Outside the theatre, less formal vehicles of comedy may consist in speech and action of every sort.

(2) Everything in existence wears its comical aspect, but this aspect is not always similarly presented and is seldom equally evident. Some things and events are doubtless funnier

than others, and are indeed more capable of exemplifying the comic than are others. The variety of presentation and of apprehension is certainly responsible for some of the wide differences that appear in comedy. Anything, however, may be the subject-matter of comedy. All actuality, from the most trivial to the most important, from the most ridiculous to the most sublime, is equally susceptible of being regarded from the comic perspective. The grandeur of a comedy has to do with the amount of existence with which it deals. Jokes aimed at current conventions are more telling than those aimed at morals, because the former are more acute but the latter broader. The former must have their effect *instanter* but the latter are of permanent value. The slightest comedy on this basis would be that which dealt only with trivial things, and the greatest comedy would be that which dealt with the whole of existence.

(3) The degree of comedy has an exceedingly wide range. With wide differences in degree, names have been arbitrarily assigned to segments of the comedy scale, so that differences in degree appear to be composed of differences in kind. The assigning of names to differences in degree, having to depend upon qualitative judgments, has largely been a normative affair. It is for this reason doubtful whether it would be possible to distinguish absolutely where one group leaves off and another begins. Any distinction between "satire" and "sarcasm," for instance, may prove to be largely verbal since that to which they refer may be the same. If this were true it would make them synonyms and thus call for the elimination of one or the other term in the interest of economy.

At the risk of laying ourselves open to error we may endeavour to arrange the names for comedy in a series, in an effort to indicate the variations in degree. Provisional hypotheses of this sort are, if taken too finally, open to the charge of dogmatism. A start, however, must be made, the main point being to work toward the establishment of an independent measure-scale for comedy. If the grouping below prove wrong, as well it may, a revision need not impair the recognition of the necessity for a measure-scale of some sort. On this plan, then, some suggestion as the following may be tentatively advanced.

> Joy
> Divine Comedy
> Humour
> Irony
> Satire
> Sarcasm
> Wit
> Scorn

Reading up in this list, we find that comedy increases the breadth of its field of criticism but lessens the intensity of the criticism. Humour, for instance, is directed at a wider subject-matter than is wit, but it is not half so biting. Reading down, we find the converse to be true; that is, the intensity of the criticism is increased and the breadth of the field is decreased. To take the same example, wit does not deal with as much material as does humour, but it is more effective in attacking that which it does deal. Thus comedy is intense over a narrow field and diffuse over a broad field. The extent of the relationship cannot be confined to anything half so simple as this; but there is sufficient evidence to reveal the presence here of a constant function.[17]

Qualitatively the justification for the scale is easily shown. Divine comedy near the top is the closest to pure comedy, while wit near the bottom has little to lose in order not to be comedy at all. The series is arranged in an ascending scale, and increases in direct ratio to the inclusiveness of the criticism involved. As this inclusiveness is increased, its sharpness is decreased in proportion, and a happy acceptance begins to take its place, until finally, at the head of the series, we have

---

[17] It must be remembered that our formulation is a standard for the judgment of the effectiveness of comedy, not a summary observation of all instances of comedy. Thus we may have attempts at intense criticism of a broad field and diffuse criticism of a narrow field, but the result would not be good comedy.

divine comedy. So excellent an example of this rare type of comedy is Dante's poem, that he has given his name to the generic term. Divine comedy criticizes almost with love, and at a very high level. Forgotten or rendered unimportant are its personal and contemporary references, and with them its bitterness has largely departed. Divine comedy consists in pushing comedy almost as far as it will go. It has judgment without criticism; laughter but above the battle; and an affirmation which is almost direct. It takes all actuality to be its province and contrasts this with the whole of the logical order. What remains is closer to tragedy; something of the tragic acceptance of the logic of events, the steady march of fate or destiny.

Finally, at the head of the list, as the mark of an upper limit to comedy, there is joy, from which criticism, and thus in a sense comedy itself, is almost totally absent. Joy lacking even a minimal criticism is pure delight. It consists in the recognition of the essential well-being of the universe: that this is the best of all possible worlds. It accounts for laughter without malice, for the happy state of childhood, and ranges to the near state of ecstasy.

The list we have given is a one-way vertical scale. But there is a lateral as well as a vertical scale for every item in the list. One example will suffice to show what is meant. For instance, joy, which stands at the top of the list because it is almost wanting in criticism, can be subdivided another way: namely, according to the degree of joy itself which is contained in an instance of comedy. Joy runs all the way from light gaiety to pure joy, from a superficial amusement to ecstasy. The gaiety of children is true comedy and is a subdivision of joy. It is spontaneous and light and easy because children have not yet learned to take the categories of actuality too seriously, as adults are wont to do. They do not see why almost anything should not be broken up, and hence they tend to laugh at almost everything. We all envy children their disregard of adult conventions, and that is why their laughter is so contagious. Childish comedy is the dawn of criticism. It consists in a comparison between what adults do and what the child himself can do in imitation. Thus arises a comparison between what is and what ought to be. All childish laughter is of the same nature. Thus the scale as we have presented it, from scorn to joy, is everywhere thick with co-ordinates which extend outward for each item with regard to its intensity as well as upward with the degree of criticism involved.

As we descend the scale, the sharpness of the criticism and the narrowing of its range of application begins to be very apparent. To drop from humour through irony, satire, and sarcasm, to wit, is to decrease continually the range of application of the criticism involved. Humour is the recognition of limitations in things and events. It is the broad range with which we are most familiar, the field of the commonest operations of comedy. Irony, satire, and sarcasm, are directed against contemporary foibles, as these are found in customs and institutions. "Sometimes," says Bergson,[18] "we state what ought to be done, and pretend to believe that this is just what is actually being done; then we have *irony*. Sometimes, on the contrary, we describe with scrupulous minuteness what is being done, and pretend to believe that this is just what ought to be done; such is often the method of humour." While this methodological difference is not the constant or only one, we can readily perceive that it is sufficient to broaden the field of humour and to intensify the criticism of irony.[19]

Wit is much the same as sarcasm, satire, and irony, but is directed at an even narrower target. Usually it chooses some one contemporary item of weakness, or even the foible of a

---

[18] *Laughter*, p. 127.

[19] The term irony, as employed here, is broad and includes similar tropes: metaphor, simile, metonymy, and synecdoche. Rhetorically, irony is the kind of trope in which what is expressed is the opposite of what is meant. It thus depends upon assistant effects, such as gesture, tone of voice, etc. The actual words employed in an ironic expression mean just what they mean unless they employ other aids to show that they are intended to indicate the opposite.

single individual, for attack. It is the most stringent form of humour, and has just enough reference to the possibility of a better order and a broader field to keep it from being pure scorn. Scorn appears at the low end of the scale to mark there the limits of comedy. There is nothing funny about scorn, which comes round again almost to the tragic attitude of divine comedy. The full circle swing from scorn to divine comedy is exemplified in the Biblical quotation, "He that sitteth in the heavens shall laugh: the Lord shall have them in derision." Comedy, then, is confined between the two extremes of pure joy, which marks its upper limits, and pure scorn, which marks its lower limits.

In order to give some slight indication of the enormous range of comedy and the extent of the field of its possible subject-matter, which the usual narrow definitions of the comedians fail to exhaust, it may be well at this point to cite a few examples of comedy. The examples are taken quite at random, and are meant to be little more than suggestive. They are unrelated to each other, and are intended merely to offer some hint of the penetration and extraordinary reach of comedy, from which nothing is inviolate. In each case, the level of criticism will be indicated.

It is reported that Chopin was invited to a fashionable dinner, and afterwards requested to entertain the other guests by playing the piano. Chopin, whose means of livelihood this was, suspected that he had been invited to the dinner for no other reason, and accordingly protested to his hostess, "*Mais, Madame, j'ai mangé si peu.*" This, of course, is close to wit, but may be labelled a sarcastic attack upon the customs of the day. Another example taken from the level of ordinary criticism is the response of Groucho Marx in one of the Marx Brothers' motion pictures. Someone asks before a large crowd whether there is a doctor among those present. Groucho stands up. "Yes," he says, "where's the horse?" The assumption that when a doctor is needed a horse must be the patient, implies that doctors who attend human beings are no more competent than veterinarians. This constitutes in effect an attack upon the alleged shortcomings of the medical profession as a contemporary institution.

Mr. Roark Bradford relates that once when working for a newspaper he was assigned to interview Ben Turpin. The interview took place in the wings of a vaudeville theatre where Turpin was playing. Bradford asked the screen comedian what in his opinion was the essence of comedy. "I will show you," replied Turpin, whereupon he walked onto the stage, with many gestures and grimaces—before a silent and unresponsive audience. Returning to Bradford in the wings, he said, "Now, watch again." This time he ran onto the stage, and fell with great force on his seat. There was a roar of applause from the audience. "That," said Turpin, when he returned to where the young reporter was waiting, "is the essence of comedy." Of course Turpin was quite right; for that too is comedy, though not of a very high order. Satires on the dignity of man and the awkwardness of walking with the gingerly balance of the upright position have their place just as much as any other type of comedy. Low comedy as well as high comedy is comedy.

In the *Greek Anthology*[20] we find the following sepulchral epigram. "Beneath this stone I lie, the celebrated woman who loosed my zone to one man alone." This is superb irony concerning human morals. A criticism of the rarity of sexual virtue, the notable thing about this epitaph is the absence of contemporary references. The tomb is unsigned, and the name of the dead woman is not mentioned. There is nothing at all to tie up the reference with date or place, and hence its generality is broader than it would at first appear.

Dialect stories are a familiar form of comedy, so familiar that no examples are required here. Relating stories, themselves funny, in dialect always seems to have the effect of heightening the comedy, because anything strange or foreign is always considered humorous by ignorant persons. The foreigner in a country is always thought to be a little mad and absurd by

[20] Vol. ii, p. 324.

virtue of the fact that his language, manners, and customs are different, i.e. not what it is felt they should be. Thus tales of incongruity are always related in dialect. In all justice, it should be admitted, however, that dialect stories are implicitly understood to be a little *infra dignitatem.*

One of the most important forms of comedy is that which involves direct social criticism. The drawings by George Grosz afford one variety. But there are many kinds of social criticism, which do not have to be directed against social injustices to be criticism. One of the best examples of this fact is the *New Yorker* cartoon of a building under construction. In the foreground two labourers are on a scaffolding, carving a name over the door of the building. One labourer turns to the other, and asks, "Does '*ex*' take the dative or the ablative?" Such a criticism of the presumptuousness of any pretension to learning on the part of workers was bound to arise in New York where the incongruous proximity of wage-slave and wealthy is so noticeable. It is basically snobbish criticism of proletarian ignorance, however, the idea conveyed being that ordinarily workers do not (or should not) speak like the decadent, the effete, and the over-civilized.

Comedy is frequently directed at logical and epistemological points. There is the man who said that his arm hurt him, that he had a pain in his stomach, that he was worried about his finances, and that besides, he personally did not feel so well. This is humour at the expense of logical error. The jibe is directed toward the absurdity of considering together things which have no logical justification for being placed on the same level of analysis. The whole person, his arm and his worries, are not at the same analytic level, a point which is best indicated by humorously considering them as though they did belong together.

Humour at the expense of the problems of knowledge is best exemplified by puns or plays on words. Woman: "Do you like children?" Man: "I cannot bear them."[21] Here we have the

---

[21] In the face of this old and atrocious pun, it should perhaps be pointed out that jokes are selected here for their usefulness as illustrations of the examination of comedy. It has not been the intention

epistemological trick of taking the datum for the referent, or that to which the knowledge refers. Its *de facto* moral is: words do not refer to anything; therefore why take them seriously? In this connection it may be pointed out that nonsense has a definite meaning in comedy. Nonsense *sub specie comedia* is the criticism of meaning, the syntactical joke.

Before leaving our list of illustrations of comedy, we may return to the *Greek Anthology*, in order to choose another of its wonderful examples. This time it is divine comedy that is being approached by the quotation. It is again a sepulchral epigram, attributed to one Simonides. The tomb reads, "I, Brotachos, a Gortynian of Crete, lie here, where I came not for this end, but to trade."[22] The superb brevity of this attack upon the vanity of all human occupations has rarely been exceeded. Here is cryptic denunciation of nearly the highest order, social criticism reposing in a nutshell.

We have listed the various kinds of comedy, selecting our illustrations at random from Ben Turpin to the *Greek Anthology*. These few examples should suffice to show that anything may be the subject of comedy, from the most trivial of things to the most sublime. The degrees of comedy listed in the scale on page 205 give some indication of how wide is the subject-matter included in comedy and how various the intensity of comedy itself. But just as any action, any feeling, any reasoning, any finite thing or event, may be the subject-matter of comedy, so numerous also are the vehicles of comedy. We may end this brief survey with three examples of comic poetry, ranging from nonsense verse almost to stark criticism.

The whole of "Jabberwocky" is too familiar to need quoting.

> 'Twas brillig, and the slithy toves
> Did gyre and gimble in the wabe;
> All mimsy were the borogroves,
> And the mome raths outgrabe.

to cause the reader to laugh but rather to help him understand what it is that arouses laughter. For this purpose, jokes which are not particularly funny have often been deliberately chosen.

[22] Vol. ii, 254A.

In Praise of Comedy

Like all nonsense verse, Carroll's poem is a criticism of meaning. It means *almost* nothing, yet depends for its effect upon the vague penumbra of meaning which it seems to retain. By contrast, Kipling's limerick begins to make a special point, but it is very special, and is amusing because of its criticism.

> There was a small boy of Quebec
> Who was buried in snow to his neck;
>   When they said, "Are you friz?"
>   He replied, "Yes, I is—
> But we don't call this cold in Quebec."

In the example which we have culled from Heine, the humour has spread out somewhat, and criticizes more. Of the "mutilated choir boys," Heine says,

> They sing of love that's grown desirous,
> Of love, and joy that is love's inmost part,
> And all the ladies swim through tears
> Toward such a work of art.[23]

The last example is only a little funny, because the social criticism is so severe that the comedy is almost entirely replaced by scorn. In the following we hear the voice of the reformer which now has triumphed over that of the comedian.

> The golf links lie so near the mill
>   That almost every day
> The labouring children can look out
>   And see the men at play.[24]

9. THE DIVINE COMEDY

One kind of comedy has been saved for the last, namely divine comedy. We have described this as comedy which takes the largest field that comedy can take for criticism and remain comedy, i.e., not lose all of its criticism through diffusion and

[23] *Von die Heimkehr*, translated by Ezra Pound.
[24] Sarah N. Cleghorn, quoted in B. E. Stevenson, *The Home Book of Verse*, p. 563.

become pure joy. The criticism of divine comedy is directed at nothing less than the whole field of the finite predicament: the glorious effort and partial failure of that which is limited as it strives to comprehend (and thus partially to transcend) its limitations. The breadth that comedy can achieve and remain comedy is, then, wider than might at first have been supposed. For limitations are nowhere as narrow as they are often conceived to be. Beyond any limited order there is always a less limited order, and so on in infinite progression. God in this sense could almost be defined as the least limited or the most unlimited order. Comedy thus has an infinite range, and the divine comedy is still criticizing something. Nietzsche had some such conception as this in mind when he said, in *Also Sprach Zarathustra*, "I could never believe in a God who did not know how to laugh." To accept actuality just as it is, even for a God, would mean not to be the ruler of the logical order.

Peirce's ethical principle of the unlimited community calls for union with infinity, to be sought not immediately by mystical affinity but mediatedly by means of limited organizations, using each organization as a stepping-stone to the next less limited, and so on, until the least limited of all is attained. This is the same principle as the one demanded by divine comedy. For the positive pursuance of an unlimited community requires two steps to each unit of advance. As we pursue the unlimited community from the limited communities we know, we must at each stage of advance recognize the limitations of those we are leaving behind and the greater positive content of that toward which we are advancing. The recognition of such positive content requires only the feeling for value which each of us to some extent possesses. But the recognition of limitations requires a certain amount of intelligence; and it is in this second step in the process that the place of comedy is found. Thus comedy paves the way for progress by pointing out at each stage of advance the limitations of all which has been so far attained. It thus calls for the abandonment of past attainments in favour of greater possible attainment. And it calls for the neglecting of intermediate successes in favour of the pursuance of still greater success. In this sense it is in sympathy with the revolutionary struggle for something better and again for something still better.

Comedy is only to a small extent an individual affair. To a much greater extent it is a property of the gregarious. "We laugh far more easily in a group than when alone,"[25] as tests made with groups and individuals seem to show.[26] Nevertheless, there is a sense in which private comedy must remain private. A private as well as a public perspective exists on comedy, which is the view of the organization of the organism from within, and the understanding of its predicament as finite. We can share the knowledge of that perspective but not the feeling, except secondarily by means of empathy. Divine comedy enters into the private perspective, for example, upon occasions of private, as contrasted with public, success and failure. In some way, the public success of the individual is always connected with his private failure: he knows that whatever he has accomplished was due in large part to favourable circumstances, and that he is not able to take himself at the same high evaluation that has been publicly accorded him. On the other hand, public failure (which is far more common) is always connected with private success: the individual knows that he has striven for what he thought to be worth striving for according to his lights and that he is not able to take himself at the same low evaluation that has been publicly accorded him. Public failure has its private success. The individual is aware that he did not lose, could not lose, in a game in which there was no such thing as winning. The deep understanding of this fact lends an aspect of divine comedy to the private predicament.

Comedy is in the fullest sense a moral principle, an ethical force. It ever reminds us that nothing thus far attained is

---

[25] Carney Landis, in Carl Murchison, *Foundations of Experimental Psychology*, p. 499.
[26] R. E. Perl, *American Journal of Psychology*, vol. 45 (1933), p. 308.

sufficient; it laughs at actual values for their manifest limitations, which it takes great delight in pointing out; and it calls
for the girding up of loins and the pressing ever forward toward
fresh values and original organizations, demanding new
victories and new achievements for the human race. Criticism,
and hence humour, belongs only to those who want to improve
the world, and not to those who are willing to accept it as found.

We have said that comedy consists in the indirect affirmation
of the ideal logical order by means of the derogation of the
limited orders of actuality. As divine comedy, its affirmation
consists in the indication here and there that the malice of
actual events may be symbolically logical. Does the recognition
of great men sometimes wait until there is no chance for
biographical details to be remembered, because the greatest
men are those who are known through their works and not
through what may be remembered of their personalities? Did
Charles S. Peirce, the only time he had any money, plan a big
attic for his new home—an attic which was to house disciples
—but run out of funds before the attic had been completed,
because he was fated not to have any disciples? Did Francis
S. Haserot's book, *Essays on the Logic of Being*, fail to be
advertised or sell, and, becoming remaindered, end up on the
bargain counters of drug stores, because it was good medicine?

It is hard to answer these questions, since here we run not
only into symbolism but frequently into unfounded symbolism
or dogma. Yet events must each have their own significance,
and we can fancy that sometimes we can detect what that
significance is. Nietzsche's god with his knowledge of laughter
would surely be much inclined to indulge himself in this sort
of comedy. But we do not need the postulation of a god with a
sense of humour in order to harbour a suspicion that events
themselves sometimes foreshadow in these cryptic symbols,
intended for those who run to read, the logic toward which
all creation is aimed and toward which events grope with
varying successes in historical time. The malice of events, which
does occasionally appear to be symbolically logical, may not

be rational or dependable enough to serve as a guide to action. However, it will be well to recognize it here and there, as it lurks beneath the surface of phenomenologically random events, and to let such recognition take the form of amusement and laughter.

CHAPTER V

Illustrations From Modern Comedians

1. IN PRAISE OF THE COMEDIAN

WE have reviewed the history of comedy by giving short sketches of examples taken both from the actual comedians of the past and from speculators who have set forth hypotheses as to the theoretical nature of comedy itself. Finally, we have offered our own theory of the nature of comedy. Now it remains only to discover some illustrations among modern comedians in order to show that comedy is always, to some extent at least, classical in its attitudes. For we shall find among the comedians of our own time the same relations to the timeless elements of truth and to highly contemporary factual elements. It should here be made fairly obvious what our contention has been all along: namely, that the comedian is a highly contemporary fellow, and yet that he is affirming truths and values which stand independent of time. For the customs and institutions to which the contemporary comedian has reference are always those which are most familiar to us; indeed they are those which have become part of the necessary conditions of our daily activities. Further, the criticism to which he subjects these customs and institutions reminds us of things as they should be but as they never have been on sea or land. The comedian thus plays essentially before our conscience; he exalts us to greater efforts and insists that we keep our highest ambitions constantly in mind.

The other day difficulties developed within the management of a travelling rodeo. It seemed that the company had not been paid salaries due for some weeks, and the whole troupe, headed by a clown who was the most enterprising and intelligent of them all, threatened to take over the show. Peace was restored only when the authorities promised to pay the salaries in arrears out of gate receipts, before turning the funds over to the financial backer and manager. At the next night's performance, when the star act, "Tony and His Wonder Horse," was announced, the clown who was in the arena remarked half under his breath, "Yes, you know why Tony calls him a wonder horse? Because he wonders when he is going to eat again." Now this is a poor joke, but it does make the function of true comedy stand out in relief, and it does exemplify the rôle of the comedian. He is one who has a tragic life indeed. His reward consists in the fact that he is allowed without punishment to tell the truth about something.

Multiply this example many times, and you have a picture of comedy in any given period and at any particular place. The comedian simply refuses to accept compromises and insists upon reminding each and every one of a duty to truth and value. The contemporary world is, from this point of view, simply a field for the operation of comedy—the comedian's raw material.

"Folly, conceit, foppery, silliness, affectation, hypocrisy, attitudinizing and pedantry of all shades, and in all forms, everything that poses, prances, bridles, struts, bedizens, and plumes itself, everything that takes itself seriously and tries to impose itself on mankind—all this is the natural prey of the satirist, so many targets ready for his arrows, so many victims offered to his attack. And we all know how rich the world is in prey of this kind! An alderman's feast of folly is served up to him in perpetuity; the spectacle of society offers him an endless *noce de Gamache*. With what glee he raids through his domains, and what signs of destruction and massacre mark the path of the sportsman! His hand is infallible like his glance. The spirit of sarcasm lives and thrives in the midst of universal wreck; its bells are enchanted and itself invulnerable, and it braves retaliations and reprisals because itself is a mere flash, a bodiless and magical nothing."[1]

[1] *Amiel's Journal*, translator H. Ward (New York, 1928, Brentano), p. 178.

Illustrations from Modern Comedians

The degree to which the criticism contained in comedy is tolerated by those at whom it may be aimed is a measure of the condition of a civilization. In days of great conservatism, the comedian is frequently himself too much involved in the implicitly accepted premises of the world in which he lives, and so he like all others may come to regard the brutal effect of comedy as an attack upon contemporary assumptions, deeming it crude and uncalled for and even uncivilized. The attitude of Meredith in this regard is a case in point. Meredith held that the only comedy worthy of the name was a kind of light banter which played upon the surface of the least important of contemporary foibles. He abhorred the "bad taste" of comedy which criticized individuals or which offended in any way. Such was the state of affairs in the nineteenth century. But in days of great social upset, of economic turmoil and political upheaval, like our own, the responsibility of the comedian is a heavy one. He is, so to speak, on the firing line; he may be either made into a king or crucified, although more often the latter. It is, however, obligatory upon him to take his stand, and to receive the praise or blame which is meted out to him, usually out of proportion to his just rewards. In this sense he is a pioneer of values.

The reward of the prophet is usually an extreme one. To campaign for values is to stand for those imponderables to which one's own times are temporarily blind, although the shortcomings of an older period are always obvious enough. Thus the pioneer tends to be a leader whose followers cannot keep up with him. They are not equal to the demands which he makes upon them; yet there he is for all that, and he has to be accounted for in some way which is not too unflattering to them. The solution is supposed to be found in labelling every comedian a crazy man and a "nut." The truths uttered by the comedian are of such serious consequence that they cannot be faced as serious. Wherefore they are dismissed as foolishness, as utterly meaningless. The comedian, the defensive populace claims, is a crack-pot who does not really mean what he says.

In Praise of Comedy

But the refutation of such a charge is easy enough. It consists in two points. The first of these is the reaffirmation of the objectivity of comedy. This can be accomplished by accepting the charge rather than by refuting it. But if every comedian is a "nut," then some "nuts" must be comedians, and the fact is that they are. The insane, who are themselves unmindful of their own meanings, are meaningful in so far as their actions or words are intelligible. It is words and not the use to which we intend to put them that carries meaning, and proof of this lies in the fact that perfectly sane persons do not always succeed in conveying in speech exactly what they mean; they are misinterpreted or misunderstood. If an insane man performs an act or says something which is funny, there is an implied criticism in his words and he is a comedian—regardless of whether he is sane enough to mean anything he says or not. The people of London were accustomed to amuse themselves some while ago by visiting Bedlam, the insane asylum, to watch the antics of the inmates.

The insane more often than not appear to us to be humorous. One doctor relates the tale of the manic-depressive he had observed standing up in his cell with a book carefully balanced on his head. The doctor became interested, and when walking into the cell, he removed the book from the patient's head he was instantly knocked down by the patient. Hearing the commotion, attendants came hurriedly to the rescue for fear that further bodily harm might be the lot of the doctor. But such was not the case. The patient paid no more attention to the doctor once he no longer constituted an interfering element, but instead carefully picked up the book and, replacing it on his head, went on with his balancing. The apparent comedy was in truth comedy, but was certainly not intended by the insane patient to be viewed in that light.

The second point consists in demonstrating that sanity requires a sense of humour. The insane are sometimes funny, but the sane to be sane must always be capable of being so. A sense of humour is, after all, only a sense of proportion, a feeling for logic in actuality. The inability to judge proper proportion would mean the taking of things as they are for things as they ought to be, or *vice versa*. The man who insists in thinking that he is Napoleon may have a very good sense of humour. The distinction lies in the degree to which the conditions of actuality are pretended to be other than they are. Delusion has its place, and is only out of place when it pretends to be the whole of truth. But a complete lack of a sense of humour would also mean insanity. The gravity of some persons who never smile, or the easy laugh of some persons who regard everything as equally funny, alike betray the complete absence of a sense of humour. Some sort of a failure of intelligence is similarly indicated. A minimal sense of humour is probably the possession of all normal persons, but there are some in whom it rides at dangerously low ebb, and these are no friends of the comedian.

The relation between the social environment of a given period and the comedy of that period is occasional rather than causal. That is to say, the particularity and the peculiar individuality of formal comedy is unique for any special time and place, but the meaning of the comedy itself, provided that it is of a high enough order, is usually more general than the conditions which gave rise to it. Comedy criticizes everything, from the most transient of local habits and customs to the relatively more permanent aspects of human nature. Indeed the faults of "human nature" are the subject-matter of the very greatest comedy. Shakespeare, for example, is often given credit for having touched in a most universal way upon the irremediable characteristics of human nature which, we are told time and again by one writer after another, "never changes." But what is this human nature? It is obviously something which most of us exhibit. Extreme persons are notoriously lacking in it; supermen and saints are commonly described as being "hardly human" because of their extreme goodness; diabolically evil men are likewise labelled for being more than ordinarily evil. The human range is properly thought to lie in the narrow band between the two extremes. "Human nature" is confined by ordinary to the search for small values and lesser truths, and to the commission of small defections and inconsiderable errors. That is why we are in the habit of saying of any absolutist scheme, that it leaves human nature out of account. Now, the comedian, like logic itself, has no use for compromises. He is an absolutist, a dealer in extremes, and has as little time for compromises as he has for the devil himself. He works for the logical order and in the name of the highest values. At the hands of the proponents of human nature in the round he meets with nothing but bafflement, disappointment and defeat.

Comedy in critical times like the present tends to be severe; it has to cut pretty deep if it is to carry any significance in times of rapid change. The revolutionary nature of comedy is recognized well enough in those countries where it meets with sharp and uncompromising dictatorial suppression. Dictators never laugh; and suppression is their way of acknowledging the critical powers of true comedy. Comedy is not necessarily political by nature, however. It may be so, as when the targets of its criticism are transformed by political change. But just as often it may not be, as when the things which it criticizes remain the same under political alteration and continue to call for criticism by showing some sort of persistency, despite radical shifts in the social system.

In general, however, we may assert that comedy tends to have some political significance. For rulers and ruling classes do not readily detect the weaknesses of the systems which benefit them. It is the vanquished and not the victors, the fools and not the kings, who are apt to want to point out through comedy the shortcomings and contradictions in the prevailing social systems. But this is only another way of saying that there is a recognizable tendency for comedy to arise from the oppressed classes and also from those whose sympathies go out to the oppressed. Thus the comedian is a reformer who is often ignorant of the fact himself but whose message of serious import passes through gates which would not be thrown open were it not for the disguise of laughter and seeming triviality. Like pioneers in other fields, the comedian faces the rather gruesome choice of being ignored, misunderstood, or suppressed altogether, But if he is a true comedian and his comedy true comedy, the extent of his success is a measure of progress and civilization.

In what follows we shall touch upon only a few of the current comedians, seeking to choose examples from as wide a variety of types as possible. Needless to say these are by no means exhaustive nor in any way complete, although they should be illustrative.

2. THE COMEDY OF EVERYDAY LIFE: THE MARX BROTHERS

Among those comedians having the greatest popular appeal must be numbered the Marx Brothers. The antics of the clown, "Harpo," the incessant talk of "Groucho" and the dialect of "Chico," have been the delight of large audiences in many countries. From their orginal act in vaudeville to their present eminence in the movies, all their work has been marked by a consistently high quality, and by a profusion which is somehow over and above the ordinary run of professional funny men. Their success is certainly due in large part to the down-to-earth character of the humour involved. Chico's dialect is among the oldest tools of the trade, as is also much of the pantomime of Harpo. We have heard before in crude joke-books the dialect in which the language that we know is mispronounced; we have seen before in the mischief of the classic clowns the troubles in which Harpo gets himself engaged. And we have even had time and again the pattern of the puns for which Groucho is so often responsible. But we have never seen so much humour packed into a single play and offered in the short span of one evening.

The comedy of the Marx Brothers is essentially that of the commonplace. Nothing in contemporary American life is safe from their jibes. The real estate business, the medical profession, horse racing, returning African explorers, the opera—we laugh because in the cock-eyed presentation of these familiar occupations we remember it all. It is all as plain and as familiar as the fact that the sun is shining, and it is equally unself-conscious. We have the impression that what we are witnessing is the good spirits of some people who, in the abundance of their feeling for life, refuse to take anything seriously.

But it is perhaps in the realm of modern business that the Marx Brothers are most at home. The pomposities of big business executives, the language and sanctity of contracts, the bold adventures in large enterprises—the Marx Brothers inimitably select the weaknesses, and tear them upon the points of a wit which is audacious by virtue of its terrific economy. The laconic language of Americans is likewise involved in the humour of these comedians. We have a habit of picking up a telephone in American hotels, and saying "Ice-water in room 412." Groucho upon one occasion, is supposed to be desk clerk in a hotel. The telephone rings, and Groucho picks up the receiver. After listening a moment, he says, "Ice-water in room 412? Where did you get it?" Groucho understands the pretensions of the modern American business man better than anyone else, and he takes huge delight in the risible aspects. When Groucho has done with him, the authority of the business man falls away and he stands there before us in his naked self-interest.

Do not, however, let the very baldness of the humour of the Marx Brothers deceive you into assuming that it is a superficial kind. For it is assuredly nothing of the sort. It is a profound and penetrating criticism of the modern way of life, and especially of the values which we here in America have chosen for our own. But although the humour is peculiarly American, its contemporaneity assures it of a wider field than anything national, and extends it to modern life in general.

Groucho is by far the most excellent of the Marx Brothers.

Illustrations from Modern Comedians

His humour may be taken as typical of their kind of comedy. The reader should perhaps be warned that in the following remarks no account has been taken of conscious intention. The question of the extent to which Groucho is aware of the meaning of his humour has nothing whatsoever to do with the case. We are considering here an objective comedy which Groucho perpetrates but for the message of which he is not entirely responsible. To know how far he is able to analyse his own humour would throw some light upon his individual intelligence but little or none upon the meaning of his comedy. It may be taken as a truism that comedy addressed to the public is public comedy, and hence absolutely available for analysis to meanings which are themselves objective meanings. It should by now be a recognized truth that the artist is not always the best aesthetician; and similarly the comedian is not always the best expositor of his comedy.

The comedy of Groucho Marx is the comedy of the commonplace. The material with which he works is largely furnished by platitudes. He is a great comedian because he understands, probably intuitively, that comic artistry centres about the issue of platitudes. Great tragedy consists in the invention of platitudes; comedy in their destruction. The utterances of the great tragic dramatists are incorporated into the language because they are the fullest and the most economic expression of truths which are universal in their application. But there comes a time when through excessive repetition these statements are rendered ineffective; their meaning seems to have worn thin, and it is no longer the meaning but only the words which are heard. It is at this point that the comedian steps in. He instinctively realizes that if the meaning is to be made clear and forceful again, the truism which expressed it must be destroyed. The destruction involves the abandonment of the original expression as well as the revivification of the meaning for which it stood.

We have all grown deaf with hearing others, and perhaps ourselves say, "don't leave a stone unturned." We have heard it so often and for so long that it no longer conveys anything. Then along comes Groucho and gives it a new twist. He and his fellow-zanies are looking for a man whom they have been unable to find in the expected places. "Don't leave a stone unturned," cries Groucho. "He may be under one of them." The trick is done, the spell broken. We may never be able to avail ourselves of this expression again; but at least we are made to realize once more what it means.

Many illustrations could be given of the use of platitudes and truisms in Groucho's comedy. In a room full of people smoking, Groucho observed, "Pardon me if I don't smoke." Here the method is slightly different; because it is no longer necessary to ask permission to smoke, so general has the habit become. Now we almost have to ask permission *not* to smoke. Groucho has pointed out how ridiculous this situation is, and he has relieved us of one more inane expression.

One of the most popular of Groucho's targets is the pretensions and failures of the medical profession. In a brilliant stroke Groucho reminds us of the lowly origins of modern medicine in magic, blood-letting and alchemy, when he points out the analogy between the stage trick of pretending to saw a woman in half and the practice of the laboratory teaching of students. The scene is a lecture on medicine. Groucho pops his head in the door and asks, "Have they sawed the woman in half yet?" He reassures one young lady, who supposedly had been his father's patient and who was still ill, "My father's patients are good enough for me." But not only the lowly history of medicine and the failure of medical practice to effect cures, are the recipients of Groucho's criticism. The attack goes much deeper to a comic analysis of medical functions and their validity. Upon one occasion when taking a man's pulse, Groucho looks at his wrist-watch, and at the man, and says, "Either this man is dead or my watch has stopped." In *A Day at the Races*, Groucho is a horse doctor who practices medicine among human beings.

From the reaffirmation of the truth contained in platitudes

Illustrations from Modern Comedians

through their acceptance or logical denial, to logic itself, is not a far step. The acceptance or denial of a truism on logical grounds alone is logical enough. But Groucho can do better than that. He is capable of taking the form of the syllogism itself as the subject-matter of his humour. He accomplishes this by starting what appears to be a perfect line of deductive reasoning and following it to an absurd and unnecessary conclusion. To one young lady who observed that it would be impossible for him to stay in a closet, he replied, "Just remember, my little cabbage, if there weren't any closets there wouldn't be any hooks, and if there weren't any hooks there wouldn't be any fish, and that would suit me fine." This exhibits the bare bones of logic itself, hardly concealed behind any actual subject-matter. Or rather, the only justification for what actual subject-matter there is, is contained in the effort to set forth an illogical chain of deductive reasoning.

There is implicit in the above joke also, a criticism of the psychological order of reasoning. Reason is never false, but reasoning frequently is. Groucho recognizes that the arguments which result from abandoning one's mind to the psychological order of reasoning, the random order in which one thought follows another regardless of any fixed plan or guide, is funny. The order in which ideas occur to us is seldom the logical order of those ideas. Groucho's presentation is a recognition of this fact. By showing us that the psychological order is absurd he is able to affirm the proper or logical order indirectly. This is pretty close to pure comedy, although not of the highest kind. Groucho, like all good comedians, is constantly reminding us of the literal meaning of the words we use. The commonest vehicle for such a reminder is the pun. But the illustrated pun is the Marx Brothers' contribution. "Get the seal," someone says in the office of the president of a university. An important document is to be signed. Harpo, it must have been, comes in with a live seal, whose physical presence at this stage renders innocuous the whole grave proceedings.

The classic aspect of the Marx Brothers' comedy is evident in its ridicule of the romantic aspects of life. All modern forms of the romantic attitudes are criticized by these clowns, in one way or another, regardless of whether the romantic be evident in love scenes (which Groucho adores to parody) or in tales of adventure. The very surprised but secretly enamoured middle-aged lady to whom Groucho is constantly making love is (or should be) a legally constituted member of the troupe by virtue of her ability to be consistently unrelaxing in the defence of her outraged dignity. Without warning, Groucho drops to his knees before her. With the most appealing of love-soft looks he says, "I mean your eyes."

But perhaps the best example of the attack upon the romantic is the long account which Groucho as "Captain Spaulding" gives of his hunting trip in Africa. The Captain is a guest at a fashionable week-end party in a Long Island home. After dinner, he lectures informally to the guests, recounting many anecdotes about his trip. "We shot two bucks," he said, "and lost. That was all I had in my pocket. But perhaps it will be better if I give you a picture of a typical day in camp. We got up at seven, washed and dressed and had breakfast, and were back in bed by eight. After a while we got so good that we could be back in bed by seven-thirty. We took some pictures of the native girls. Of course they're undeveloped. But then we hope to go back next year. One morning I woke up and there, staring right into my tent, was a huge rhinoceros." It was a tense situation, and Groucho's attitude and tone of voice indicate the fact. "What did you do then, Captain Spaulding?" some one of the guests asks breathlessly. "Captain Spaulding" relaxes and flips the ashes off the end of his cigar. In a very matter-of-fact voice, he answers, "Well, what could I do? I had to marry his daughter."[2]

The arts come in for a goodly share of criticism, especially the performers and interpreters. "When you get near a song

---

[2] Neither the order of these quotations nor the exact wording is correct. But both are near enough to give the required indication of the humour.

play it," Groucho tells Chico when the latter is busy performing at the piano. And when Chico goes through the same song twice, Groucho observes, "When it comes round again jump off." The most hilarious instance of the comic approach to the interpretation of music is the scene in which Groucho is talking with the leader of the orchestra (Chico) at the country home where he is a guest. Groucho is plainly dissatisfied with the music. The conversation went something like this.

"How much do you charge to play for an hour?" Groucho asks.

"A thousand dollars."

"And how much would you charge me to play for a whole evening?"

"Ten thousand dollars."

Groucho drops back into his matter-of-fact tone. "And how much would you charge not to play at all?"

"You couldn't afford it," replies Chico.

The Marx Brothers have a wonderful ear for the overtones of American speech and ordinary American attitudes. They are especially clever at catching the platitudes in the serious conversation of important people. But they also know the value for comedy of all sly references to sex. Upon one occasion Groucho is seated at a coffee-table talking with a big executive. Groucho turns to him, and asks casually, "Tell me, Professor, what do you think of the political situation?" He does not wait for an answer but goes on to a more important item, "What do you think of the European situation?" Still he does not wait for an answer, but this time almost whispers in the Professor's ear. "What do you think about when you go to bed at night?" And, changing his voice, "You beast!" The Marx Brothers give us comedy almost in the grand manner, and with all the classical elements which we have come to expect from our survey. It lacks only the formalism of written comedy, available to all comedians, to be of permanent value. As it is, the evanescent methods employed, and the changing nature of many of the objects criticized, make its permanence a matter of question. It certainly has, however, helped to over-throw the objects of its criticism, affirmed certain values which have not been experienced, and made life a little more bearable and valuable for many of us who have had access to their popular art.

3. THE COMEDY OF MYTH: JAMES JOYCE

The problem of what place to assign to the works of James Joyce in contemporary literature has always been a matter of grave concern and has never been satisfactorily settled. Of course this statement could be made about almost any such obviously important living author, but the case of Joyce is particularly vexing. He has been recognized almost from the very first by a small but alert group of serious readers as a highly pivotal figure. But each of his books marks such a radical departure not only from the rest of contemporary literature but also from his own earlier work, that his readers are left in constant amazement, a state alternating between extreme appreciation and considered bewilderment.

Joyce was born a rebel. He rebelled in *Portrait of the Artist as a Young Man* against the Catholic tradition in which he was presumably raised. He rebelled in *Ulysses* against the provin-cialism of the Irish, the imperialism of the British, and the standards of the contemporary world in general. Equally important from another point of view is his rebellion in the same book against the fixed and formalized traditions of methods in classic English literature. For certain aspects of his work, he has been compared with previous rebels, such as Swift and Rabelais, with whom it was found he had something in common. Indeed in this book Joyce established himself as the leader of a school of modern writing which adopted after him the "stream of consciousness" technique, the method of setting down thoughts without punctuation exactly as they might occur, in their psychological rather than their logical order. But Joyce is not one to rest content with achievement; he must always go on ahead. Therefore he rebelled against the tradition which he himself had started. In a little book of verse, *Pomes Penyeach*, he proceeded to rebel against those who had assumed that he was a methodological rebel and not primarily an artist. For this time he composed a volume of poems as conventional and traditionally faultless as possible.

The present book upon which he is engaged is unfinished and therefore very difficult to assess. Several parts of *Work in Progress* have been published separately, however, and are more or less complete in themselves. They give us a pretty fair indication of what the completed work will be. It is the present thesis that Joyce is primarily a comedian, a very great comedian indeed, and for the purposes of defending this position two books chiefly will be discussed: *Ulysses*, and *Work in Progress*, particularly the latter.

Like all exemplars of the divine comedy, Joyce is a myth-maker. By availing himself of the full value of the material of modern life, he has tried to set up a number of myths. His method is primarily the method of comedy: humour evoked by the indirect affirmation of the eternal values resulting from a comic criticism of the shortcomings of the world as his contemporaries see it and as they have changed it. The special method employed, however, is parody. In *Ulysses*, Joyce has written a parody on the Homeric poem, but it is a parody the vastness of whose conception lifts it above the ordinary triviality of that method. Aside from the analogy, Joyce is closer to Aristophanes than to Homer. For he has used the wanderings of Ulysses as symbolical of human history; "in this grain of sand, this banal day in the life of an inglorious Dubliner, we may discover an entire synthesis of the macrocosm and a compelling symbol of the history of the race."[3] *Ulysses* is concerned with the adventures of one Leopold Bloom in the course of his compromises with actuality. At first glance, all is confusion within the book. There are words, phrases, and

[3] Stuart Gilbert, *James Joyce's Ulysses* (New York, 1931, Knopf), p. 41.

even whole sentences and paragraphs which are upon first reading almost meaningless. But this confusion is not what at first it appears to be; since it has a purpose. It is not confusion at all but fragmentary revelation, essential to the comedy of life itself, for "the Joycean method of fragmentary revelation corresponds to the manner in which nature herself disposes the clues to her discovery. The consequences of universal law lie scattered before our eyes in apparent confusion."[4]

Joyce is a self-conscious classic artist. He spurns the romantic, and reaches back into the past only so far as he longs to reach into the future. "Michael Robartes remembers forgotten beauty and, when his arms wrap her round, he presses in his arms the loveliness which has long faded from the world. Not this. Not at all. I desire to press in my arms the loveliness which has not yet come into the world."[5] The romantic laments the passing of those aspects of things which he has come to know and love; the classic celebrates those imponderable aspects which cannot change or be changed in time. Joyce is a classic artist. Like all comedians, he is thinking always of an ideal order in contrast with which the failures and disvalues of actuality appear funny, and, like all great comedians, he takes the whole of existence as his subject-matter and compares it with the whole conception of an ideal order. If the greatness of a comedian consists in the amount of existence with which his comedy deals (as it surely must), then Joyce stands with the greatest and *Ulysses* is divine comedy. Since, however, the Joycean method is carried forward somewhat and intensified in *Work in Progress*, it will be to our advantage to study it in more detail there.

Four separate parts of *Work in Progress* have been published thus far,[6] but we shall have space here to consider only two of them, *Anna Livia Plurabelle*, and *Two Tales of Shem and Shaun*.

[4] Op. cit., p. 39.
[5] *Portrait of the Artist as a Young Man.*
[6] These are: *Anna Livia Plurabelle, Two Tales of Shem and Shaun, Haveth Childers Everywhere,* and *The Mime of Mick, Nick and the Maggies.*

Illustrations from Modern Comedians

Anna Livia Plurabelle[7] is, as Padraic Colum tells us, concerned with the flowing of a River. "Two washerwomen tell her story: as it begins, the evening sun, we fancy, is dabbling the water; as it closes, night is closing in. Voices become remote. Metamorphosis comes upon all that has been looked upon and talked about. . . . In the uncompleted work it belongs to a section called 'The Book of Life.'" In *Anna Livia*, Joyce deals with all the romantic themes, in their most romantic aspects. Romance itself, time, change, and sex, all are treated romantically by Joyce the classic artist. The contrast furnishes the comic aspect of the work. The two washerwomen gossip over their tubs, discussing the tales they have heard concerning the owners of the clothes they are washing, and the evidence offered by the dirty clothes themselves. In their talk, every river in the world is mentioned—there are said to be over five hundred—and the onomatopoetic sound of the prose keeps the reader constantly in mind of the sound of a river flowing. Out of this material Joyce has compounded a myth. He is in his references "as local as a hedge poet," but he is also as universal as a metaphysician.

Three passages at least must be quoted. The first is taken from the pages relating the sources and early cavorting of the river, given in its analogy with the youth of Anna. "She says herself she hardly knows whuon the annals her graveller was, a dynast of Leinster, a wolf of the sea, or what he did or how blyth she played or how, when, why, where who offon he jumpad her. She was just a young thin pale soft shy slim slip of a thing then, sauntering, by silvamoonlake and he was a heavy trudging lurching lieabroad of a Curraghman, making his hay for whose sun to shine on, as tough as the oaktrees (peats be with them!). . . ."[8] Then Anna Livia comes of age (i.e. the river grows to its full size) and has her first experiences with sex, that eternal theme of comedy. "Two lads in scoutsch breeches went through her before that, Barefoot Burn and

---

[7] (New York, 1928, Crosby Gaige.)
[8] *Anna Livia Plurabelle*, pp. 20–21.

In Praise of Comedy

Wallowme Wade, Lugnaquillia's, noblest picts, before she had a hint of hair at her fanny to hide or a bossom to tempt a birch canoedler not to mention a bulgic porterhouse barge. And ere that again, leada, laida, all unraidy, too faint to buoy the fairest rider, too frail to flirt with a cygnet's plume, she was licked by a hound, Chirripa-Chirruta, while poing her pee, pure and simple, on the spur of the hill in old Kippure. . . ."[9]

Surely this is poetry of a very high order, and comedy too. It is the closest approximation in our time, and in a very long time, to the divine comedy. The last page is devoted to the finality of nightfall. The washerwomen are tired; we hear night on the river. "Can't hear with the waters of. The chittering waters of. Flittering bats, field-mice bawk talk. Ho! Are you not gone ahome? What Tom Malone? Can't hear with the bawk of bats, all the liffeying waters of. Ho, talk save us! My foos won't moos. I feel as old as yonder elm. A tale told of Shaun or Shem? All Livia's daughtersons. Dark hawks hear us. Night! Night! My ho head halls. I feel as heavy as yonder stone. Tell me of John or Shaun? Who were Shem and Shaun the living sons or daughters of? Night now! Tell me, tell me, tell me, elm! Night night! Tell me tale of stem or stone. Beside the rivering waters of, hitherandthithering waters of. Night!"[10]

Joyce is essentially a parodist. Few if any of his tales there are that do not have their basis in some old accepted legend. *The Two Tales of Shem and Shaun*[11] contain the tale of "The Ondt and the Gracehoper," a parody of Aesop's fable, "The Ant and the Grasshopper." The reader is advised to go through both, beginning with Aesop. For here the motif is candidly classic: no more romance, time and change, but the cold moral of the imponderable values. We are told that "the sillybilly of a Gracehoper had jingled through a jungle of love and debts and jangled through a jumble of life in doubts. . . ."[12] The tale is made into a presentation of the eternal contradiction between theory and practice, between the perfection of the

[9] Op. cit., p. 25.
[11] (London, 1932, Faber & Faber.)
[10] Op. cit., pp. 60–61.
[12] Op. cit., p. 38.

ideal and the compromises of actuality. We may suppose that the ant said to the grasshopper (according to Aesop, at least), "Since you could sing all summer, you may dance all winter." Whereupon the "Gracehoper" replies, in verse

> I pick up your reproof, the horsegift of a friend,
> For the prize of your save is the price of my spend.

and further

> Your genus its worldwide, your spacest sublime!
> But, Holy Saltmartin, why can't you beat time?[13]

And he closes "In the name of the former and of the latter and of their holocaust. Allmen."

All the furniture of comedy is at Joyce's elbow: parodies, platitudes revivified, puns. The "portmanteau word" is peculiarly effective in his hands, where it receives a poetic treatment never envisaged by Lewis Carroll, or any of the later users of the method. Nor is Joyce unaware of his work as a sort of modern version of the divine comedy. Like Dante, he has resorted to the vulgar tongue as an instrument for presenting a universal parody upon the predicament of humanity. He is aware, too, as internal evidence in *Work in Progress* as well as reliable authority informs us, that he is endeavouring to follow out some of the implications of Vico's *Scienza Nuova*: to write a universal history in mythological language. Myth is the truth of history effectively presented in symbolical form.[14] Joyce takes the common actuality of the workaday Dubliner and presents it as symbolic myth; his is the language of the modern Gods, as Homer's was in his day, which is to say the

---

[13] Op. cit., p. 45. Cf. the answer in Rabelais made by the Limousin scholar to Pantagruel.

[14] Samuel Beckett, "Dante . . . Bruno . . . Vico . . .Joyce," in *Our Exagmination Round His Factification for Incamination of Work in Progress* (Paris, 1929, Shakespeare & Co.). See also in this same volume the extremely illuminating essay by Stuart Gilbert, and the remarkable parody of the parodist himself, entitled "A Litter to Mr. James Joyce," by Vladimir Dixon.

deified fundamental needs of the man in the street. There is no break in the tradition which stretches from Homer's language of the Gods, through Dante's raising of the vulgar language to divine comedy, through Vico's observation that humanity is divine although there is no divine human, to the social mythology of James Joyce. The comedian at his greatest is the myth-maker and the dreamer of the common dreams of humanity; and because Joyce is both a myth-maker and a comedian we must accord him a very importance place.

4. The Comedy of Literature: Gertrude Stein

Gertrude Stein takes her work very seriously, and so do some of her critics. She is regarded, at least for the present and in certain quarters, as one of the outstanding writers of the period. There is, of course, some justification for this evaluation. That she has exercised a considerable influence upon such writers as Sherwood Anderson, Ernest Hemingway, and perhaps even James Joyce, there can be little doubt. Until quite recently she was regarded as a writer's writer, and remained comparatively unknown to the wider public. It is only since she has taken to writing intelligibly that she has become known to a general audience. From the evidence offered in her later books we are forced to conclude that she is capable of writing intelligibly about only herself and her own adventures. In the *Autobiography of Alice B. Toklas*, and *Everybody's Autobiography*, she has found her public style in the subjective, discursive kind of writing. Needless to say, any reputation based upon these two books must be of the most evanescent kind. Like the utterances of Shaw in his dotage, it rests chiefly upon the effect to shock by the exaggerations of self-conceit, and this is not the kind of appeal that will wear well.

For our purposes, the later Stein must be dismissed, and we must return to an examination of the earlier period, the period of *Tender Buttons* and *Geography and Plays*. The Stein which is represented by these works is essentially the comedian.

Illustrations from Modern Comedians

That Gertrude Stein would probably not agree with this estimation is nothing to the point. When we consider artistic accomplishments, we can ignore the intentions of the artist, which may have been in direct contradiction with what was actually accomplished. In all likelihood, Miss Stein began her career as an iconoclast, like so many of her "lost generation." She wrote with her tongue in her cheeck and an ambition to *épater le bourgeois.* But whether such was her intention or no, we may assert that it is what her books reveal, and thus it is all we need be occupied with considering. Fortunately or unfortunately for the artist, works of art once delivered to the public are public property, and there are many who are more equipped to assign them their proper place than the artist himself. Thus we are justified in calling Miss Stein a comedian provided only that we can show wherein the comedy lies.

Miss Stein's own special brand of comedy is devoted to the problem of discontinuity. She is a defender of reason who has chosen as her method the exposition of the absurdities of extreme irrationalism. There was a university professor who once announced to his class, "This course is devoted chiefly to study. Last week the lecture was on projective geometry. Next week, metals." He neither saw nor tried to show his students any connection between the two subjects. Yet his course was in perfect conformity with the kind of discontinuity which is demanded by the widespread authority of an implicit nominalism and, moreover, deeply accepted by the modern mind. No topic has anything to do with any other; and every existent is discontinuous with every other. Next week, metals. This is thoroughgoing irrationalism. It is the kind of irrationalism Miss Stein makes fun of by herself taking it seriously and asking us to do the same, in order to demonstrate that such serious consideration is quite impossible.

One joke and one alone underlies the Stein writings, although there are many implications. The juxtaposition of words in sentence form, which tantalizingly sound as though they had a meaning when they have none, in an effort to ridicule meaning itself, is the formula. It is a subtle variety of the comedy of meaninglessness. In one kind of writing it relies upon sheer monotony.

"The same examples are the same and just the same and always the same and the same examples are just the same and are the same and are always the same. The same examples are just the same and they are very sorry for it."[15] The monotony becomes unbearable, whereupon we are presented with a bewildering kind of half-truth which we may or may not be expected to take seriously; this is the familiar trick which is employed over and over. It can of course be equally effective if reversed:

"Supposing no one asked a question. What would be the answer.

"Supposing no one hurried four how many would there be if the difference was known."[16] These passages are characteristic. Fragments of meaning are found, distorted, broken, and utterly simple; but we can make nothing of them. The gamut of meaninglessness is run, all the way from pages of unbearable repetition, such as the following:

"Yes and yes and more and yes and why and yes and yes and why and yes. A new better and best and yes and yes and better and most and yes and yes and better and best and yes and yes and more and best and most and yes and yes."[17] And so on, to passages of beauty which are almost intelligible poems, such as this, for example:

If you hear her snore
It is not before you love her
You love her so that to be her beau is very lovely
She is sweetly there and her curly hair is very lovely
She is sweetly here and I am very near and that is very lovely.
She is my tender sweet and her little feet are stretching out well
which is a treat and very lovely

[15] Gertrude Stein, *Useful Knowledge* (New York, 1928, Payson & Clarke), p. 71.
[16] Op. cit., p. 51.   [17] Op. cit., p. 76.

Her little tender nose is between her little eyes which close and are very lovely.
She is very lovely and mine which is very lovely.[18]

The trick of putting together ideas which do not belong together because they are not on the same level of analysis, used so often by Miss Stein, is an old one but always effective, because it ridicules the commonest error of bad thinking. *Tender Buttons, Geography and Plays*: the pointed meaninglessness is so effective that it could hardly have been accidental. The practice of considering together ideas which do not belong together, and of making fun of them thereby, has been noted by other theorists of comedy as well as by other comedians. It is what Freud calls "the comic of speech or of words,"[19] but it is rather the comedy of erroneous logical analysis. Freud quotes two examples of this kind of comedy: " 'With a fork and with effort, his mother pulled him out of the mess,' is only comical, but Heine's verse about the four castes of the population of Göttingen: 'Professors, students, Philistines, and cattle' is exquisitely witty."

Another variety of comedy employed by Stein is the use of platitudes in a way which is capable of restoring their original powerful meaning. We have in the last section seen this take superb form at the hands of a master, as when used by Joyce, but Miss Stein's method is slightly different. She falls back more upon meaninglessness of an orthodox nature. The phrase "before the flowers of friendship faded" is so trite and disgustingly sentimental an expression that nobody would think of taking it seriously. Gertrude Stein uses it with her trick of repetition, and it is funny. "Before the flowers of friendship faded friendship faded." Again meaning aggravatingly looks out and we are almost tempted to avail ourselves of a serious reading.

There is an aspect of Stein's writings which leads us to the assumption that she is attempting to work only through the

---

[18] Op. cit., p. 93.
[19] Sigmund Freud, *Wit and Its Relation to the Unconscious*, p. 343

connotation of words, avoiding any real detonation. Her close connection with the magazine, *Transition*, and with its editor, Eugene Jolas' "revolution of the word" would convict her of aiming at the deepest kind of irrationalism. The group of writers in Paris which centred about this periodical flirted with all the Chthonic deities. Various methods of writing, such as Joyce's stream of consciousness, automatic writing, and "the language of night," have doubtless had their effect upon Stein.

Yet, as we have pointed out before, it is not what she may have set out to do but what she did that matters. In poker it is not the betting but the cards which count. Over against the influences we have mentioned it should also be noted that Stein studied under William James, and she has been friendly with Alfred North Whitehead. However, these direct rationalists (we can count James a rationalist in so far as he was a philosopher at all) seem to have exercised no influence upon her. There can be little doubt that Stein considers herself a proponent of irrationalism. Actually, her work itself has little to do with irrationalism or the Chthonic deities. What she may be said to have demonstrated is that irrationalism will not work; that the extreme irrationalist position is untenable. Thus she is a comedian in the deepest sense of the word, and this because she accomplished the opposite of what she set out to do. She really succeeded in defending reason; she has reaffirmed by implication the infinite and necessary relatedness of all things in a certain order, and thus refuted the nominalism with which she started.

Stein's comedy of meaninglessness has been very useful. It has served as an instrument of liberation. She has freed modern literature from the sterile formalism and Victorian smugness and outworn pretence with which it was encumbered when she first appeared upon the contemporary scene. This was a task which very much needed doing. Her books have helped to reacquaint us with the naked sound of our language, hitherto only available to foreigners, and allowed us to examine its connotations in isolation.

Illustrations from Modern Comedians

It is hard to forgive her, though, simply because she does not know what she does. Her ignorance of her own function is illustrated by the two meaningful autobiographies in which she talks chiefly about herself and in high seriousness. We are at last allowed to see the meaning, we are taken behind the scenes and permitted to hear Miss Stein talk in a normal tone of voice. It is quite an *exposé*, because we learn for the first time, and after much puzzlement, that there is no meaning at all. And we are angry with ourselves for not having guessed as much. Having nothing else to talk about, after years with gibberish, she talks about herself: her own life and her genius. And we long for the gibberish again, for that at least was self-contained. It is like looking inside a balloon after having for some time admired its shining surface, only to learn that there is nothing to it but surface. What a clever trick it was after all, and how amusing. For Miss Stein is a comedian and nothing else, and her words have a meaning only when she is talking nonsense.

5. THE HUMAN COMEDY: CHARLIE CHAPLIN

Film comedy is as old as the film. Among the first comedies to be made in Hollywood were the old Keystone affairs. As crude as these were, there is much to be said for them. It has been related that the Keystone comedies were made without benefit of written script. The scenario writers sat about in a room, and between them built up through conversation the plot of the next Keystone opus. The result was something which is rough and obvious yet very human, and, even more strange, rigidly within the classical comic tradition. There were few subtleties and fewer innuendoes in the pie-throwing, rough-and-tumble of the Keystone approach, yet the comic spirit which hovered over these efforts is the same one which also watched over Aristophanes (although perhaps then with a better education!) and later on, the Mummer's Play in the Middle Ages. The rough-housing that has come down to us in the classic dramas of Aristophanes and the Mummer's Play has a broader social meaning and is more obviously profound and rational; yet fundamentally the Keystone points deal with the same topics. It is not claimed here, of course, that there is anything like a comparison to be made in value between the classical and the Keystone comedies; but only that they both employ something of the same method and the same material.

The Keystone comedies refuse to take death seriously. A shot in the rump—and these are frequent enough—is never the occasion of serious injury, but merely forces the person who is shot to jump into the air several times while grasping the injured part. The dead are not dead, as we are led to suppose, but arise to fight again. This, surely, is the modern version of a hallowed tradition. Comedy, as we have noted in an earlier chapter, had its origins in the primitive fertility rites of archaic Greece; and ever since then it has been a constant function of comedy to show that the tragedy of death is not final, and mortality not to be taken seriously. The tradition of the magic doctor, the comic character who comes upon the stage in time to restore the protagonist to perfect health after his supposed slaying, was changed somewhat by Molière, who placed the burden of the comedy upon the doctor himself and made the point a satire upon the insufficiencies of the practice of medicine, and it is changed again by the Keystone comedies which dispense with the doctor in this sense altogether and simply refuse to allow the instruments of death, the thrown weight and the gun, to have their logical effect in death. The dead are not restored to life; the living simply do not die when they should. It is the same point, only somewhat differently scored.

There are other similar comic instances which could be pointed out, although few are as obvious. In general the Keystone comedies followed the traditional and true meaning of comedy: to employ the expression of T. E. Lawrence, which has become a sort of *leitmotiv* for this work, they spelled their words anyhow to show what rot the systems are. The nonsense was acted anyhow, it was directed aimlessly against the foibles of any prevailing custom and against the peculiarities of any existing institution, but always with the same end in view: to show what rot the systems are. But, alas, the difference between a good comedian and a bad one is the relative importance of what he criticizes as well as the depth of his criticism. The Keystone comedies were not aimed at anything very fundamental; they took for their target the surface of things, the familiar objects of contemporary life. Their method was almost good enough; polished a little it might have been great. The trouble was with their aims; they tried to amuse, and succeeded, but they did not do so by criticizing anything that mattered in a very profound way.

Many important film comedians, afterwards famous in other rôles, were given their start and moulded in a certain tradition by the pattern of the Keystone comedies. Among these was the greatest film comedian of them all: Charlie Chaplin. The mark of the Keystone manner is upon him forever. It is his source for material as well as for method. But with what a difference does Chaplin employ both! With an instinctive eye (since there is little reason for believing it conscious altogether) Chaplin seized upon the essential verities behind the Keystone pictures and made them something altogether inimitable and his own. He uses the same devices: his comedies are crude; they are rough-and-tumble; he defies the same authorities, among which may be numbered the laws of nature; he criticizes customs and institutions. But there is a fundamental difference, in fact a number of differences, between the Chaplin and the Keystone comedies. These are based primarily upon the peculiar emphasis which is brought out by Chaplin's own personality.

In many pieces of criticism, critics from the journeyman essays of Gilbert Seldes to the gilded prose of Elie Faure, much effort has been devoted to the task of analysing the art of Charlie Chaplin. It is a complex art and therefore in all probability is susceptible only to a complex analysis. The film rôle of Chaplin is that of a beggar. His costume is significant: the old derby hat, the oversized shoes, the baggy clothes, are all obviously meant to portray the cast-off clothes of others, the "hand-me-downs" of somewhat larger men. Thus the costume alone is an indication of presumption: the Little Man (as Charlie Chaplin has himself designated his stock character) is attempting to fill the clothes (the place) of a larger man. But this is not all. The larger man is not only larger physically; he is also and very obviously a personage of some importance. His clothes include a derby (in America the mark of a banker, a man of fashion, or an industrialist), and a cane, and the latter is a mark of fashion. Thus the Little Man is trying to fill the clothes of a large man of considerable distinction, as the standards go.

To Chaplin, if to any comedian, belongs the special appellation of critic. He seems to be capable of making fun of current errors in evaluation exactly in the order of their importance. Surely in the field of comedy this is what we mean when we call a man a genius. A good example is the way in which Chaplin is able to disregard the ordinary taboos of his craft. For instance, it is generally considered bad sportsmanship to ridicule the aged and the infirm for their feebleness. Yet in one of his early pictures Chaplin finds a palsied old man in a department store near the toy counter. He quickly picks up a drum and holds it under the old man's hand so that the movement of his palsy causes him to beat the drum with his fingers.[20] The audience bursts out laughing and is not offended. Why? The answer lies in the peculiarly logical manner of Chaplin. He twists his moustache; he is indeed a little bored by his own antics; that is part of the character of the Little Man. What he does is done by order of the logic of events; it is what seemed expected at the time. Therefore the pattern is carried out. But obviously, therefore, the Little Man is as incapable

[20] I am grateful to Mr. Jasper Deeter for calling my attention to the fact that there is an element of "usefulness" here, also an important value.

244

of hurting feelings as he is of enjoying the infliction of personal injury on others. He is simply doing what he has to do. He is, so to speak, acting for the logic of events, and is thus himself placed above good and evil.

The wonderful walk which we have come to associate with Chaplin has many meanings. The shrugging of the shoulders indicates indifference to the adventures imposed by fortune. Be the fates kind to him or no, he can shrug off happenings; he knows how to cast them aside. He is the captain of his own adventures and not susceptible to the will of others. The angle of the walk, the jaunty handling of the cane, the sprightly manner of the feet which face the side as much as the front, all indicate the character which is the chief source of Chaplin's humour. This humour consists in a contradictory attitude toward society: an impudence and a cringing alternately presented. The Little Man sees an opening whereby he can gain some advantage in his dealings with others. He takes the chance; but if he is caught or in any way rebuffed, immediately the other attitude is assumed. He is no longer impudent but, on the contrary, so cringing that it is hard to believe that he was ever self-assertive enough to do anything. He is not as good as anyone else: he is either better—or worse. Shy impudence, or arrogant cringing. He is the master of others or he is their slave; but he is never their equal.

The similarity between the art of Chaplin and typical Jewish comedy has often been shown. It is especially true of the point just discussed. The alternation of impudence and cringing is exactly that of the Wandering Jew, whose differences have caused him to be so unjustly kicked about and whose abilities have been so extravagantly praised that the speedy change from an impudent to a cringing attitude has come to be of necessity a part of his equipment. He lives either in a Ghetto or in a palace; he is either a second-class citizen or the master of history. Thus he constitutes a sort of living satire on his own times, their habits, customs and institutions. Chaplin is exactly in this tradition in so far as the Little Man by his very attitude toward others reveals the same scars, the same marks of injury and triumph. He is working against great odds, which lie in his difference from others. He has no place in the world; he does not really want one; yet that is what he schemes for all the while.

What has happened to the traditional defeat of negation, the failure to take death seriously, which we found transformed in the Keystone comedies into what we may term impotent wounding? Chaplin, with the unerring instinct of the great artist, has suffused it with value. He has no need for a gun, since he has turned the target into an object of love. For the traditional pseudo-death has been transformed into a personal optimism doomed to failure. Nothing discourages the Little Man. He is defeated in his humble plans time and again. He thinks he has found a place to sleep: a bench in the park. He lies down and covers himself with newspaper, even pretending to find great comfort and luxury in the cramped position, only to have a policeman order him to move on. Again, he makes a home in a shack of crooked planks, thinking to settle down to a blissfully monotonous married life—only to be arrested and thrown into jail through a series of inevitable circumstances for something that was not at all his own fault. Still he is never daunted, but always hopeful of the eventual proper outcome. His dogged optimism somehow does not seem to arise out of stupidity but rather out of an implicit faith in the logic of events. It is difficult to explain just how such a distinction is conveyed by Chaplin's actions and manner, but it is, nevertheless.

Few, if any, of Chaplin's films have omitted the note of tragedy, which is always somewhere in them. The homeless waif, a boy, or a girl, who is picked up and must be sheltered against the hostile or indifferent world, is a typical pattern repeated again and again. The Little Man seeks wealth and is met with failure; he wants only a humble labourer's work, but is met with defeat again. And his failure is a tragedy because it is so often not his own fault but the effect of inexorable forces which are constantly operating against him. And even when it is his own fault, we are somehow more overcome by the warm human sympathy which pity for his condition calls forth than we are by anything else. It is laughter with which we are then involved, but not simple laughter: rather the complex laughter which comes through tears. Lesser comedians try to make everything funny, with the result that nothing is very funny; but Chaplin knows that comedy has a profound meaning if it is genuine comedy, and he appreciates the value of contrast. Comedy is never very far from tragedy; and Chaplin constantly reminds us of this, and thus heightens his comedy.

The social implications of Chaplin's comedies have of late been made more apparent by Chaplin himself. *Modern Times,* for instance, is a veritable sermon against the injustices of economic inequality. But Chaplin's comedies always contain values which go farther than the economic; and, like all great comedians, he is inveighing against the predicament in which humanity finds itself. To aspire so high; yet remain so low: this is the finite predicament, of which human beings of necessity must partake. It is what the great comedian shows us vividly, and none more vividly than Chaplin, except perhaps those few supremely great geniuses, who may be ranked with Dante (if indeed there are any others). *The Divine Comedy* of Dante is not funny; it is rather an ideal limit for comedy. But the art of Chaplin has carried him far toward this goal, even if he has not reached it. He has shown us what comic situations there are in our own actual world. For there are no truly comic persons who are funny always and in every situation; there are only true comic situations which some persons are able to get themselves into more often and more easily than others. The course of human life is the path of a pencil on a graph, by which each of us is trying to trace a particular pattern. The pattern will not be complete until the tracing is done. The end of several of Chaplin's pictures show the Little Man ambling jauntily down a long road, pitting his tiny might against the emptiness and discouragement of this actual world, describing a zigzag path toward an unknown destination which inevitably awaits him but which we know he is none the less ready to greet with that optimism which maintains an infrangible faith in the nature of things.

6. THE COMEDY OF ADVENTURE: "PRINCE" ROMANOFF

There is no more extraordinary tale of adventure in our time than that related of "Prince" Mike Romanoff in the pages of the *New Yorker*, in its issues dated from October 29 to November 26, 1932. "Prince" Mike was an adventurer and comedian in the grand manner. Born Harry Gerguson, soon an orphan, he managed to live through forty years as an impostor of the great: he was an English captain, he was for a while Rockwell Kent, the artist, but mostly he was "Prince" Michael Romanoff of the Royal Russian House. In the latter rôle he appealed to the snobbish instincts of the super-wealthy in America. Whenever exposed, his personality and charm came to the rescue, and he managed to survive the unmasking. "The Prince had a glittering career in New York, Boston, Newport, on Long Island, in high-caste settlements along the Hudson, and among the aristocracies of a dozen American cities.[21] Undersized and ill-favoured, he often makes an unfortunate first impression. He has, however, a rare power of attracting attention and sympathy. . . . He is widely admired to-day not for his title but for his own sake. He has convinced a fairly large public that a good impostor is preferable to the average prince. Some of those who have been victimized by Romanoff treasure the experience. Some who know him to be a fraud, a confidence man, and a pilferer, consider him the salt of the earth."[22]

Mike was taken out of the orphanage in New York by various kindly persons, but he always ran away from them because

[21] *New Yorker* for October 29, 1932, p. 19.   [22] Op. cit.

of his contempt for work. By a series of adventures he landed in Paris, as the son of Alexander III of Russia and brother of the late Czar. "At the Ritz Bar he later became the son of the man who killed Rasputin."[23] Now become a prominent figure, no wonder that he had "cultivated an infinite contempt for the lower aristocracy."[24] In America, "He lectured at Pelham Manor and elsewhere, on 'Russia, Past and Present.' During his brief career as a lecturer Mike demanded a police body-guard because of threats against his life by the local Bolsheviki."[25] Once he escaped from Ellis Island and the romantic tale has been built into a legend comparable to Casanova's escape from the Leads. He acquired along the road a perfect Oxford accent and often fooled old graduates with his reminiscences. He got himself sent to Harvard and Yale and Princeton by wealthy patrons. At Harvard he was in jail a few days (one of many such occasions) for defrauding a Harvard student. When visited by his old friends, he said, " 'You must all be with me in the hunting season on my Galician estate.' He asked forgiveness because they would find no wild boar; the war had driven them from his preserves."[26]

" 'Chuck this Romanoff business,' a friend once advised him. 'With your talent you can become rich in any legitimate line.' 'But,' replied Mike, 'I *am* a Romanoff.' " In a way he was, or tried to be. Certainly money was needed to live like a king, and Mike obtained it, mostly by issuing bad cheques and travelling to another city when the cheques were due back from the bank. But money was not his main objective. "Mike had certain traits that go with the sceptre. He loved to reward merit. Once, on a night shortly before Christmas, after witnessing some gallant rescues by firemen in an apartment house fire, Mike lifted a holly wreath from a peddler's stand and presented it to the battalion chief. 'With the Mayor's compliments,' said Mike. It pleased the Romanoff in him to exercise absolute power."[27]

[23] *New Yorker* for October 29, 1932, p. 21.   [24] Op. cit., p. 20.
[25] Op. cit., p. 22.   [26] *New Yorker* for November 5, 1932, p. 29.
[27] Op. cit., pp. 31–32.

In Praise of Comedy

Mike was in jail in New York the winter of 1926. "He is still remembered there as the only prisoner who ever carried a walking-stick during the exercise hour."[28] One of the rich men he fleeced in New York observed of him, "He is not a criminal, he is a remarkable man. I believe he will go down in history. Perhaps my name will go down in history with him."[29] "The Prince divided all mankind into two classes; charming people who do nothing, and the dromedaries. It was his studied opinion that a man who worked was a pack animal. He was not yet prepared to become one."[30] Mike's explanation of his own position in the world, to a supervisor of probation officers who had presented him with definite evidence of his own fraudulency and advised him to reform, is wonderful. " 'I'll explain,' said Mike, after a pause. 'Have you ever been in a bare room in a new house with a view overlooking a park? You look at the park and it is marvellous. You look at the bare walls, and you find them absolutely repulsive. They cry for adornment. That is I. I don't lie because I desire to be a crook and a thief, but because I wish to associate with persons whose lives I believe to be adorned. Frankly, I will lie to you as long as you know me. If I told you the truth, I would feel like a bare wall.' "[31]

To those who meet him "Prince" Mike appears as a very tragic figure, which indeed he is. There is something romantically and warmly sympathetic about his personality. Since he is essentially a comedian it appears at first glance to be a strange thing that he is also a tragic person. But the paradox is a necessary one which the true understanding of the nature of comedy cannot help but illuminate. Comedians are generally sad in private life because the effects of their actions are comic, and comedy depends to a certain extent upon contrast. Tragic rather than comic or ridiculous actions are most apt to give rise to comedy. The comic effect is objectively effective, but the tragedy is psychologically present. This is clearly illustrated

[28] *New Yorker* for November 12, 1932, p. 24.
[29] Op. cit., pp. 24–25. [30] Op. cit., p. 25. [31] Op. cit., p. 23.

in the passage quoted above the from the "Prince" himself. Comedians with serious intent give rise to comedy. Comedians with comic intent must inject elements of tragedy into their conscious comedies in order to provide the necessary contrast, as the comedies of Chaplin exemplify. Without the conventional make-up, it is not an easy thing for a clown to laugh.

Mike's false pretensions were unmasked time and again, yet he managed to survive the unmasking, because the depth of his pretence was always underestimated. He has a gigantic faculty for fraud because he is a comedian of a very high order. It is always known that he has been unmasked, but what is not so well known is that at the same time he is unmasking others. Mike, like all comic adventurers, is a sort of walking commentary on the pretences of his own times. By feigning to belong to a social strata to which he could lay no legitimate claims, Mike managed to explode, indirectly, the falsity and pretensions of that strata itself. For instance, while he was still believed to be "Prince Michael Romanoff," he was invited to Pittsburgh by Paul Mellon to be his guest there for the marriage of his sister Ailsa to David K. E. Bruce. Now, had Mike gone through with it in proper fashion, there would have been no comedy, only a fraud. But Mike is a comedian—so he stole Mellon's gold-fitted suitcase and departed.[32] Thus his visit was, so to speak, a sell on the custom of American millionaires of trying to establish themselves on a level with European aristocracy.

"Wit belongs to a spirit that denies," says Carritt,[33] and Mike's whole career may be said to be an illustration of this prominent aspect of comedy. His life has been an implicit criticism of the foibles of his times. For instance, "In Paris he lived well for a while by borrowing from Americans to finance a trip to America. Having no passport, he could not buy a ticket, but he obtained loans on the pretext that he had

[32] *New Yorker* for November 19, 1932, pp. 25–26.
[33] E. F. Carritt, "A Theory of the Ludicrous," in *The Hibbert Journal*, vol. xxi (1923), p. 556.

to bribe ship's officers. Mike found it easier to borrow money when he said he had a crooked use for it."[34] The essence of the moment consists in a criticism of its failures, and in that sense Mike has been more contemporary than anyone else. In the last analysis he is a reformer, because by playing pander to all the snobbish weaknesses of Americans, he has exposed them, and so taken one step toward their abolition. The sordid appeal of the British aristocracy and of the Russian nobility hangs like a pall over the native democracy of American life. "Prince" Mike has unwittingly aided us in disposing of these baleful European influences.

Unfortunately, we cannot class Mike with the greatest comic adventurers. He did not rise to the heights of Casanova, who ran a lottery for the French Government; Mike's frauds were perpetrated upon individuals rather than institutions, and so he did not have the same magnificent range as the great Venetian. There is a definite pattern which the adventurer must follow, and it includes being a consummate Don Juan, a master of many women. Here again is where Mike fails to attain the greatness of a Casanova. Finally, despite an occasional insight, he lacked Casanova's gift for self-expression. He had not the sweep of a Casanova, even if he did have the ingenuity. "Romanoff squandered his genius on petty objectives. Some of his greatest strokes were planned merely to finance himself over the week-end."[35]

Yet there is something wonderful about the prospect of an adventurer in our own day fighting with personal appeal the handicaps of rapid communication and hence easy exposure which former adventurers did not have to face. We learn something, from this Odyssey of snobbish struggle, about our own people and about mistaken aspects of their ambition, and hence about ourselves; and we are the better for it. Certainly the advance in means of communication is a good, but if we are to follow it and to have nothing concealed by distance,

---

[34] *New Yorker* for November 26, 1932.
[35] *New Yorker* for October 29, 1932, p. 19.

then we must conceal nothing from ourselves either. The contemporaneity of comedy in the past, if it is not treated seriously as sentimental, is regarded as absurd. What can be more anomalous than Russian nobility clinging still to its claims of nobility? Mike, as the comedian, shows us that, and so forces us into new ways and new ambitions. He turns us from admiration of the past to new hopes for the future, and so fulfils the rôle of the true comedian by being a benefactor of society.

7. THE COMEDY OF HISTORY: SELLAR AND YEATMAN

A good example of the kind of function comedy can perform and the kind of purpose it can serve is afforded by the satire on history contained in the little book by Sellar and Yeatman, *1066 and All That*.[36] This is not a great work nor one likely to be remembered for ever. It is aimed at a particular error, and is likely to be forgotten just as soon as that error has been corrected. It does not reach above and beyond the narrow field which it has chosen for itself, and therefore contains few implications which penetrate to all aspects of existence, as great comedy assuredly does. Yet just for this reason it is a good example of at least one type of comedy.

1066 is a satire on history. It is first of all an attack upon the fashion of teaching history as a meaningless collection of names and dates. The learning of history, as some important modern historians have succeeded in pointing out in at least a few enlightened universities, does not involve merely the committing to memory of the dates of birth and death of the world political leaders and the places and dates of a few important battles which they caused to be fought. The second target of the attack in *1066* is the partisanship of history as it is now taught. The history of Europe, for instance, as taught in the schools of any nation in Europe is always given from the

[36] (London, 1936, Methuen.)

narrow point of view of that nation. Each nation strives, consciously (as in modern Germany) or unconsciously (as in nineteenth-century England), to inculcate in her subjects the supreme worthiness of her own historical cause. Sellar and Yeatman take the history of England as their topic, and attempt to show that British history is written from the point of view of the "right little tight little isle."

The average college graduate if examined some ten or twenty years after graduation would reveal some curious ideas of history. Fragments of what he had learned, combined with whatever references to historical events he had noted since, whether in books or newspapers, on stage or screen, would combine to yield the most meaningless jumble of historical notions imaginable. It is this conception of history common to the innumerable half-educated of to-day that Sellar and Yeatman show us as funny. And funny it undoubtedly is.

The book begins with a "Compulsory Preface," from which several passages may be quoted.

"Histories have previously been written with the object of exalting their authors. The object of this History is to console the reader. *No other history does this.*

"History is not what you thought. *It is what you can remember.* All other history defeats itself.

"This is the only Memorable History of England, because all the History that you can remember is in this book, which is the result of years of research in golf-clubs, gun-rooms, green-rooms, etc.

"For instance, 2 out of 4 Dates originally included were eliminated at the last moment, a research done at the Eton and Harrow match having revealed that they are *not memorable.*

"They [the Editors] take this opportunity of acknowledging their inestimable debt to the mass of educated men and women of their race whose historical institutions and opinions this work enshrines.

"Also to the Great British People without whose self-sacrificing determination to become top Nation there would have been no (memorable) history."[37]

It is unfortunate that considerations of space do not permit us to quote the whole of *1066*. The bitter dislike of insularity and all that it entails, of what A. J. Toynbee has called "British Israelitism," shines through its pages. And in the course of outlining history as it is remembered, Sellar and Yeatman find opportunity to attack many human weaknesses. But we must content ourselves with quoting a passage here and there.

Chapter I deals with Caesar's invasion of Britain.

"The first date in English History is 55 B.C. in which year Julius Caesar (the *memorable* Roman Emperor) landed, like all other successful invaders of these islands, at Thanet. This was in the olden days, when the Romans were top nation on account of their classical education, etc."[38] Caesar attacked, but "the Ancient Britons, though all well over military age, painted themselves true blue, or *Woad*, and fought as heroically under their dashing queen, Woadicea, as they did later in thin red lines under their good queen, Victoria."[39]

The authors pause, as do most historians, to give a section on the culture of the times. "The Ancient Britons were by no means savages before the Conquest, and had already made great strides in civilization, e.g., they buried each other in long round wheelbarrows (agriculture) and burnt each other alive (religion). . . . The Roman Conquest was, however, a *Good Thing*, since the Britons were only natives at that time."[40] This is a fierce attack indeed, so fierce that the laughter which it at first occasions is pulled up short. It burns out a truth like words written upon skin by a caustic. All primitive customs, however cruel, however savage, are still human and a level above the animals. Though we do not like to think of it as human, it remains true that no animals are capable as yet of burning each other alive. The cultural privilege of exquisite torture, as well as certain advantages which we prefer to think

[37] Op. cit., pp. vii-viii.
[38] Op. cit., p. 1.   [39] Op. cit., p. 2.   [40] Op. cit., p. 3.

of as human, such as art and science, are alike closed to the lower animals, who know only how to kill. The reader of *1066* will find that all historical events are divided into "good things" or "bad things" according as they proved to be Britain's advantage or disadvantage.

There is in *1066* a wonderful account of the founding of the British navy. "The latter invention occurred as follows. Alfred noticed that the Danes had very long ships, so he built a great many more much longer ones, thus cleverly founding the British Navy. From that time onwards, foreigners, who, unlike the English, do not prefer to fight against long odds, seldom attacked the British Navy. Hence the important International Law called the Rule Britannia, technically known as the Freedom of the Seas." Incidentally "Alfred compelled the Danes, who were (of course) beaten, to stop being Danes and become English. . . . For this purpose they were made to go back and start again at Thanet, after which they were called in future Thanes instead of Danes and were on our side and in the right and very romantic."[41] The whole of British insularity is in this passage. That the attack is justified may be borne out by the weather notice which was printed some years ago in a London paper. There had been a terrific storm for some hours in the Channel, and all boat and airplane passenger services had been suspended between England and the Continent. The news account of the weather was headed as follows, "Storm Over Channel. Continent Isolated."

One more quotation must be permitted. Sellar and Yeatman describe the reign of Charles I as the "utterly memorable Struggle between the Cavaliers (Wrong but Wromantic) and the Roundheads (Right but Repulsive). Charles I was a Cavalier King and therefore had a small pointed beard, long flowing curls, a large, flat, flowing hat and *gay attire*. The Roundheads, on the other hand, were clean-shaven and wore tall, conical hats, white ties and *sombre garments*. Under these circumstances a civil war was inevitable."[42] In the struggle,

[41] *1066 and All That*, p. 11.   [42] Op. cit., pp. 63–64.

as this occurs, at any time and place, between the revolutionary and the conservative forces of society, the conservatives though wrong always appear romantic and the revolutionists though right always appear repulsive. Old institutions always carry with them a penumbra of age-old and custom-sanctified values; whereas new institutions, since they exist only as possibilities in the future, have nothing but their logical structure. Old values that have been felt are opposed by new ideas that must be thought through and evaluated abstractly. No wonder that the old appears romantic, although wrong, and the new appears repulsive, although right, at least for a while.

From Julius Caesar and the early culture of Britain to Queen Victoria and the "wave of justifiable wars," the authors of *1066 and All That* have exposed all the vicious prejudices that haunt the field of British history, and incidentally set a model whereby other nations can discover their own errors in the reading of history. As is the common method of comedy, by doing something even more erroneously than is usual, the usual error has been indicated. There is comedy but behind the comedy there is a moral, and neither suffers on account of the presence of the other. The moral is indicated only, but it lingers; the comedy is foremost, but it dies. And the work is no less comedy for that, but rather manages to be comedy because of it. *1066* is a plea for the abolition of nationalistic ways of looking at history, for the elimination of all prejudice. It is a plea for the writing of broader social history and for a better understanding between peoples.

8. The Comedy of Art: Surrealism

So numerous are the current instances of comedy that it has been found quite impossible in the space of a single chapter to give examples of them all. From the casual humour of accidental situations to the formal comedy of dramatic presentation on the stage, we find comedy covering the entire range, which is a broad one indeed. Unable to do justice to so wide a field, we have chosen to show types of comedy regardless of the current vehicle rather than to attempt to illustrate all of the types of vehicles themselves. Now, it so happens that romantic comedy is best exemplified in the current art movement known as surrealism. Surrealism represents a conscious attempt to break with the past. With the understanding of comedy that has been developed in the foregoing chapters, however, it will not appear strange if surrealism appears to be a new movement only in the sense that it makes rearrangements of the materials and attitudes of the classic past. Let us examine it with this in mind.

We have said that surrealism makes a break with the past. It is a consciously irrational movement. Dissatisfied with the traditions of most of the great historical art periods, it has attempted to set out anew, by waiving all influences. That it has succeeded in doing so only in part is due to a professional sanity which inheres in the artistic method. Dali, one of the better known of the surrealist painters, is generally acknowledged to be a fine, gifted and careful draughtsman. Apart from his subject-matter it would be difficult to single him out as a surrealist; and the same is true of many of the surrealist painters.

The classic method of comedy is evident in the technique of the surrealists. The juxtaposition of objects and hence of relations which do not seem to have any good reason for belonging together lies at the bottom of all the surrealists' work. To paraphrase Lawrence, they paint their objects anyhow, to show what rot the systems are. This is not very far from the literary method of Gertrude Stein. Like Stein, they end with exactly the opposite moral of that which they set out to convey. The want to prove the world fundamentally irrational; they succeed in proving its inescapable rationality. All objects are related to all other objects, but some objects are related more closely than others. If, however, random objects can be assembled without any preconceived plan and shown to exhibit some unity, the case for a complete relationality, and hence for a final rationality, would appear to be well established. This is course is very far from the intention of the surrealists. It is, however, in a sort of back-handed way, what they actually do. That the method is back-handed would follow from the nature of comedy, as set forth in the preceding chapter. According to Herbert Read, André Breton, one of the doctrinal leaders of the surrealists, is fond of quoting a distinction made by Pierre Reverdy.

" '*L'image est une création pure de l'esprit.*
" '*Elle ne peut naître d'une comparaison mais du rapprochement de deux réalités plus ou moins éloignées.*' "[43]

Surrealism aspires to an intense subjectivity, of an exclusiveness which is obviously beyond the scope of any creative method. The very platform which surrealism espouses relies upon a certain amount of objectivity, in that the relations which it brings together must have the required objective lack of justification for being brought together.

Surrealism is frankly an appeal to the romantic principle. It employs all the furniture of romanticism and of irrationalism in its modern form: the romantic twinge of old and elaborate over-decoration, the characteristics of dream and dream-inspired conceptions, the world of the madman, the testimony of the subconscious, and finally Bergson's old comic character in a new dress: not mechanism but "automatism." A motley crew indeed, and whether seriously intended or no, one sure to produce a kind of comedy. Fortunately, the surrealists are not as mad as their material. Breton's definition of humour, although conceived vaguely along subjective lines, is not half as mistaken as we might have supposed it would be. "Humour," he says, is "a paradoxical triumph of the pleasure principle over real conditions at a moment when they may be considered to be particularly unfavourable. . . ."[44] Hence the fur teacup

---

[43] Herbert Read, *Surrealism* (London, 1936, Faber & Faber), p 75.
[44] André Breton, quoted in op. cit., p. 103.

and the clock in the stocking, failures if taken too seriously, are successful as instances of comedy.

The surrealists have taken leave of their reason—on principle. They have followed the signs and symbols of irrationalism, but with what a deadly deductive logic! Surrealist efforts at utter confusion must meet with defeat, as they generally do. No such absolute is absolutely attainable. The effect is to lead serious painting to be mindful of its rational goal, to accept nothing on faith, to challenge everything traditional to justify its claim to continuance, and largely to clean the highways and byways of the artistic pursuit of all its litter of pretension and cant. There is something essentially right with the practice of art, something deeply reasonable which does not allow the artist, if he truly is an artist, to stray very far from the path which leads to his appointed goal. Surrealism, although adopting the wrong aesthetic philosophy, has been forced by the necessities of art itself to follow the correct philosophy which always was, and evidently must always remain, implicit in the artist method.

9. THE POPULAR COMEDY: IDOLS OF THE MARKET-PLACE

There are a number of comedians whose popularity is enormous, and we must consider samples of them here. Popularity of their sort is fleeting, of course, and it is quite possible that although their names are on every tongue in America, they will be almost forgotten in a few years. But since they will be replaced by others who will be just as popular, it may be concluded that they do fill a certain function, even though thay have to be often changed. They evidently reflect certain evanescent moods to which the public is susceptible, and they pass with the passing of these moods. They are so highly contemporary they that seem to *be* the moment rather than to reflect it. They ride upon the surface of the changing scene; and since they are more of the moment than anything else they are forgotten when the moment is gone.

Illustrations from Modern Comedians

Will Rogers, the screen and radio comedian and columnist, belongs to this class of popular idols. Rogers was very popular indeed, and the attempt to sentimentalize him since his accidental death has constituted little more than a public scandal. Although he had his limitations, he was a clever man, and did represent something in America. He came closer than anyone else in the country to filling the rôle of official fool. The place he sought was an official one indeed; for he wanted to be the Congressional and Presidential fool, corresponding to the court fool of the Middle Ages. To this end he always cultivated the friendship of the Presidents, and attacked Congress whenever he could. That he had anti-democratic leanings and admired power in whatever form, there can be little doubt. His attacks, repeated again and again under the guise of humour, on the idiocies of Congressmen, were really aimed at democracy and representative government. As additional evidence, there is the piece he wrote for the papers in praise of Mussolini.[45]

From his envied coign of vantage as public comedian, Rogers was able to point out the truth about many things which might not otherwise have been accepted so pleasantly. In a letter to a friend, Rogers revealed that he saw the point, for he says, "Don't take what a comedian says to heart, if anyone ever starts taking me serious I am sunk."[46] Will Rogers was full of contradictions. He was, for instance, a fearless critic at times. He attacked everything, from business ("Gentlemen, you are as fine a group of men as ever foreclosed a mortgage on a widow. I'm glad to be with you Shylocks.")[47] to Christianity ("I tried to find out who the Barbarians were. From the best I could learn, Barbarians were people who stole from you. If you stole from the Barbarians you were indexed in your history as a Christian").[48] He observed the effect of the absence of liberalism in Soviet Russia in its proper perspective, when he said, upon the news of the execution of some public official,

---

[45] Will Rogers, *Wit and Wisdom* (New York, 1936, Stokes), pp. 68–72. [46] Letter to Courtney, in op. cit., p. 15.
[47] Op. cit., p. 73. [48] Op. cit., p. 46.

that "Russia doesn't have what you might call a constant critic," and he wrote an epitaph for the unfortunate:

> Here lies the body of Nicholas Vimsky,
> He tried to criticize Stalin, but Stalin outlasted himsky.

He was even keen enough to observe that fame and position were often the result of events, and that events continued to occasion the fortunes of the great. He observed that "Being great as President is not a matter of farsightedness; it's just a question of the weather, not only in your own country but in a dozen others. It's the elements that makes you great or that break you."[49] The Rogers pose, however, was a pose, and so his words of wisdom had to be spoken in an ignorant language, abounding in grammatical errors.[50] Rogers also said proudly that he was ignorant of art and disliked it.[51] He used to dress like a cowboy; to that end he wore his hair carelessly, and often boasted that he never owned a "dress suit."

The Achilles heel of Will Rogers was his respect for big business and big business men. He spoke of the American Government as "the biggest business in the world,"[52] and intimated that the rich would make better Congressmen than the poor, on the grounds that only the rich were accustomed to dealing in large sums of money.[53] Frequently in his syndicated newspaper paragraphs, Rogers had something good to say about some wealthy person whom he was visiting or knew. He wanted written on his epitaph, "I joked about every prominent man of my time, but I have never met a man I didn't like."[54] Rogers might have been a wiser man, and therefore a more permanently valuable comedian, had he lived through the long years of the trade depression. As it is, there is little worth remembering, for his own ambition has been fulfilled:

[49] Op. cit., p. 100.
[50] "Maybe ain't ain't so correct, but I notice that lots of folks who ain't usin' ain't, ain't eatin'." (Op. cit, p. 26.) Many who used ain't weren't eating either.
[51] Op. cit., p. 116.
[52] Op. cit., p. 54.
[53] Op. cit., p. 50.
[54] Op. cit., p. 124. ❧

Illustrations from Modern Comedians

"I hope to be like a good bookkeeper: when my volumes are finished my accusations and denials will balance so even that I haven't really said a thing."[55]

Another good example of highly contemporary humour is offered in the pages of the weekly periodical, the *New Yorker*. The *New Yorker* has been very successful, although there is no way to tell just how long such successes will last. *New Yorker* humour is very easy to analyse because the *New Yorker* really has only one joke. One particular joke, repeated over and over, and in many different varieties and ways, fills its pages. This joke consists in the spectacle of the worker speaking like a scholar. We have already given two examples of *New Yorker* humour; we may restate them briefly. Two stonemasons are working on a scaffolding on the side of a large building that is being erected. One turns to ask the other, "Does 'ex' take the ablative or the dative?" Again, a man in overalls is eating in a cheap restaurant. Behind him we can see a sign, 'Watch your lid.' The customer turns to the waiter, who is in shirt-sleeves, and says, "These peaches are good, really they are." To which the waiter replies, "We think they're amusing."

The assumptions behind these jokes stagger the imagination. First, that every worker is ignorant is a proposition which it is pretty hard to accept. More than likely it can be demonstrated absolutely untrue. We may guess that the *New Yorker*, as highly contemporary as it seems, has never caught up with the times, for its jokes are more appropriate to the period before the trade depression than they are to the period since. The second assumption is as silly as the first, for it consists in the proposition that all the wealthy are gentlemen and scholars. It requires no comment. The appeal of the *New Yorker* is thus strictly on a snobbish basis.

We may give the *New Yorker* a different moral than the one it ostensibly boasts. We may urge that the comparison between the ignorant but ambitious worker and the rich gentleman scholar is meant to be not detrimental to the worker but rather

[55] Op. cit., p. 22.

serviceable to his interests. The worker, says the *New Yorker* joke, is not merely a wage slave; he is also an ambitious human to whom also belong all the accretions of culture which his labour has helped to build up. It is ludicrous indeed to find one who has not had the opportunity to acquire an education behaving like an educated person, and this is undoubtedly the candid form of *New Yorker* humour. But to limit this humour to snobbery is to take only the most superficial view of the matter. Undoubtedly the table is turned in the *New Yorker*. For its snobbish humour marks the recognition of the fact that however imperfect from any point of view one may be, one is still, compared with others, a little farther along on the path to perfection. The humour thus reduces finally to the recognition of the fact that progress is possible.

There are any number of popular idols who might be considered had we more space to devote to them. Mr. Roark Bradford has observed that in its hour of need America's favourite comedian is—a wooden dummy: Charlie McCarthy. Charlie (it might be remarked that the wooden dummy is also a radio comedian) is a constant critic, but not of anything important, and a dissembling pretender himself. His popularity, subject to change without notice, as all such reputations are, is probably due to the skilful construction of his personality. He is a pretender who is trying to "get by" in the world, while at the same time keeping his eyes open to the innumerable pretensions and follies of others.

The comedy of Burns and Allen, equally popular radio performers, is that of logic, parading as foolishness. Gracie Allen is a silly woman who gives utterances to many truths because of her artless literal interpretation of spoken statements and traditional saws. George Burns is the disgusted male, who because he is forced to endure the absurdities of Gracie's conversation is also able skilfully to bring out its logical meanings. Such people as Charlie McCarthy and Burns and Allen are superficial combinations of popular idol and court fool. It is unfortunate indeed that the vested restrictions of one kind or another put upon them, not all from the outside, do not allow them to criticize the current scene at a more profound level. Were they able to do so, American life might be better than it is.

We have been speaking thus far of comedians whose effect is gained indirectly through criticism. We shall close this section with one whose criticism is indirect and whose effect is positive. The short film comedies of Walt Disney and his company, the Mickey Mouse films and the "Silly Symphonies," are affairs purely of delight. They do not criticize what-is in favour of what-ought-to-be, which is the usual method of comedy; thay rather affirm what-ought-to-be as though it were, which in itself constitutes an indirect criticism of what-is. This was ever the method of phantasy. The world in which we move in the Walt Disney pictures is one of sheer delight. For a while it appears to be the way we should like to think that things are: a dream world in which animals speak, always kindly, trees come alive, and everything has interesting adventures. It is the kind of story-book world which adults in an open conspiracy have always persuaded children is for them alone.

But the kind of world Walt Disney presents to us goes deeper than that. Its make-believe is logical and consistent. It is an animistic world in which everything not only comes alive, but in which Disney tries to persuade us and often succeeds, everything that lives acts according to the dictates of its own logic. Creatures that we dream of and tell children about, witches, dwarfs, giants and ogres and talking birds, suddenly appear in a natural world and prove that they are not impossible by moving before us without loss of self-consistency. We remember these people and this environment because we have heard of it in another connection, but we do not see that it is strange to find ourselves living in their world. There is indeed nothing strange about their world; it is not out of time or place and it suits them.

In Praise of Comedy

We have accepted their premises, for the moment anyway, and we are drawn to make their conclusions. And we are all at home with non-contradiction, and feel that we are still receiving safe-conduct by the syllogism.

So many of us imagine that in the world of phantasy we are escaping from the so-called inescapable logic of the real world. Nothing could be farther from the true situation. We do not escape from the exigencies of logic; we merely exchange our old premises for new ones. The logic itself remains, and applies the new premises with all the vigour which characterized its application of the old. Robert Nathan reports that his step-daughter, aged four, "looked up suddenly from her spinach and remarked in a dreamy voice:

" 'I know a little boy who turned into a flower.' "

Her little brother, aged six, exclaimed with energy:

" 'That's silly. You have to say what he ate that made him turn into a flower.' "[56]

The world of imagination and phantasy may be different from our own but its logic is emphatically not. The greatness of Mickey Mouse is due in large part to the fact that he does not try to challenge the law of the excluded middle.

Disney's comedies are not so obviously criticism; they are called comedies because they present us with sheer delight. But there is a sense in which delight constitutes the deepest kind of criticism. By having to depart from what we know, by having to leave our familiar actual world and travel to a world which is strange and where many of the conditions are new, in order to achieve logic, a criticism of our actual world is implied. The feeling of joy and the knowledge of non-contradiction: value, and logic, reside more abundantly in the world of the imagination than they do in the field of our experiences, the actual world. This is the message which phantasies have to give us. It would be idle to deny the indirect criticism. Phantasies are ideal goals, limits after whose image we are urged by hope and aspiration to want to model our actual world. As

[56] Quoted by Lewis Gannett in the *New York Post* for June 27, 1938.

266

long as any disparity exists between them, we are sure to compare them and to criticize what we have because it is not what we know we ought to have, and thus to take cognizance of the comic perspective.

10. CONCLUSION

We have reached the end of our essay on comedy. We have tried to show in historical theory and practice as well as in modern theory and practice, that a certain kind of understanding of comedy is indicated. We have come a long way, although nowhere have we done more than barely to point out the field of observation. Whole books could be written—and have been—upon particular periods of comedy which we have covered in a few pages. And as for the leading theories of comedy, it would not be difficult to compose comprehensive commentaries; indeed it would involve little beyond the inhibition of self-restraint, for the temptation is surely present. But our object has been merely to suggest something of the nature of comedy. If our premises have been correct, then the definition of comedy set forth herein should not be soon set aside and never aside entirely, but only taken into account as a special case of some wider truth. In the meanwhile it is the humble claim of this book that its central hypothesis is more or less correct.

Comedy *in esse* is indestructible. Short of a change in the relation between actuality and the logical order, it cannot be amended. Since comedy has been defined as the indirect endorsement of the ideal by means of a criticism of the temporal, or the derogation of actuality in favour of the logical order, comedy cannot become superannuated until the ideal becomes entirely actual. On this day, as the Good Book observes, all will be one and His name will be One. There will not be comedy because there will not be anything else. All will be what C. S. Peirce has said infinite unity must be: one continuous feeling. But in the meantime comedy makes distinctions, and will

itself continue to be a distinction. It is of permanence because
it rests upon the most permanent of distinctions: (by definition)
that between actuality and the logical order.

It has been wondered what would happen if a philosopher
were some day to be taken at his word and carried to infinity.[57]
There would, of course, be no more comedy. But this is not
the situation with which we are confronted. We are face to
face with error, evil and ugliness in proportions which must
make the most unobservant and insensitive stand aghast. We
are asked to decide whether the very high civilization which
we have succeeded in attaining is to perish by the instability
from which it suffers or go forward to greater attainments.
Is it to fall a victim of its own efficiency perverted to the uses
of destruction? The decision lies at present in the balance, a
balance from which the careful guarding of sanity is sure to
extract the correct reward. There is something which whispers
that we must go forward and not backward; an echo, perhaps,
of the logic underlying events.

Certainly the weapon of logic is comedy, so far as the purposes
of actuality are concerned. We have said that the dictators of
fascism, Mussolini and Hitler, never laugh. But laughter at
current institutions has been prohibited before; it was Plato
who set the style, that very same Plato who gave to comedy its
realistic and objective basis. He says:

"Neither ought our guardians to be given to laughter; for a
fit of laughter which has been indulged to excess almost always
produces a violent reaction. . . . Then personages of worth,
even if only mortal men, must not be represented as overcome
by laughter, and still less must such a representation of the
gods be allowed."[58]

Plato, it appears, counted too much upon conformance
and thereby set aside the implications from his own valuable
conclusions as to the nature of comedy. Nietzsche, who held
to some extent at least to the truths represented in the Greek
pantheon, said that he could never believe in a god who did

[57] Mr. Roger Sergel, in conversation.   [58] *Republic*, 3. 71.

not know how to laugh. We can understand now what that statement means. But the dictators are not gods; at the very best they are no more than institutions, and these inevitably become changed at the behest of comedy when the contradictions contained in them prove insupportable. The conservative forces of inertia compel us to put up with a great deal of superannuated abuse; but nevertheless every contradiction has its day. We have our shortcomings over which the few of us who are the least involved ponder and the wisest ponder the most. Future generations will glance backward and laugh, deeming our difficulties to have been a little childish and their later solution a mere matter of common sense. But they will have difficulties of their own, and the gadfly critics will follow them in the guise of their own comedians, because comedy is imponderable and cannot be saved because it cannot be destroyed.

When the mediaeval guild watchers kept the sepulchre light from Good Friday to Easter morning, they sang songs, "and it is an example of the irrepressible mediaeval tendency to *mimesis* that they were sometimes accoutred like the knights of Pilate."[59] There was nothing peculiarly mediaeval about the "irrepressible tendency to *mimesis*"; it can be postulated for all persons always and everywhere. Everyone is to some extent a mime, and the mimic has a universal appeal which is unlikely ever to be abrogated. For comedy, and consequently the rôle of the comedian, is essential to change; it can on occasion render service to the forces of reaction by ridiculing the novel aspects of anything new and valuable, yet is indispensable to progress.[60] Comedy, as we have noted, was present when

[59] E. K. Chambers, *The Mediaeval Stage*, ii, p. 23.

[60] The revolutionary nature of comedy does not mean that it approves of everything new and ridicules the old. It is indifferent to this problem since it is concerned with values and not with time. Comedy makes fun of everything actual for its shortcomings and limitations, without partiality. There is also revolutionary comedy in the conservative attitude, when confronted with overwhelming change. In general, however, comedy works for the revolutionary rather than the conservative forces, because only the virtues of the former, whereas the vices as well as the virtues of the latter, are in evidence.

men first learned to think and feel and do. It is present also to-day, and has been inherited in a straight line through history; inherited not through learning as knowledge but through being as organization. We do not have to be much to note that others are not all that they should be; we feel that a change is in the air; and we make signs to indicate the fact. Thus comedy is an object to be reckoned with in any situation. Where there is smoke there is fire; laughter is an indication of the presence somewhere of comedy.

Comedy should not be hard to find; it is never very far away. It furnishes the gaiety of the critic, and makes tears possible. Its artistic nature is affirmed in the fact that it manages to exhibit external and timeless values by means of the most instantaneous of contemporary manifestations. Nothing is more local than a joke—and yet the jokes never change. Not that they are patchwork jobs; the man who invents a joke does so, we may be sure, without erudition or even borrowed scholarship. He may be a pedant or an everyday kind of ignorant man, but he makes up his pun or his satire upon the spot *instanter*, and the forms of comedy will not permit him to be any exception to their inflexible rules. His spontaneity turns out the most traditional kind of product. It is an occupation in which every scholar is made a fool and every fool a scholar. The comic doctor and his evidence of the unimportance of death, for instance, is a comic pattern that survives, albeit in highly local form, throughout historical time. This pattern was probably, as we have noted earlier, one of the forms of primitive comedy, antedating even classic civilization. The "Lord of Misrule" who reigns for the day of *Mardi Gras* in the carnival at New Orleans in 1938 is the same Lord of Misrule or "Abbot of Unreason" who was crowned in the thirteenth century, the same who led the festal processions in the fertility rituals conducted by the primitive inhabitants of archaic Greece. Mr. Roark Bradford had never read *The Arbitrants* of Menander when he wrote his short story, *The Ring Sing Twins*.[61]

[61] In *Let the Band Play Dixie* (New York, 1934, Harper).

Illustrations from Modern Comedians

Very obviously, the comic patterns are not imitated from generation to generation; they are not inherited; and neither are they a product of "race-memory." From the primitive fertility dramas to Molière is a long time indeed, yet the character of the magic doctor survived; from Menander to Bradford is also a long time, yet the plot of the girl who is seduced and made pregnant at the holiday celebration and who later, through a set of intricate circumstances, discovers that her seducer is not the man she did not want but thought she had to take but rather the man she loves, has survived the long period. Such persistent patterns must have some basis in the comedy of existence itself, whereby they can be discovered independently at any given time, and moreover are almost sure to recur again and again. Investigation along these lines must undoubtedly reveal certain basic patterns of a cultural anthropological nature which are integral parts of human action. Comedy at this point is very close to mythology. For what are myths except the symbolic expression of certain values which have been abstracted from time and given affective denotations and wide connotations?

The calm amusement of resignation which has traditionally characterized the Chinese attitude toward existence lies at one end of the comic scale, and the revolutionary comedy of Westerners at the other end. Mr. Graves tells the story of "an influential mandarin who by the machinations of certain of his enemies was reduced from a position of affluence and security to one of infinite misery. He retired to a cell on the To mountain, where he spent the remainder of his life inscribing with a burnt stick upon the walls of his apartment: 'Oh, oh! strange business!' "[62] Could such calm amusement be retained with the adoption of dynamic action rather than passive resignation? Very likely it could. But meanwhile the Western comedy is more volatile, for it has to do with the drama of life and more especially of death. Comedy is dangerous, as are all activities that engage in fundamentals. The comedian is, as Faure says,

[62] Robert Graves, *The Future of Humour*, pp. 48–49.

271

an acrobat, and "The acrobat marvellously symbolizes the position of man confronted with the problem of giving order to the universe."[63] There is a sense in which he is the image of God.[64]

Comedy is a game but an extremely hazardous one, for like all art "it is a matter of dancing on the edge of the abyss or hiding it with flowers."[65] It results in a feeling of "enthusiastic security," however, because it succeeds in making actual the apprehension of those truths and values in which alone finite things are at home. For the moment that man is shown his participation in that which never changes, he cannot feel lost. This is precisely what Western comedy does with its violence. The magic doctor who restores the dead to life and thus cheats death, the film comedian whose wounds in the seat of his trousers do not break his spine, but merely cause him to jump up and down with fearful anticipation of serious injury, are typical of the Western perspective on comedy. But in either way of looking at things some sort of resolution has taken place. We are all comedians to some extent, a property which manifests itself at one time or another and to more or less degree. And to say that we are all comedians is to say that we are artists, for "to appreciate the comic aspect of real life implies that we have already exercised the aesthetic activity upon it; have in some sense reflected upon our brute experience."[66]

Comedy is always what we should to-day describe as realistic. It has its feet on the ground. It is mindful not only of death but of taxes, and its perennial barbs are always aimed at the same targets throughout the life of a given culture. It gets to handle, so to speak, the traditional and ever-present irritations which people know as evils but which they also find themselves powerless to eradicate. Thus we find recurrent jokes about the quarrelsome and interfering mother-in-law, the familiar wife,

[63] Elie Faure, *The Spirit of the Forms* (New York, 1937, Garden City), p. 175.

[64] See above Chapter III, p. 26.　　　　[65] Op. cit., p. 460.

[66] E. F. Carritt, "A Theory of the Ludicrous," in *The Hibbert Journal*, vol. xxi (1923), p. 556.

the inevitability of taxation, the deceitfulness of politicians, bad cooking, and so on. These are, so to speak, its bedrock, its foundation-stones, the fundamental units upon which it must depend and from which alone it can hope to build. But comedy does not stop there. It rises to heights which Dante has shown us are divine, to the point where comedy and tragedy meet and become indistinguishable, fused in the fulness of actual value. This is only made possible, however, so long as its feet remain upon the ground. Mr. Graves once asked a friend, " 'How could one write a legend about an angel and a cuckoo?' to which the friend wisely replied, 'One would have to build it up from the cuckoo.' "[67] Like all successful enterprises, it must start at the bottom and build surely if it hopes to rise to any heights.

For build it always will, as long as there is a moment to pause from the day's work or an evening to devote to contemplation under the spell of rational aspiration. Such are the perspectives upon existence, that we are enabled to compare them and thus to note that each to some extent reveals an actuality which is not what it ought to be but only what it is; and it is then that we laugh. As long as human existence is a limited and finite affair, as long as actuality pursues a dialectic course, as often as organizations are set up or discovered and customs and institutions taken as final entities, there will echo the sound of laughter, a sound reminiscent of an indefinitely repeated round of humour and improvement stretching on into the boundless future of an unlimited community.

[67] Robert Graves, *The Future of Humour*, p. 95.

Primitive Comedy

IT was found impossible to place primitive comedy historically, since the early cultures of which we have present knowledge are in their modern form probably older than more advanced civilizations, yet exist still to-day. They could accordingly be dated before archaic Greece—or in the twentieth century. Fortunately, they possess logical differences which justify giving them a separate mention.

A culture consists in a system of institutions taken together with their implements of myth. The application of an implicitly accepted dominant ontology of a people to actual circumstances of place and date must be modified in proportion to the difficulties presented by the total environment. By total environment here is meant the social level of diverse cultural traits acquired by contact with other cultures, as well as the level of purely physical influences such as temperature modifications.

The comedian in this broad connection may exercise one or two functions. His function in the culture may be to stand a little to one side in order to indicate to other members of the culture that their pattern is not the only pattern, and that in terms of the selection of some other pattern their own institutions and myths would appear inadequate and hence funny. This is the function of the greatest comedians in highly advanced civilizations.

The other function of the comedian may be to institutionalize comedy itself in order to integrate it within the culture. This is the function of the surest comedians in the primitive cultures. We cannot here afford the space to write a lengthy essay on primitive comedy. It must suffice to quote several examples in order to show that primitive comedy, like its more sophisticated brother, enjoyed and continues to enjoy an enormous range.

Among the Zuñi of the New Mexico pueblos there are regular clowning cults. Comedy is a social affair, a regular obligation upon certain members of the tribe. Like many other Indian ceremonials, and also like more civilized peoples, dancing for rain can be a comic as well as a solemn occasion.[1] It is a joyous occasion whenever the dance has its desired effect. "The clowns make merry in the deep adobe mud, sliding at full length in the puddles and paddling in the half-liquid earth. It is their recognition that their feet in the dance have the compulsion of natural forces upon the storm clouds. . . ."[2] Primitive dancing of comic nature runs all the way from the sober performance of the highly integrated Zuñi culture to the Dionysiac frenzy of certain other Indian groups.

Dancing is the more familiar form of primitive comedy but it is far from being the only one. William Seabrook has pointed out in a recent article[3] that primitives enjoy considerable humour. They laugh at anything and they mimic everything, from their own customs and rituals to our more civilized ways. Much of what we take solemnly in primitive arts is ritual comedy to the primitive. We label a dance, for instance, religious or comic. The combination of the two, so familiar in primitive life, baffles our efforts at classification simply because we try to force the primitive behaviour into our own familiar categories. We have the habit of saying of a comedian whose criticisms are particularly sharp, that he "holds nothing sacred." A primitive might as easily make just the reverse comment, for the primitive comedian holds everything sacred. The facile comparison between children and primitives in this

[1] See J. G. Frazer, *The Golden Bough* (London, 1926, Macmillan), "The Magic Art," vol. i, p. 301 n., for comparison with the French Italians, Japanese, and Chinese.

[2] Ruth Benedict, *Patterns of Culture* (Boston, 1934, Houghton Mifflin), p. 93.

[3] "The Lighter Side of Primitive Art," in *Town and Country*, vol. 92 (1937), p. 93.

connection is misleading. We like to discourage laughter at those institutions in which we believe, and suffer children to do so only until they are grown old enough to "know better." The primitive, on the contrary, makes his laughter over into an institution. There is a profound difference.

Even when living in contact with civilization, as the American negroes do, primitives have a resistance to other standards which is sometimes amazing. The civilized world, for them, is a world of upset standards, and the white man someone not always to be trusted. This is not true of course of any but the most primitive negroes.

Mr. Lyle Saxon, the journalist, has related that every Christmas he has been in the habit of treating the negroes on his Louisiana plantation to a ride into the nearby town, with a motion picture there and whiskey to drink on the way home. One Christmas, the movie to which he took his faithful share-croppers was *King Kong*, the film in which cities were depicted as being terrorized by a giant ape many times larger than a man. In the picture, the mechanical ape destroys elevated railways and performs other feats of strength which make the human beings beside him appear very small by comparison.

On the return ride to the plantation, Mr. Saxon noticed that the negroes in the big van were very quiet. They were not talking or even drinking the whiskey with which he had provided them. He was riding in front with the driver, and was very much concerned over the subdued state of affairs. Calling Henry, the most intelligent of the negroes, forward, he inquired what the trouble was.

"Well, you see, Mr. Saxon," Henry replied, "they think that you have tricked them and they are very hurt that you could do a thing like that."

"Tricked them? But how?"

"Well, they don't believe there is any such giant ape, and they never suspected you would be the one to try to make them believe that there was."

"Henry," Mr. Saxon said, "you've got to do something.

Fix it up for me in some way. You know I wouldn't hurt their feelings for anything in the world."

Henry returned to the others, and in a little while all was normal. The negroes were laughing and drinking and singing. Mr. Saxon became curious again, and again sent for Henry.

"What did you tell them?" he asked.

"It's all right now, Mr. Saxon. I told them that the ape in the picture was a regular size ape, but that the people were tiny people."

We may laugh at the primitive and his odd misunderstanding of our own culture, but when we do so we are laughing at another, albeit a lower, culture. Malinowski and Lips have edited a book entitled *The Savage Hits Back*, in which our own culture becomes the target of the primitive. The satire on Western ways is not always complimentary and is often truly aimed. Much can be learned concerning the nature of the comic from a study of the comparative comedy of different cultures, including the primitive.

Index

279

Index

Index